CICERO, MARCUS TULLIUS (106–43 B.C.), Roman orator and statesman, was born at Arpinum of a wealthy local family. He was taken to Rome for his education with the idea of a public career and by the year 70 he had established himself as the leading barrister in Rome. In the meantime his political career was well under way and he was elected praetor for 66. His ambitious nature enabled him to obtain those honours which would normally only have been conferred upon members of the Roman aristocracy, and he was duly elected consul for 63. One of the most permanent features of his political life was his attachment to Pompey. As a politician his greatest failing was his consistent refusal to compromise; as a statesman his ideals were more honourable and unselfish than those of his contemporaries. Cicero was the greatest of the Roman orators, possessing a wide range of technique and an exceptional command of the Latin tongue. He followed the common practice of publishing his speeches, but he also produced a large number of works on the theory and practice of rhetoric; on religion, and on moral and political philosophy. He played a leading part in the development of the Latin hexameter. Perhaps the most interesting of all his works is the collection of 900 letters published posthumously. These not only contain a first-hand account of social and political life in the upper classes at Rome, but also reflect the changing personal feelings of an emotional and sensitive man.

MICHAEL GRANT has been successively Chancellor's medallist and Fellow of Trinity College, Cambridge, Professor of Humanity at Edinburgh University, first Vice-Chancellor of Khartoum University, and President and Vice-Chancellor of the Queen's University of Belfast. Until 1966 he was President of the Virgil Society. He has also translated Cicero's *Selected Political Speeches* and *Murder Trials* and Tacitus' *Annals* for the Penguin Classics; his other books include *The World of Rome* (1960), *Myths of the Greeks and Romans* (1962), *The Civilizations of Europe* (1965), *Gladiators* (1967), *Roman Readings* and *Roman Literature* (both published in Pelicans), *The Climax of Rome* (1968), *The Ancient Mediterranean, Julius Caesar* (both 1969), *The Ancient Historians, The Roman Forum* and *Nero* (1970), *Cities of Vesuvius, Roman Myths, Herod the Great* (1971), *Cleopatra* (1972), *The Jews in the Roman World* (1973), *The Army of the Caesars* (1974), *The Twelve Caesars* (1975), *The Fall of the Roman Empire* (1976), and *Saint Paul* (1976).

D0057758

CICERO

SELECTED WORKS

AGAINST VERRES · I

TWENTY-THREE LETTERS

THE SECOND PHILIPPIC AGAINST
ANTONY

ON DUTIES · III

ON OLD AGE

Translated with an Introduction by
MICHAEL GRANT

PENGUIN BOOKS

Penguin Books Ltd, Harmondsworth, Middlesex, England
Penguin Books, 625 Madison Avenue, New York, New York 10022, U.S.A.
Penguin Books Australia Ltd, Ringwood, Victoria, Australia
Penguin Books Canada Ltd, 2801 John Street, Markham, Ontario, Canada L3R 1B4
Penguin Books (N.Z.) Ltd, 182–190 Wairau Road, Auckland 10, New Zealand

—

First published 1960
Reprinted 1962
Reprinted with revisions 1965
Reprinted 1967, 1969
Reprinted with revisions 1971
Reprinted 1974, 1975, 1976, 1977

—

—

Made and printed in Great Britain
by Richard Clay (The Chaucer Press) Ltd,
Bungay, Suffolk
Set in Monotype Bembo

CONTENTS

INTRODUCTION

PART ONE: AGAINST TYRANNY

PART TWO: HOW TO LIVE

APPENDIXES

INTRODUCTION

I

CICERO AGAINST TYRANNY

AMID the recurrent crises of the twentieth century there is a curious topicality in the spectacle of this highly intelligent but far from super-human personality, first struggling to eminence in a great state, and then having to face, as well as he could, a crushing series of almost world-wide emergencies and convulsions. Very few other men have both stood at the centre of world events and written so well and fully about the part they played. The character that emerges is a complicated one, composed of brilliant but discordant and sometimes contradictory qualities.

His story which will be told – largely by himself – in this book essentially consists of his repeated efforts, in spite of frequent and for-midable discouragements, to oppose the autocratic modes of rule which were gradually throughout his life encroaching on the Republican system: and which reached their climax in the wholly authoritarian dictatorships of Sulla (82–79 B.C.) and Caesar (49–44 B.C.), and the scarcely less formidable committee regimes, both cynical and the second efficiently ruthless, of the two sets of Triumvirs (60–50 and 43–31 B.C.).[1]

Cicero was not often a very successful politician, but he derives un-mistakable greatness from his insistence, against odds, that such dicta-torial rulers were in the wrong because they unjustifiably curtailed the freedom of the individual: whereas the ultimate authority should be not themselves but certain unchangeable moral principles which they are incompetent to annul or amend. His own words on the subject, in his treatise *On the State* (III. 33), written during a period of profound political disappointment, represent an early and fundamental statement of one side's position in a perennial controversy.

True law is Reason, right and natural, commanding people to ful-fil their obligations and prohibiting and deterring them from doing wrong. Its validity is universal; it is immutable and eternal. Its com-mands and prohibitions apply effectively to good men, and those uninfluenced by them are bad. Any attempt to supersede this law, to

1. Pompey, Caesar, Crassus (d. 53); Antony, Octavian (Augustus), Lepidus (dismissed 36).

7

repeal any part of it, is sinful; to cancel it entirely is impossible. Neither the Senate nor the Assembly can exempt us from its demands; we need no interpreter or expounder of it but ourselves. There will not be one law at Rome, one at Athens, or one now and one later, but all nations will be subject all the time to this one changeless and everlasting law.

That is to say, right and wrong are irreconcilable, and no legislation can make one into the other. But Cicero was not content to enunciate moral principles from the study. For he was one of those politicians, never too numerous and in his day outstandingly rare, who have proposed, in their finest and most unhampered moments, to put their moral principles into practice in the conduct of political affairs.[1] True, when he came to write his treatise *On the State* – as the government was visibly collapsing – he was prepared to envisage a 'guide' for the Republic. Though the conception was general and ideal, his own qualifications as well as Pompey's (or those which he had once hoped that Pompey might possess, p. 78), cannot have been wholly absent from his mind. But this was to be a constitutional, philosophical sort of guidance from the sidelines: dictatorship was and remained the negation of all that he stood for. Indeed, he attempted, at decisive moments of his career, to prevent such regimes from taking root and suppressing the free operation of Republican institutions – which alone, in his opinion, could supply the ideal of a stable and balanced state where human beings might express themselves as social creatures.

However, a description limited to those terms does not show the peculiar nature of Cicero's political achievement. The austerely grand picture of a high-minded man resisting tyranny was what he would have liked the world to accept, but the truth is more complex and more interesting. Any consistently straightforward, high-minded approach was, for Cicero, ruled out by insuperable obstacles. The ruthless, cut-throat politics of the late Republic did not allow success to come at all easily to men like him who were excluded by birth and resources from the cliques of great and rich families which, in shifting combinations, traditionally dominated the Senate and the state.[2]

Cicero was only able to fight against these difficulties at all because of his incomparable eloquence, which was as welcome a support to poli-

1. Rex Warner, in *The Young Caesar*, makes Caesar say that Cicero 'looked for perfection and wished to find in this period of utter and necessary revolution the balance and dignity and organic structure of his own prose'.

2. For Cicero's origins and early life, see p. 35.

tical leaders as the backing of a leading daily newspaper would be to-day. But Cicero's struggle to utilize this asset to the best effect was seriously impeded by his own personality; for his extraordinary talent was matched by equally conspicuous faults and weaknesses, including snobbery, vanity, extravagance, vacillation and a too emotional and rancorous judgement of political problems – not to mention a tendency to make enemies by injudicious jokes. In the recurring dilemmas of a hideously disturbed national situation he was obliged to accept many humiliating failures and compromises. 'Matched as in single duel,' as de Quincey described him, 'with a strong temptation to error growing out of his public position,' Cicero repeatedly changed direction, laid himself open to many charges of insincerity, and not infrequently despaired. His practice abundantly fell short of his principles and pronouncements.

Yet these, in regard to totalitarian rule, came genuinely from the heart; and, obstructed by the imperfections of the political scene and of his own character, Cicero recurrently though in the end unavailingly sought the means to carry them into effect. His permanent political value lies in the attempts which this all too humanly unheroic man made to realize his right idea. This despite every discouragement he never altogether abandoned, and once or twice, at critical moments, supported at great personal risk – indeed, finally, at the cost of his life.

Of the violence and greed besetting the decaying Republic, he was constantly aware; and from an early stage of his career he attacked them when opportunity arose (Chapter 1). However, like his contemporaries, he did not know of any changes that could radically improve matters. In effect, Cicero felt that his ideal state might be achieved by the existing Roman system, reformed a little by a return to ancient practices, as seen in the idealized colours of Macaulay's *Lays* (Chapter 5). But this view took fatally inadequate account of the fundamental flaws in the contemporary scene: the narrowness and political barrenness of the dominant groups, the dangers to public security from armies, gangs, and mobs, the competition between all classes in plundering the provinces, and the general unfitness of a government designed long ago for a city-state to rule what had become an enormous multi-racial empire. Cicero did not fully realize that this government, without far-reaching administrative reforms such as those later introduced by Augustus, had no hope of keeping pace with the large, grim new world for which it had never been intended.

In public life, as John Morley observed, the choice is constantly between two evils, and action is one long second best. Cicero's choice, given the current failure to think of anything better, was between in-efficient and incomplete freedom, and the tidier and possibly (though not certainly) more efficient solution of dictatorship. Whatever the drawbacks of the former, he found it preferable, since the alternative was incompatible with his belief that governmental powers must be limited. That is why, in spite of the allurements of an unprovocative ac-quiescence, he summoned up the courage to attack Antony, at a time when Antony was powerful and menacing (Chapter 3).

True, it would be oversimplifying Cicero's motives to interpret them as straightforwardly altruistic. All his past humiliations, mistakes, and evasions – including most recently a prompt withdrawal after Caesar's murder, when his guidance might have been very valuable – must have come to his mind and pricked him towards this desperate action. Pos-sibly, too, he may have felt that the invective he was addressing to An-tony, for which precedents existed, need not be irreparable, and that oratorical violence need not lead to physical violence; although there was clearly a risk that it would. The risk became a fact: Cicero proved to have staked his life, and he lost it. Whatever the complexity of his mo-tives he had taken a deliberate decision, when he need not have done so, to oppose the threat of a dangerous tyranny. His adoption of this course, in spite of all the familiar temptations to quietism and all the excruci-ating doubts which, at every crisis of his life, his active brain suggested to him makes his essential moral courage all the more remarkable; as he himself aptly remarked, 'I am timid in attempting to guard against dangers, but not in facing them'.

In comparison with this basic achievement of resistance to autocracy, a precise definition of the varying nuances of his political views at differ-ent stages of his career is of less importance. Cicero was very often speaking for the Italian 'knights', the largely middle-class non-senators from whose ranks he came – the business community of Italy and the empire. His political programme, if so it can be called, was 'Harmony between the Orders' – cooperation, in the interests of the Republic, be-tween the knights and the Senate, of which he became a member. He started his career on the left – interested not indeed in Revolution (he calls the proletariat 'leeches that suck dry the Treasury'), but in the ex-tension of privileges beyond the senatorial class to the knights (Chapter 1). Later, in the fifties B.C., his emphasis shifted towards a more general and universal 'harmony', based on a new conception of the harmonious élite, less now as a political or economic grouping than as a category of men distinguished by a sense of moral responsibility – a category which included many of his good, moderate fellow-countrymen from the Italian towns. This development of Cicero's thought was prompted by disillusion with the governing class, and yet in another sense Cicero had moved towards the right: his mind was no longer on attacking vested interests, as in the *Verrines*, but on desperately endeavouring to conserve what good might be found in them. Men often move to the right as they grow older, when their temperaments cool and they acquire vested interests in the *status quo*. But in Cicero's case the change was due not only or even principally to this general tendency but to alterations in his political environment. When he was young, the dangers to the Republic came from the right: the dictatorship of Sulla had favoured the aristocracy against the middle classes, and then the misgovernment of men like Verres, which so discredited the Republican system, was still supported by the same traditional elements. In those days, therefore, Cicero had stood to the left of the regime. When he was older, however, the threat came from Caesar, who aimed to put a revolutionary stop once and for all to the free operation of the consuls, Senate, and other Republican institutions; so Cicero, standing with those who opposed Caesar, found himself (with misgivings) the associate of the traditionalists and the right.

But fundamentally, at all times, he was a moderate, a 'middle-of-the-road man'; to the two tyrannies, reaction and revolution, he was equally opposed, and whenever either of them became menacing he was on the other side. That is to say, he was a liberal; indeed he is the greatest ancestor of that whole liberal moderate tradition in western life which is at hazard today. Though he had much else to give the world, this aspect of his character and literary production – his role as an early, thoughtful, articulate, and ultimately self-sacrificing enemy of oppressive and unparliamentary methods of government – is so important, both in his own life and in the subsequent history of the world, that it must be chosen as one of the two leading themes of this volume. The other, that will now be discussed, relates to the principle which – along with temperamental preference and enlightened self-interest – encouraged him to this course of action: namely the necessity (because it is natural) of cooperation between human beings.

2

HOW TO LIVE: HUMAN COOPERATION

True to the ancient belief that politics and ethics were part of a single philosophical whole, Cicero's morality was by no means limited to the relationship between governments and subjects. 'If the man lives,' he declared, 'who would belittle the study of philosophy, I quite fail to see what in the world he would see fit to praise.' For all his passion for public life, he is said to have expressed the hope that his friends would describe him not as an orator but as a philosopher. He had felt this devotion from boyhood, encouraged by his father in spite of their anti-Greek municipal background. And by philosophy – in spite of his immense contributions to European epistemology, logic, and theology – Cicero primarily meant moral philosophy.

He enthusiastically accepted the belief of the Greek Stoics [1] that high moral standards, the determination to live up to them, and the emotional self-restraint needed to do so (which Romans so admired, and Cicero knew well to be hard of achievement) were the most important things in the world – probably the only important things: this being the imperative command of a Law of Nature, identical with divine Providence – which is universally applicable to human relations, because a spark of this divinity is universally distributed among mankind. And that is why, according to Cicero's *Tusculan Disputations*, virtue joins man to God. From this belief two things follow: first, all human beings, however humble, must count for something, must have some inherent value in themselves – the basic assumption in that humanism which is so fundamental to western thought – and secondly, this spark of divinity supplies an unbreakable bond of kinship between one man and another, irrespective of state, race, or caste, in a universal Brotherhood of Man; and it is right and necessary that brothers should receive decent treatment from one another.[2]

This conception, so far from being the meaningless platitude which debasement has often made it in later centuries, was fundamental to Cicero's attitude and runs continuously through the writings in which he endeavours to explain the human condition and, simultaneously, to guide human behaviour (Chapter 4). In the works of the later Greek philosophers he found material to reinforce his conviction that one of the first impulses in man is affection for his kind: this is natural, nature is good, and accordingly man's first rule must be regard for his fellow men, and the avoidance of any personal gain when this can only be acquired by harming another.

In his presentation of this view Cicero stands about halfway between

1. For these and other philosophers, see below, pp. 17–20.
2. Like his contemporaries, Cicero accepted slavery, but there was much affection between him and his slaves, and his writings greatly contributed towards the humanizing of the institution.

the agnostic who asserts that man can be truly good without whole-hearted adherence to a clearly defined religion, and the Christian who denies it. He is concerned first and foremost with men, he throws moral responsibility upon man's shoulders, and he believes that man can make decisions without detailed interference by gods or Providence. And yet he denies complete self-sufficiency for human beings, since he assumes the existence of this supreme power – belief in the gods being established by almost universal consent – which endows all men with the divine spark, and makes them brothers. His essential belief was that, because of the presence of this divine element in every human being equally, 'it is by helping others that man approaches closest to divinity'. Such interest in theology as he possesses, then, is related and even subordinated to his prime concern, which is human cooperation: his specific contribution is the idea of humanity.

Since, however, this idea is based on the divine spark which humanity shares, theology has its place: and it is the subject of the treatise *On the Nature of the Gods*. In this, after the Epicurean and Stoic systems have been described, the Academic spokesman Gaius Aurelius Cotta[1] is careful to say that he upholds the traditional religion of Rome, and that his philosophical standpoint, for all the apparent contradiction, does not infringe on this. In the same way Cicero's own religion varies between the patriotic godliness of the Forum and the more detached philosophizing of the study. The former is an interest in religion because this is applicable to national politics; the latter is none the less profound because it never reaches a solution. That is because, true to his distaste for dogmatic assertion, Cicero refrains from definite conclusions concerning the nature of the divinity. Likewise, when he speculates about the life beyond the grave – as he does with increasing intensity after the death of his daughter Tullia – he still qualifies by reserves, with Cato the Censor as his spokesman, an evident inclination to believe that the soul is immortal (Chapter 5).

His interest in the human cooperation which was his principal concern is eminently practical. He is writing for educated Romans, and the way of life and method of cooperation which he proposes were deliberately designed to be adjustable to their potentialities and circumstances. They were not temperamentally suited for contemplation; they were public men – following the careers of statesman and soldier, which, whatever the future of the soul might be, could bring a man immortal fame – and Cicero, reacting against the 'ivory tower' ideal of the later Greek world, was the last person to suggest that they should cease to

1. For these philosophical schools, see below, pp. 18ff.

be public men. So the contemplative or mystic virtues were clearly beyond them. That does not mean that Cicero wants them, or himself, to aim low. On the contrary, the target he sets them is at the very limit of their capabilities. But it is not beyond that limit. And this confers a special and modern interest upon his discussions of such subjects. Both we and Cicero live in times of ludicrous or tragic disparity between the standards which the great religions demand from their adherents and the infinitely smaller degree of goodness which most of those adherents, individually or banded together in governments or other associations, are able to achieve. Noting this the Stoic Panaetius, in mitigation of the austerities of his predecessors, had tried in the second century B.C. to bring their creed within reach of human and Roman possibilities. Cicero drew upon and adopted his writings, as well as upon the practical experiences of Scipio Aemilianus's circle to which Panaetius had belonged, in order to present a way of life which, although fine and idealistic, was nevertheless (in contrast to many of his aims in the political sphere) *possible*: for example for orators, to whose exalted art or science he believed – with some partiality, owing to his own interest – that philosophy, as well as law and history, was of the utmost assistance. 'One should know', he tells his son, 'what philosophy teaches, but one should live *civiliter*' – and this untranslatable word means: like a citizen, like an educated Roman, like a civilized man living as a member of his community. Among those of the world's codes of behaviour which are within the bounds of practicability, few if any deserve more careful consideration than Cicero's.

He would not have minded our calling attention to a note of vagueness, and even inconsistency, in his interpretation of the ultimate sanction – or of anything else. For the dogmatic creeds such as Stoicism had, by his day, become overlaid by a certain element of suspended judgement or scepticism, and that was particularly apparent in the New Academy (the descendant of Plato's Academy) of which Cicero regarded himself as a disciple. Accordingly, in spite of his admiration for the Stoics (an admiration regarded as legitimate by the New Academicians) he refused to subscribe wholeheartedly to dogmatic statements of their case. Cicero did not venture to claim certainty: the highest that he aspired to achieve was the most probable opinion. This could best be reached by considering and criticizing current theories in a spirit of free inquiry which should pursue the argument wherever it led. Let us not, certainly, lose our tempers; but 'let each man defend what he believes: judgement is free'.

Cicero – herein resembling all other Romans – was not a philosophical thinker of any marked originality. He, himself, dismisses his treatises as mere copies, but this modesty, which presents a notable contrast to his political self-estimates, does not do him justice. It is true that works such as *On the Greatest Degree of Good and Evil* (*De Finibus*) only aim at being impartial expositions of doctrine, but *On the State* and *On Laws* have some claim to be regarded as original works, and in *On Duties*, III (Chapter 4) his varied reading enables him to strike out some distance on his own. In general Cicero may be inscribed as an acute reader of a wide range of Greek philosophers, well equipped to extract from them what suited him, adding shifts of emphasis appropriate to his character, nation, and environment. In his capacity to do this, and to transform his conclusions into words (with astonishing rapidity), he is very much a figure for the twentieth century, the effective popularizer of knowledge and doctrine – a popularizer so skilful and successful as to leave modern portents such as H. G. Wells' *Outline of History* far behind: though the comparison is of limited application, because Cicero's popularizing was conducted with that great regard for tradition which was not a component in the brilliance of Wells, admirer though he was of Cicero's speeches and letters.[1]

Cicero's task was not an easy one; the Greek philosophies to which, with the added infusion of his own personality, he gave eloquent expression – far more eloquent than that of their original authors – contain much that was complicated and difficult, especially to unphilosophical Romans. Besides, Cicero wanted to present them accurately, for he had a keen regard for the truth. Though humanly eager to present his political actions as favourably as he could, in matters of the spirit he knew that no such concessions were possible, and in one of his lost works, the *Hortensius*, he praised the pursuit of truth as the worthiest aim of mankind and the source of real happiness.

There is no reason to doubt his own assertions of a lofty motive. One of its elements was a vigorous patriotism which helped to direct all his activities. 'Tully taketh much paynes,' said Sir Philip Sidney, 'and many times not without poetical helpes, to make us knowe the force love of country hath in us.' The wealth of illustrations from Roman history in Cicero's treatises recalls his conscious mission to make available to Rome the best and most applicable of Greek thought, and particularly the guidance to living designed by the Stoics and other later Greek schools. That, and his public life, were his principal contributions to the human cooperation in which he believed. It is true that there were also more pri-

1. Several more of these treatises are translated in *Cicero: On the Good Life*, Penguin Books, 1971.

vate and personal motives impelling him to write. One, at the peak period of his production (45–44 B.C.), was insomnia; 'the amount I write', he says, 'is beyond belief, because I work in the night as well since I cannot sleep.' Moreover at that same time he was working to distract his thoughts from the recent loss of his beloved daughter – and, in addition, to compensate for his enforced exclusion from politics. 'Could I have kept alive', he says, 'if I had not lived with my books?' But as in other authors the personal and the idealistic motives were interfused and reinforced each other.

The task he set himself was particularly attractive to Cicero because of his heartfelt admiration for Greek thought. Admittedly, there was a certain difference, as in the case of his religious utterances, between what he said in the law-courts and what he wrote in the study. When prosecuting Verres before a Roman audience it was advisable to affect a certain philistine vagueness regarding the Greek sculptors whose works the proconsul had stolen (Cicero's own grandfather had compared Romans to Syrian slaves: the better they knew Greek, the worse their characters). Yet even in speeches Cicero could drop this mask: his defence of the minor Greek poet Archias (though ostensibly concerned with the confirmation of his client's Roman citizenship) includes sustained and heartfelt praise of the intellectual life and its nourishment on Greek literature. In this passage, it is true, he first of all characteristically praises these cultured activities because of their practical, character-building, and so career-building advantages. But then he goes on to say (*Pro Archia*, 16):

Yet even if these great benefits were not apparent, even if the object of these studies were pleasure only, even so you must agree, I believe, that no other mental activity is so worthy of a civilized human being [*humanus, liberalis*]. All other pursuits depend on particular times or ages or places, but these studies are as stimulating for young people as they are a source of pleasure for old: they grace success, and they provide comfort and refuge in adversity. They are a delight in the home; they are no hindrance to public life; in the night watches, on our travels, on our holidays in the country, they give us companionship.

This was from a man whose naturally gregarious tastes, as well as his principles as a believer in human relations, made him unsympathetic to withdrawals from society. But he knew his practical debt to the superior culture of the Greeks; 'whatever I have achieved', he declares, 'I have achieved by means of the studies and principles transmitted to us in Greek literature and schools of thought.' This errs on the side of modesty, since the oratory to which he owed his public success, as barrister and statesmen, was largely due to his unequalled personal talent, developed within a Roman tradition of able speaking in a society where tremendous issues depended on oratory. Yet it is also true that he would never have scaled such heights without his training in Greek studies and particularly Greek rhetoric. He was not exceptional in this, seeing that the whole contemporary system of higher education was based on Greek theories of public speaking – the activity which was all-important to the Roman politician's career. Some of Cicero's finest works, particularly *On the Orator*, *The Orator* and the *Brutus*, are devoted to analyses of this institution and its history and techniques, which he approached with the liberal conviction that only the man of fine moral qualities could succeed as an orator and therefore as a statesman. As the Athenian Isocrates and the Roman Cato the Censor (p. 211) had already stressed, in this noblest of professions to have a well-stored mind was not enough.

A few notes on the principal Greek philosophical schools to which he refers may be of assistance. Towards the end of his treatise on *Old Age* (Chapter 5), quoting Greek beliefs in the immortality of the soul, Cicero cites two philosophers, Pythagoras and Plato.

PYTHAGORAS of Samos (6th century B.C.), the quasi-mythical leader of a strictly disciplined religious community at Croton in South Italy, believed in the transmigration of souls. He interpreted the soul as a fallen divinity confined within the body as a tomb, and condemned to a cycle of reincarnation as man, animal, or plant, from which it can win release by purity. When the historian Herodotus (*c.* 480–425 B.C.) writes of certain Greeks, 'some in former times and some in later', who believed in the immortality of the soul, it is thought that one of the earlier philosophers to whom he is referring is Pythagoras.

PLATO (*c.* 429–347 B.C.), disciple of Socrates (469–399 B.C.) and founder of the Academy, was influenced by this Pythagorean doctrine of transmigration. In the *Republic*, the *Phaedrus*, and especially the *Phaedo*, he deduces the immortality of the soul from his Doctrine of Ideal Forms. Dividing the soul into three parts – the rational, the spirited, and the appetitive – he regards the rational part (the soul in its true being as it is apart from mixture with the body) as immortal, i.e., existent both before birth and after death. Plato implies the eternity of reason, but it is doubtful to what extent he believed in what is now understood by 'personal immortality'. The *Dream of Scipio*[1] in Cicero's treatise *On the State* is a revelation of immortality adapted from Plato's *Republic* and other sources.

1. See below, p. 26, for its influence.

In certain of his other works not translated here, Cicero devoted himself to those speculations about the universe which had comprised the characteristic activity of Greek philosophers before Socrates. But, in this typically Roman, he followed with particular keenness the ethical preoccupations which Hellenistic philosophers derived from Plato – the inheritor of Socrates' interest in the human personality – and from Aristotle (384–322 B.C.). What – the Hellenistic schools had asked – in this new world of great states in which people felt terrifyingly alone, would make a man impervious to the hazards of fortune? What, that is another way of saying, is the supreme Good? Diogenes the Cynic (*c.* 400–*c.* 325 B.C.) held that the answer was to renounce all material possessions; but this was a solution unlikely to find favour among Romans. In the third book of his treatise *On Duties* (Chapter 4) Cicero, who is our oldest and most considerable source of information on post-Aristotelian philosophy, mentions the following additional Hellenistic schools which sought to provide answers:

The Cyrenaics, led by Aristippus (the grandson of a companion of Socrates), taught that the only proper aim is immediate happiness. Another philosopher to whom reference is made, Anniceris, who was probably a contemporary of Alexander the Great, provided a link between the Cyrenaics and a further non-moral school which Cicero finds equally unattractive –

The Epicureans ('The Garden'), founded by Epicurus of Samos (341–270 B.C.). Epicurus accepted the guidance of the senses, and believed that they indicate the supreme good to be happiness, which he mainly identified with the absence of pain and trouble. Cicero disagreed and also recoiled from Epicurus' belief that, the world being composed of material atoms obeying their own laws, there is no evidence for divine intervention or interest in human affairs. As a boy, however, Cicero had admired the Epicurean professor Phaedrus; and Cicero's close friend Atticus (p. 58) obeyed the Garden's injunction to shun public life (though he conspicuously contravened their further instruction to 'flee from all forms of culture').

The Stoics ('The Porch'), established in *c.* 300 B.C. by Zeno (335–263 B.C.), who since he came from Cyprus (Citium) may well have been at least partly Semitic in origin and culture. Zeno and his successors Cleanthes and Chrysippus taught belief in Divine Providence, and in Virtue as the Supreme Good – a creed of a new ethical urgency. Panaetius of Rhodes (*c.* 185–109 B.C.) of the 'Middle Stoa' modified the rigidity of this doctrine for Roman society by leaving room for imperfect virtue, 'progression *towards* virtue'. A further Stoic idea, that of the Law of

Nature (p. 12) which joins the human Brotherhood in the 'world-state' (*cosmopolis*), was adapted to Rome by Posidonius of Apamea in Syria (*c.* 135–50 B.C.). He identified the 'world-state' with the Roman empire; a summary of his book *On Duties* was in Cicero's hands while he wrote the third book of his treatise with the same name.

Cicero had studied under Posidonius, and before that under another distinguished Stoic Diodotus. The moral emphasis of Stoicism (when its dogma was toned down) was very acceptable to him, and indeed the basis of a great deal of his thought and feeling on such problems. But he found Zeno too mystical, and he humanized Stoic morality; we do not know enough about the 'Middle Stoa' to decide how far he modified its doctrines, and it is not always clear whether the Romanization of Stoicism is taken straight from Panaetius or comes from Cicero's adaptation of his views.

The Peripatetics (Peripatos – 'Covered Arcade'), the followers of Aristotle, expounded their master's science and philosophy and propagated his belief in 'the Mean', which Cicero, like Horace after him, admired as a doctrine of moderation. In admiring the Stoic view that virtue is the *only* Good, Cicero mentions, without entirely or finally rejecting it, the less urgent Peripatetic opinion – exemplified by his son's tutor Cratippus at Athens – that virtue is, if not the only Good, at least the best of Goods. But he scarcely recognizes the Peripatetics as a separate school, treating them as barely distinguishable, in some passages from the Stoics, and in others from the Middle and New Academy.

The Middle Academy. The Academy of the last three centuries B.C. claimed to be the heir of Plato's Academy; but Cicero knew little about its development before the Middle Academy, of which the leaders were Arcesilaus of Pitane (315–241 B.C.) and Carneades of Cyrene (214–129 B.C.). Influenced, like Arcesilaus, by the Sceptics – who, claiming to go back to Socrates' pupil Pyrrho (*c.* 368–270 B.C.), refused to admit that real knowledge could be acquired – Carneades introduced Rome to criticisms of Stoic and Epicurean dogmatism about life and philosophy; Cicero accepted this undogmatic approach.

The Fourth Academy of Philo of Larissa (*c.* 160–80 B.C.) and *Fifth* of Antiochus of Ascalon (*c.* 130–68 B.C.), teachers of Cicero, adopted a more positive attitude, seeking to select and blend together the good points of various schools. Their general aim was towards the modification of contemporary Stoicism in harmony with what was now regarded as the Academic tradition. This current tendency enabled Cicero, for all his enthusiasm for Stoic ethics, to claim that the Academy was nevertheless the school to which he belonged. It is sometimes suggested that Philo, as the less dogmatic of his two teachers, had the greater influence upon his thought.[1]

3

CICERO AS WRITER AND SPEAKER:
TRANSLATOR'S PROBLEMS

Cicero's combination of native oratorical and intellectual gifts with a very thorough education endowed him with every weapon that a pleader in Roman lawcourt, Senate, or Assembly could need.

> *You, most eloquent of Romulus' descendants,*
> *Those now living, or dead and gone before them,*
> *And those still to be born in future ages,*
> *To you, Cicero, gratefully Catullus*
> *Gives his thanks – he, the worst of living poets,*
> *Just as surely the worst of living poets,*
> *As you, Cicero, are the best of lawyers.*[2]

Cicero's gifts, whether they made him a conspicuously good man or not, enabled him to speak and write the unprecedentedly eloquent language which is the foundation of all subsequent European prose. An ancient critic, author of the essay *On the Sublime*,[3] sees his style in terms of combustion. 'Like a spreading conflagration,' he says, 'Cicero ranges and rolls over the whole field; the fire which burns is within him, plentiful and constant, distributed at his will now in one part, now in another, and fed with fuel in relays.' Augustus, coming upon one of his grandsons attempting to hide a work of Cicero that he had been reading, summed up the man for whose death he had been partly responsible not only as a patriot but as a master of notable words (the Greek *logios*) – as befitted an emperor who used Ciceronian clichés in his propaganda. Cicero was also a masterly anecdotist and wit (in whom a German scholar sees foreshadowings of the English sense of humour – although he was more ironical, with increasing effectiveness). These

1. The fourth section of this Introduction will say something about the enormous influence exercised on subsequent ages by Cicero's popularization of Greek philosophical doctrines.

2. Catullus, XLIX. For this English version (in the same metre) acknowledgements are due to Gilbert Highet, *Poets in a Landscape* (1957), p. 51.

3. It used to be attributed to Longinus, a well-known critic of the third century A.D., but is now usually ascribed to the first century.

manifold talents made him one of the most persuasive public speakers who have ever lived; this is conclusively proved by the successes that he achieved.

We are able to study this phenomenon by reading Cicero's fifty-eight surviving speeches, more than half his total output. Nevertheless, this aspect of his versatile genius is not the easiest for a twentieth-century reader to enjoy. In the first place many of his speeches (including unfortunately some of those habitually selected for use in schools) contain legal technicalities and references to contemporary minutiae that were not very important at the time, and are less so now. His private speeches (in addition to a great deal that is valuable) inevitably have their share of such esoteric obscurities. Instead, therefore, of specimens of these, I have included here two orations – those against Verres and Antony [1] (Chapters 1 and 2) – which possess an exceptionally great general significance for one of the main themes of this selection, Cicero's resistance to tyranny. But even these speeches – especially the former of them – requires a certain mental adjustment from the modern reader, who is generally not susceptible to oratory. There has never been a generation, in Britain at least (the situation is very different in, say, the Arab world or the West Indies), so unappreciative and suspicious of the sort of rhetoric of which Cicero was the master.

One of the translator's principal duties is to be readable: since otherwise he will not be read, and he will then have failed in his task of communicating the writer whom he has translated. And he will not at the present day be readable or be read, if he writes rhetorical English. This consideration adds, for a translator of Cicero, a new and special reason for believing the often-repeated assertion that translation is a task which cannot succeed. The linguistic as well as the other qualities of his speeches are truly daunting. 'A single page of them contains the results of more concentrated thought, active experience, and training in language than most modern speakers can command in a lifetime'.[2] Cicero's rhetoric is the product of his training in language; it is part and parcel of his style; leave it out, and you have lost one of the things he has been most admired for, and much else besides. Leave it in on the other hand, and, as I have said, you have lost something else – contemporary and readable English. There is no compromise solution to this dilemma. Since therefore I am not prepared to forgo the attempt to approach as

1. This decision should not obscure the fact that, apart from a few great lawsuits such as these, Cicero rarely appeared as prosecutor: see *Cicero: Selected Political Speeches*, Penguin Books, 1969, p. 29.

2. Gilbert Highet, *The Art of Teaching*, p. 99.

closely as I can to adequate modern English, I am obliged, with full consciousness of what the reader is losing, to forgo the rhetoric.

This decision, necessary though I believe it to be, will make any translator's task singularly vulnerable and exacting: for he has to deny himself precisely those rhetorical means by which Cicero himself captivated his contemporaries – readers and hearers alike – attuned as they were to his methods by native taste and Greek educational influences. Without these stimulations, the modern reader may well become uncomfortably aware of threadbare or irrelevant arguments – Lord Brougham remarked that only one-sixth of the speech defending Archias kept to the point – from which the orator himself, brilliantly haranguing a susceptible and emotionally charged gathering, was evidently well able to distract attention. In these circumstances the translator will have accomplished all that can be expected of him if, in addition to reproducing the Latin as readably as his respect for the original text permits, he manages to acquire just a little of the persuasiveness which was Cicero's peculiar gift – if, that is, his readers like Cicero's audiences go away believing that Antony and Verres are really as black, or at least almost as black, as he has painted them!

Yet even if the translator has somehow evolved a method of dealing with the speeches, he has by no means solved his whole problem. For there is a remarkable diversity in Cicero's style, ranging from the solemn rotundity of his oratorical perorations, through the pellucid but still formal rhythms of his treatises, to the various degrees of colloquialism in his letters. In general, the difficulties encountered by translators of prose have received much less recognition lately than those faced by translators of poetry, though the two sets of problems are different and equally absorbing. Each activity, for example, is faced with its own peculiar difficulties created by the Latin word-order. In prose and poetry this obeys different rules and customs; but in neither case can it be rendered into English without extensive transpositions. And the translator of Cicero, in particular, is faced by quite another problem as well. That is to say, he is easily lulled into an entirely misplaced confidence by the superficial resemblance of Cicero's language to a certain outworn kind of English:

> that easy Ciceronian style,
> So Latin, yet so English all the while.

When Alexander Pope wrote that, and even a good deal later, Cicero's 'abundant' and rhythmical prose was by no means alien to contemporary fashion. Now the situation has changed. The translator is still insidiously tempted to utilize these analogies with the English that used to be, and to produce a Ciceronian English. But this is unquestionably not the sort of English which is, or should be, written today. On the contrary, if contemporary readable English is to be written, these blandishments must be resisted and sentences cast in an entirely different mould; to take a single example out of many, a row of rhetorical questions is nowadays scarcely acceptable. In view of the strong temptation which constantly invites the translator to ignore the steady widening of such divergences during the past century and a half, it is in certain respects harder to attempt a version of Cicero than to translate from some language so alien that no such misleading analogies suggest themselves, such as Turkish.

The same seductive familiarities beckon in the case of vocabulary, and these too have to be kept at arm's length. *Res publica*, for example, though on occasion it can and should be translated 'republic', is more often better rendered as constitution, or government, or state, or nation, or country, or social system. I also mentioned earlier (p. 14) that a good deal of thought is needed before the right word can be found for *civiliter* – whatever this means in Cicero, it does not often mean 'civilly'. I then referred to an even more important word *humanitas* – the ideal which he exemplified himself and handed down to Europe. Now there are occasions, as one might expect from Cicero's views, when this seems to mean just 'humanity' – or at least humaneness, or humanism, or humanitarianism, or human relations, or knowledge of how human beings behave. But much more often quite a different English word has to be found. A recent discussion [1] offers a further series of possible equivalents for *humanitas* from the whole range of moral, intellectual, and social life, the whole process which civilizes a man and makes him a true man – kindliness, helpfulness, consideration for others, tolerance; the liberal arts, culture, and education; as well as those social graces of easy manners, wit, and urbane polish, which are mistaken by some for the main essence of Ciceronianism. When Cicero writes of *humanitas*, as he frequently does, it is only translatable by context; and although there is a strong Roman element in its total significance, the word is sometimes – like many other abstractions in Cicero – only translatable after it has been decided which of several Greek terms he had in mind when he was writing.

Indeed, the creation of such fruitfully comprehensive ideals as *humanitas* was partly due to Cicero's pioneer difficulties in adapting the smaller vocabulary of his native tongue to Greek philosophical *finesses* with

1. M. L. Clarke, *The Roman Mind*, pp. 135–9.

which it was unfamiliar. He invented the terms '*qualitas*' and '*quantitas*', and excuses the description of philosophy as '*moralis*'. But on occasion he employs vocabulary with a certain insouciant vagueness that does not facilitate the translator's task. The same applies to the structure of his writings. This is often inorganic, repetitive, and illogical; at times suggestive of the after-dinner monologues which, without their underlying seriousness, they might be. The casual development of one point or topic from another makes easy, attractive reading, but also makes it hard to follow some of the Greek arguments which Cicero is intending to reproduce.

Here the translator is in a dilemma: is he to fog the sequence of thought as effectively as, on occasion, Cicero does himself? At first sight it might seem to be his duty to do so – indeed, with distinguished exceptions, this has been the usual practice. But then the reflection recurs that Cicero held the attention of his readers by miraculous stylistic assets which are far beyond the reach of those endeavouring to translate him. Besides, he was writing (as indeed were a number of his translators) for readers of whom many already had some acquaintance with the arguments that he was placing before them. Perhaps then the translator ought after all discreetly to clear up, as best he can, a few of the more insignificant ambiguities along his path. He must not interfere with the construction of a work or with the order of ideas, but he may be justified in inserting a word or two here or there to clarify their sequence. This, it appears to me, is particularly necessary in the treatise *On Duties*; and if my version of that work seems to some readers not literal enough, I would ask them to consider whether the more literal character at which translations have customarily aimed has not made it unduly difficult to follow the sequence of thought.

4

THE FAME OF CICERO [1]

The influence of Cicero upon the history of European literature and ideas greatly exceeds that of any other prose writer in any language. In most of the literary, political, religious, ethical, and educational conroversies that have gravely agitated western mankind he has been passionately and incessantly quoted – usually by both sides.

Though his immediate following was not very extensive – for in-

1. For the dates of those mentioned in this section, see Index.

stance his younger contemporary Pollio thought his speeches exuberantly insincere – it was soon declared (by Livy) that only another Cicero could praise him adequately. He was canonized, as a model of superlative eloquence, character, and citizenship, by the greatest of Roman educationalists, Quintilian; and the satirist Juvenal, though mocking his poetry and his timidity, speaks of the Second Philippic as 'divine'.

Lactantius, known as the 'Christian Cicero', declared that in his treatises Cicero 'contributed a great deal of his own', and found *On Duties* adaptable to the needs of the Church; Ambrose's *On the Duties of Ministers* owes very much to the same source, and his *Epistles* deliberately imitate Ciceronian diction and form. For Jerome and Augustine Cicero symbolized the pagan culture whose vanities Christianity had rejected. Yet Jerome, in a dream, saw himself arraigned before the Seat of Judgement as more Ciceronian than Christian, and Augustine, though the *City of God* was written to oppose Cicero's conception of Providence, writes of his treatise the *Hortensius*: 'this book quite altered my affections, turned my prayers to thyself, O Lord.' [1] At that decisive moment of transition from the ancient to the medieval world the Fathers kept alive, and transmitted, the classical philosophy that they had learnt from Cicero: whose works thus became an important ingredient in Christian doctrine and scholastic logic.

Pope Gregory the Great, however, wanted to destroy his writings, since they diverted men's attention from the Scriptures. This heralded a period, during the last half of the first millennium A.D., when – though exceptions occur – there was a partial eclipse of Cicero's influence. From the eleventh century onwards, however, it rose again steadily. His idealized Republic, good sense, public spirit, and portrayal of a civilized community appealed to the rising urban peoples of the later Middle Ages – merchants, professional men, administrators – in their struggles for an independent, stable, and rational life. *On Duties*, almost as much as Augustine's *City of God*, now figured as a support for the Christian Faith and a guide for the development of the western mind. More and more readers felt profoundly attracted to Cicero, first as a writer of popular stories and anecdotes, and secondly as the plain man's interpreter of ancient thought: and medieval and modern philosophy owe him a great amount of its terminology. When schools grew in size and scope in the twelfth century, and systematic rhetoric was increasingly taught, a juvenile work by Cicero on rhetoric, *On Invention*, occupied

1. Certain of Augustine's views on the classics are translated in *Roman Readings* (Pelican Books), pp. 454 ff. For Quintilian's praise of Cicero, ibid., pp. 338–40.

a dominant place in education.[1] John of Salisbury, whose favourite Latin author he was, declared that Cicero would have been one of the greatest of the great, if his conduct had not fallen short of his wisdom. The typical medieval Cicero had formerly been the teacher of a flight from the active life, but now, when civic responsibility was again beginning to play a part in literary culture, St Thomas Aquinas could point to the Cicero of On Duties as sole champion of a life of activity.

By c. 1290 Italian versions of certain of his speeches had begun to appear, but his essays On Old Age and On Friendship were what contributed most largely to his reputation as a good, wise man. The same two works were likewise the chief Latin sources of the most important of love romances, the thirteenth-century Roman de la Rose. This begins, however, with an allusion to the Dream of Scipio in Cicero's treatise On the State – a Platonic revelation of immortality well-known to medieval writers from Boethius to Chaucer, who founded upon it his Parliament of Fowls; Cicero's Scipio Africanus became a hero to the later Middle Ages. Henry de Bracton, author of the first comprehensive treatise on English law, relied on principles derived, through Papinian, from Cicero's definitions of Natural Law. Dante described On Friendship as his chief philosophical guide, and the classification of sins in the Inferno (Canto XI) is based upon a passage of On Duties.

The astonishing outburst of creative vitality which dazzled the eye in the fifteenth-century Italian city-states was believed by the Italians themselves to be a rebirth, a Renaissance, of classical antiquity. Although there were no complete precedents for their own progressive vigour and feeling for abstract order, they found in the ancient classics many things which helped to stimulate their colourful and ebullient civilization: a sense of style and harmony, an individualistic belief in human achievements and potentialities (within the framework of the divine plan), a desire to be rational. One of the very strongest forces contributing to this Renaissance ideal, and through it to the whole intellectual, scientific, and social development of Western Europe, was the character of Cicero as interpreted by Petrarch. Though he was fired by him because of what was already existent in his own mind, the novel element in Petrarch's humanism [2] was his devoted determination to use Cicero as his guide in interpreting the present through the past: Cicero as the paragon of eloquence, the writer on friendship and civilized leisure, the

1. Also a treatise on the same subject To Herennius which was then believed to be by Cicero, but is now attributed to another, unknown, author writing in Cicero's youth.

2. Though this word was not coined until 1808, when it occurs in German.

delineator of an idealized Roman way of life, and, in particular, the stimulating thinker on moral questions – for Petrarch, though like later Italian humanists a devout Christian, preferred ethics to theology, and felt that salvation must come through right conduct. In this sphere – he believed – as in eloquence, Cicero was superior to Aristotle (now reaching the climax of his dominance in Italy), on the grounds that the latter, though more skilled in defining virtue, was less effective in urging its cultivation. Led by Petrarch, then, the Renaissance became, above all else, a revival of Cicero, and only after him and through him of the rest of classical antiquity.

After becoming devoted to Cicero (as well as to Virgil) as a young man, in 1333 Petrarch with much excitement read and transcribed two speeches which he had come upon at Liège, inaugurating a series of such 'discoveries' which added, dramatically rather than substantially, to the corpus of continuously inherited works. Then, in 1345 (two years after the establishment at Bologna of a Lecturership in Cicero and in Ovid's *Metamorphoses*), Petrarch rediscovered, in a library at Verona, Cicero's letters to Atticus, Quintus, and Brutus – with their self-revelations of their writer's political life. These at first came as a shock to him. Cicero's reappearance from philosophical retirement in order to resist Antony seemed madly rash to Petrarch who, although exalting – against medieval renunciations of this life – the desirability of renown (*fama*) won by inborn merit (*virtus*), himself lived in exile at Italian courts and as 'the hermit of Vaucluse', and was divorced from the public life of his native Florence.

The next generation of Italians, on the other hand, found this same patriotic responsibility of Cicero the fulfilment, not the negation, of his moral teaching: Cicero's experiences and arguments, between them, had laid the foundation for an age-long analysis of the conflicts between freedom and despotism. Florence was one of the last Italian city-states to remain free of dictatorial rule; and its Chancellor, Coluccio Salutati, who identified at Verona (and claimed to have learnt political lessons from) a manuscript of the *Letters to Friends* (1390), as well as Leonardo Bruni, professor at the same city and one of the founders of modern historiography, resembled Machiavelli and Guicciardini a century later in seeing their city as the heir to the Roman Republic and champion of individual liberties: a fact to which they attributed her cultural pre-eminence.

Cicero's ideal of the whole man, combining mastery of language (including invective) with a sense of public responsibility and a cultivated employment of leisure, humanized philosophical studies and also became the basic education of the Renaissance upper class, through the colleges of Guarino at Ferrara [1] and Vittorino da Feltre at Mantua. The former resembled a University department, but in the latter, with its pupils (drawn from a variety of classes) for whom knowledge of Cicero was the avenue to a political or diplomatic career, the roots of the English public-school system can be discerned.

In 1418 the Florentine humanist Poggio Bracciolini, himself a discoverer of manuscripts, visited England for four not very productive years. The great patron of letters Duke Humphrey of Gloucester, who possessed and presented to Oxford an influential library, unavailingly invited Bruni to England (c. 1433), where he enjoyed a high reputation as translator of Aristotle. In common with other Englishmen, Duke Humphrey also admired Guarino. The latter's pupils at Ferrara included William Grey (c. 1445–6), the later Bishop of Ely, in whose palatial library (as in Duke Humphrey's) Cicero occupied the main place; Grey's protégé John Free of Balliol, the leading fifteenth-century English humanist, who attributed his literary inspiration to Guarino's lectures on Cicero; Robert Flemmyng, who while at Padua had already transcribed On Duties, and John Tiptoft Earl of Worcester, the princely translator of On Friendship. Then Thomas Chaundler, pioneer of humanism at Oxford, was a fervent admirer of Cicero, from whose treatise On Duties he frequently quoted.[2]

Cicero's overwhelming reputation in the later fifteenth century is also illustrated by the early history of printing. Within the very first year in which classical books were printed (1465), On Duties was published twice, at Subiaco and at Mainz – the latter edition being the first book to print Greek works in Greek type – and Subiaco in the same year also published Cicero's treatise On the Orator, of which a manuscript had come to light fifty-four years previously. Before the end of the century, printers in Italy had produced more than 200 editions of Cicero. In 1481 Caxton published an English translation, from a French rendering, of On Old Age – very popular again in this and the next century – and also

1. Guarino himself attributed the popularity of Cicero in Italian schools to another humanist Gasparino da Barzizza, whose volume of model Latin letters was the first printed book published in France (1470).

2. The humanist Thomas Linacre and his pupil John Colet were guided by the Florentine Politian (critic of too meticulous Ciceronians) and Marsilio Ficino (founder of the Platonic Academy) respectively. The views of Vittorino da Feltre reached northern Europe through the Czech, J. A. Comenius, whose mission to England in 1641, to reform schools, was interrupted by the Civil War.

a version of *On Friendship*. This was an age of translation: the Renaissance view was that if great thoughts can be communicated – across whatever obstacles and difficulties – they will produce great thoughts. Yet Latin, untranslated, was the language of royal courts, chanceries, embassies, churches, and universities; its model was Cicero, and controversy raged concerning the desirability, or otherwise, of achieving an exact copy of his style.

The sixteenth century was the time when these influences spread massively northwards from Italy, to which royal courts elsewhere owed so much of their style, culture, and self-will. Between 1553 and 1610 there were sixty-three editions of *On Duties*, a figure equalled by no other book. To Erasmus this work seemed to embody every principle needed by a youth undertaking a public career; in spite of his *Ciceronianus* satirizing too pedantic an imitation of the model, he was more devoted to Cicero than to any other writer, and owed him much of his skill as a storyteller. Erasmus praised him for bringing philosophy within reach of the common man, and declared his moral doctrines to be more truly Christian than many discussions by theologians and monks. Martin Luther regarded his treatises as superior to Aristotle's, and Melanchthon described *On Duties* as a work of perfection; while another product of the Reformation, Polish Socinianism, was directly derived from Cicero. This favour was reflected in Protestant teaching programmes; yet *On Old Age* and *On Friendship* remained equally prominent in the curricula of Jesuit colleges. Montaigne, though he complained of verbosity in the philosophical essays, quoted Cicero 312 times, loved his eloquence and his letters, admired *On Old Age*, and derived from *On Duties* much of his emphasis on discovering and remaining true to one's own self. At the age of sixteen, Queen Elizabeth I had read nearly all the works of Cicero, of whose style her tutor Roger Ascham, like the preacher Richard Hooker, was a master.

Yet the most truly Ciceronian phase in England is not the Elizabethan but the Jacobean age; the increased efficiency of classical learning led to a more understanding admiration of Cicero's complex style. The dedication introducing the Authorized Version of the Bible is directly based upon his rhythms. Milton, whose prose is as deeply pervaded by Latinity as his poems, was another master of his rolling periods; though his own structure was looser, as befitted the far less inflected English language.

Edward Herbert, John Locke, and Bossuet owe a very great deal to Cicero's writings. 'A beautiful soul always,' said Montesquieu of him, 'when it was not weak.' Humanists, deists, believers in natural religion, rationalists, free-thinkers – all turned to his essay *On the Nature of the Gods*. 'I desire,' wrote David Hume, 'to take my Catalogue of Virtues from Cicero's *Offices* (*On Duties*), not from the *Whole Duty of Man*.' [1] Diderot was another admirer, and so was Voltaire. He praised *On Divination* for its attacks on superstition, declaring that 'Cicero taught us to think', especially in *On Duties* (p. 157); while his associate Frederick the Great, claiming 'infatuation' for Cicero – whose works he took on his campaigns – proclaimed the same treatise to be the best book on morals that had been or could ever be written.

Perhaps the periodic structure of Cicero's style is best reproduced in the eighteenth-century abundance of Samuel Johnson, William Robertson, and Edward Gibbon, who praised the orator's language as well as his freedom-loving spirit and 'admirable lessons', with their enlightenment concerning 'the public and private sense of a man'. The adaptation of forensic prose to Ciceronian rhetoric is illustrated by Burke: when Johnson was asked by Boswell if he thought Burke had read much Cicero he was wrong to answer 'I don't believe it, Sir', since Burke, whose attack on Warren Hastings explicitly refers to the *Verrines*, owes much of his balance, symmetry, and resonance to Ciceronian oratory. Chatham, Sheridan, and Fox again all echo in varying degrees the same elaborate rhythms; and the younger Pitt developed his oratorical powers through methodical exercises in translating them. Through the agency of such men Cicero's influence was stimulated in England by the House of Commons debates, as well as by the growth of trial by jury.

Kant, the youthful Schiller, and Herbart were all influenced by *On Duties*. John Adams, quoting Cicero extensively in his *Preface on Government* (1786), observed that 'all ages of the world have not produced a greater statesman and philosopher combined'; and Thomas Jefferson, though critical of Cicero's political life, infused the American Declaration of Independence with his Natural Law and 'unalienable' rights of man, and filled his own commonplace book with references to the *Tusculan Disputations*. [2] Meanwhile Cicero, long the model of spiritual dissatisfactions as well as of the 'establishment', was ever in the minds of young Frenchmen fired by the Revolution: Camille Desmoulins described *On Duties* as a masterpiece of common sense, Mirabeau based one of his speeches upon three of Cicero's, and the Girondin Louvet drew upon the orations *Against Catiline* for his speech against Robes-

1. Published 1659, ascribed to Richard Allestree and Dr Fell.

2. One of at least seven American towns called Cicero became the home of the gangster Al Capone.

pierre, whose reply, based on the speech *For Sulla*, earned him the accusation of comparing himself to Cicero.

Among those born at the turn of the next century Cicero still had powerful, though critical, supporters. Macaulay, though he deplored his 'girlish vanity' and egotism and accused the panegyrist Middleton of 'composing a lying legend in honour of St Tully', particularly admired *On Duties* – recommending his nephew Sir G. O. Trevelyan to read it while attending mathematics lectures. Cicero's cadences could still be detected in the speeches of Gladstone and – whether he knew it or not – Abraham Lincoln. Cardinal Newman regarded Cicero as irresolute and inconstant, but admired his campaign against Catiline: 'other writers,' he concluded, 'write Latin. Cicero writes Roman.'

During the nineteenth century, a good deal of his influence is still apparent in the patriotic nationalism of Germans, the public-school morality of the English, the taste for rhetoric among the French. Yet the survival, in this way, of individual elements in his many-sided personality was now often accompanied by unprecedentedly sharp critical reactions. Drumann, in praise of monarchy, had attacked his Republican politics with what was described as 'inquisitorial harshness, finical casuistry, and brutal inconsiderateness'. Then Theodor Mommsen, another admirer of Hohenzollern Caesarism, again deplored Cicero's Republicanism, and with it by implication not only the Junker aristocracy against whom his own assault was primarily directed but also the whole very different liberal tradition of European humanism which Cicero had so largely created – a significant development in the rise of imperial Germany. In England, J. A. Froude agreed with Mommsen, and Dean Merivale's damping epithets for Cicero are 'discreet and decorous'. While, as a whole versatile man, his merits far outweigh his defects, an age of specialization was bound to find fault individually with each of his various activities.

Since then Cicero's reputation has been lower than ever before. In particular, those who associate classical studies with the now suspect élite culture of the nineteenth century are inclined to misinterpret the practical, moral stimulus of his *humanitas* as the mere social elegance of an effete ruling clique, and so to underestimate the authentic belief in human brotherhood from which his hatred of men like Verres and Antony stemmed. Moreover, irreligious and religious people alike are discontented with his non-dogmatic attitude to divine intervention, misunderstanding his philosophical standpoint (p. 13); the former think he only dragged in Providence for the sake of conformity, whereas the latter, ignoring his traditional stimulus to the churches, are inclined to misconceive (as the Renaissance did not) his humanism as the atheism for which nowadays this word popularly stands.

Moreover, although during the present century a sharpening dislike of Caesarism in many quarters removed one of the chief reasons for attacking Cicero, his political compromises have, in the darkening political scene, continued to cause irritation. So, upon the same suspicion of insincerity, has his rhetoric, from which J. K. Huysmans sought to lead the readers of *À Rebours* (1891) towards the un-classical charms of later Latin. School-teachers have not, in general, followed his lead, but their persistence with Cicero has somehow lacked conviction, and in recent years, despite successes with other authors, they have largely failed to commend Cicero to their charges. Partly as a result, contemporary thought, literature, and criticism, even when they are aware of other classical writers, take little account of him. The year 1958, therefore, was the first of twenty centenaries of his death in which relatively few educated people concerned themselves with this absorbingly significant builder of western civilization – significant to its past history, and highly relevant also to the problems which it faces today.

PART ONE

AGAINST TYRANNY

CHAPTER ONE

ATTACK ON MISGOVERNMENT
(AGAINST VERRES · I)

There is great force about this speech. Cicero had not attained that perfect mastery of the whole art of rhetoric which he possessed at a later period. But on the other hand there is a freedom, a boldness, a zeal for popular rights, a scorn of the vicious and insolent gang whom he afterwards called the 'boni', which makes these early speeches more pleasing than the later.

THOMAS BABINGTON MACAULAY

Born in 106 B.C. at the central Italian hill-town of Arpinum (Arpino), Marcus Tullius Cicero received his education at Rome in rhetoric (public-speaking – the basis of higher education of the day) and philosophy, as well as in law which, combined with politics, was to be his career. After a courageous speech at the age of twenty-six, in which he criticized an agent of the dictator Sulla, he proceeded to Athens, and then to Rhodes, for more advanced courses in philosophy and rhetoric; he cured himself of a bad habit of shouting the most important passages in his speeches. At Athens he cemented his friendship with Atticus, whose name derives from his close association with that city. During the seventies B.C. Cicero embarked on the first stages of a Roman official's career – serving for a year in Sicily – and married his first wife Terentia, who bore him a daughter Tullia (their son Marcus was born about twelve years later).[1]

He also undertook a number of important briefs culminating in his first major triumph, against Verres. In 70 B.C. Gaius Verres, governor of Rome's oldest province Sicily during the past three years, was prosecuted at Rome by Cicero, as a result of serious complaints from the Sicilian communities. Since the restoration of large sums was demanded, his charge came before the court reserved for cases of extortion;[2] but it was widely understood to involve

1. For Terentia, Tullia, and Marcus, see below, pp. 65, 84, 157.
2. Established by the Calpurnian law of 149 B.C., regularizing procedure established twenty-two years earlier. Verres' rapacity caused fears at Rome that the Sicilians would cut their wheat production, and the Roman state lose its rich tithes.

accusations of general misgovernment, and the citizen rights of Verres were at stake. So, in an important respect, was the position of the Roman Senate. The dictator Sulla (83–79 B.C.) had arranged for the extortion court to be entirely composed of members of the Senate, whom the democratic reformer Tiberius Gracchus, half a century earlier, had debarred from this service – and source of patronage – in the hope of securing less lenient verdicts against Roman provincial governors (these being of senatorial rank) accused of dishonesty in their province. By the time of the present cause célèbre, Sulla had abdicated and died; the Senate, as strengthened by him, was still in command, but its general supremacy was beginning to weaken, since two men indisposed towards respect for its authority, Pompey and Crassus, had been elected consuls for the year. Cicero devoted all his efforts to the case, for a number of reasons. First, he genuinely hated dishonest administration; and, as he pointed out, 'the solidity of a state is very largely bound up with its judicial decisions'. Secondly, though himself a Senator since 74 B.C., he was consistently sympathetic to the 'knights' among whom he had originated, the non-senatorial class of business-men whom Sulla's reforms had excluded from membership of the court and from other positions of power; Cicero honoured the memory of his own unaristocratic fellow townsman and kinsman by marriage, Gaius Marius, who had been Sulla's enemy. Thirdly, this was a great opportunity for Cicero to defeat and supersede the most distinguished orator of the day, Quintus Hortensius, who was briefed by Verres and his noble supporters: 'luxurious without taste or measure, the advocate got a name for high living and dishonest earnings, for his cellar, his game-park, and his fish-ponds'.[1]

Taking advantage of the Roman custom by which a prosecutor was not required to confine his onslaughts to the particular charge he had brought, Cicero violently attacks Verres' entire record. The tactics of the opposition, on the other hand, show the hindrances with which a young lawyer had to contend. First, the opposition tried to put up a false prosecutor, Quintus Caecilius Niger – probably an ex-slave of the Caecilii Metelli (p. 45) – who was really on their own side. Then they attempted to occupy the court with another case altogether, in the hope that Verres' trial would be postponed until the following year, when more complaisant judges would be available. This endeavour, as well as others, is disposed of in the speech of which the written text (probably not very different from the version actually delivered) is translated here. Cicero was entirely successful. Without waiting

1. Ronald Syme.

for the second part of the trial – in which, according to the normal procedure (p. 57), the advocates should have tried conclusions with each other again – Verres retired to Massilia, in voluntary exile (a course open to a defendant up to the last moment before the verdict), and was then condemned to outlawry and a fine of twice, or two and a half times, the amount of his extortions.[1]

Subsequently, Cicero published a series of five further speeches containing the additional material which he had proposed to bring forward. The Senate duly lost its monopoly of the court's membership by a measure passed later in the same year (the Aurelian Law) which obliged them to share these duties with the knights and also with another, slightly less wealthy, class. Cicero cannot have been disappointed – in spite of the prologue to this speech in which he claims to speak as his fellow Senators' best friend.

JUDGES: At this grave crisis in the history of our country, you have been offered a peculiarly desirable gift, a gift almost too opportune to be of human origin: it almost seems heaven-sent. For you have been given a unique chance to make your Senatorial Order less unpopular, and to set right the damaged reputation of these courts. A belief has taken root which is having a fatal effect on our nation – and which to us who are Senators, in particular, threatens grave peril. This belief is on everyone's tongue, at Rome and even in foreign countries. It is this: that in these courts, with their present membership, even the worst criminal will never be convicted provided that he has money.

That, then, is the dangerous crisis with which your Order and your courts are faced. Speeches have been prepared, laws drafted, with the purpose of inflaming still further this hatred that already rages against the Senate. And at this very juncture Gaius Verres has been brought to trial. Here is a man whose life and actions the world has already condemned – yet whose enormous fortune, according to his own loudly expressed hopes, has already brought him acquittal! I, gentlemen, am his prosecutor, and the people of Rome are strongly and confidently on my side. To increase the unpopularity of your Order is very far from my intention. On the contrary, I am eager to remove your bad reputation – which is as much mine as yours. And the

1. Like Cicero himself, he was executed by the Second Triumvirate (43 B.C.); the story was that Antony wanted one of his works of art.

defendant whom I am prosecuting, being the man he is, provides you with your opportunity to recover the lost prestige of these courts and to regain the favour of Romans and the outside world alike.

Verres has sacked the Treasury.[1] He has devastated Asia and Pamphylia. His tenure of the city-praetorship was a record of robberies; and the province of Sicily found him an annihilating pestilence. Pronounce a just and scrupulous verdict against Verres, and you will keep the good name which ought always to be yours. Let us imagine, on the other hand, that his great wealth succeeds in undermining the conscience and honesty of the judges. Well, even then I shall accomplish one thing. For the general conclusion will not be that the judges failed to find a guilty defendant – or that the defendant lacked a competent prosecutor. On the contrary: the deduction will be that there are no good judges in the land.

I have a personal statement to make. On land and on sea, Gaius Verres has set me many traps. Certain of them I have avoided by my own precautions; others my loyal and vigilant friends have helped me to escape. But I have never felt so conscious of danger, never so apprehensive, as I do in this court today. The keen hopes that are invested in this speech of mine, the great crowd that is assembled here – these are disturbing enough. Yet it is not because of them that my anxiety is so great. No: what alarms me is the fresh series of criminal plots that Verres has laid. By their means he proposes to ensnare, at one and the same time, myself, yourselves, the presiding praetor Manius Acilius Glabrio: indeed the whole Roman people itself, and its allies, and the other nations of the world – not to speak of the Senatorial Order and everything for which it stands. The people who have reason to fear prosecutions, Verres assures his friends, are those who have only stolen just enough for their own use: whereas what he, on the contrary, has stolen is enough to satisfy many people! Nothing, he declares, is too sacred to be corrupted by money; nothing too strong to resist its attack. If the secrecy with which his projects are put into effect were comparable to the criminality which inspires their

1. As quaestor to Gnaeus Papirius Carbo, in Cisalpine Gaul, 84 B.C. Verres was in Pamphylia (to the south-east of the province of Asia) as legate to Gnaeus Cornelius Dolabella, governor of Cilicia, 81 B.C. He became city-praetor (see Appendix C, praetor) in 74 B.C., just before going to Sicily as governor. See also Appendix D (maps).

design, he might, to some extent or at some stage, have kept them from my notice. But so far, conveniently enough, his unbelievable unscrupulousness has been matched by a peculiar degree of folly. He has grabbed his wealth without any attempt at concealment; and he has let everyone see the schemes and intrigues by which he hopes to corrupt his judges.

Verres says he was only seriously frightened once in his life; and that was when I announced that I was going to prosecute him. He had recently arrived from his province. The blaze of virulent hostility, though itself far from new, had only just begun to rage around him – and he had struck a bad moment for bribing the court. That is why, when I requested a very brief period to make inquiries in Sicily,[1] he created a diversion by finding someone to ask for a duration two days shorter in order to make inquiries about another governor, in Achaia. I worked hard to complete my mission, but he had not the slightest intention that his nominee should carry out an equally painstaking and industrious job. Indeed, this Achaian investigator never even reached Brundisium! I, on the other hand, spent fifty days on a careful investigation of the entire island of Sicily; I got to know every document, every wrong suffered either by a community or an individual. Anyone could see, therefore, that this other investigator was not put forward with any genuine idea that his ostensible defendant from Achaia should be prosecuted. Verres' real aim was that the time I needed for the case against himself should be occupied by other business.

And now listen to this demented scoundrel's present intention. He realizes that my preparation and documentation of this trial have been thorough: and that I can consequently pin him down, in your hearing and before the eyes of the world, as a thief and a criminal. He sees the

1. The chronology of these events of 70 B.C. has recently (though without certainty) been interpreted as follows: 10 January, prosecution announced, 20 January, speech against Quintus Caecilius Niger (p. 36), 20 January–20 April (a period which in this year may have included an 'intercalary', i.e. additional, month after 23 February). Cicero's investigations (perhaps 20/25 days studying case in Rome, 15/20 in Sicily, 10/12 back in Rome), end April–early July abortive Achaian inquiry, between 14 and 26 July challenging of judges in Verres case, 5 August, this speech, 13 August, adjournment, mid-September, Verres retires into exile, 20 September, his conviction. For the Games during the later part of the year, see p. 48.

many Senators and knights who can bear witness to his misdeeds. He sees the crowds of Romans and allies whom he has grievously wronged. He sees also the numerous, highly responsible deputations, from communities in the friendliest relations with Rome, which have assembled here bearing the official credentials of their governments. Yet, in spite of these facts, his estimate of all right-minded men must indeed be low – and his belief in the ruinous corruption of the senatorial courts unbounded. Indeed he habitually asserts, in public, that his passion for money-making is justified – since he finds money such a wonderful protection! He has bought something which was by no means easy to buy – namely the date for his own trial: and now that this has been bought, it will be simpler to buy everything else in future! Meanwhile, granted that he cannot permanently evade his impending charges, he can at least avoid meeting them at the stormiest season.

Now if he had felt the slightest confidence in the strength of his case, or in any honest defence, or in the eloquence or reputation of his supporters, he would surely not have had to chase up and scrape together all these expedients. Nor would he have revealed his utter scorn and contempt for the Senatorial Order indicated by the arbitrary selection of this other Senator from Achaia to stand his trial first, so that Verres could have time to prepare his own defence.

I can quite clearly see his hopes and intentions in all this. It is true that with you on this bench, gentlemen, with Manius Acilius Glabrio as your president, I do not understand what Verres can hope to achieve. But what I do understand is this – and when the judges' names were challenged [1] the people of Rome came to the same conclusion: his hopes of salvation were based on his money and his money only. If this protection were removed, he was thoroughly well aware that nothing else could save him. For the greatest brains, fluency, and eloquence in the world could not even begin to defend the life this man has led. His innumerable vices and misdeeds have long since received passionate and unanimous condemnation from the entire world. I will leave unmentioned the shames and disgraces of his younger days, and turn to his quaestorship, the first stage of his official career. This is a story of Gnaeus Papirius Carbo having public

1. See last note. Under a law of the dictator Sulla both parties had a right to reject judges.

funds stolen from him by his own quaestor. Consul and commanding officer, Carbo was left stranded and defenceless; deserting his army, abandoning his province, Verres spurned the official lot by which he had been appointed – in violation of his sacred duty.[1]

Then came his tenure as provincial legate: upon Asia and Pamphylia, in their entirety, it brought disaster. Household after household, cities in great number, holy shrines one and all, succumbed to his depredations. Moreover, he revived and repeated, during this period, that original scandal of his quaestorship – this time at the expense of Gnaeus Cornelius Dolabella. As his legate and acting quaestor, he was guilty of criminal disloyalty to his superior, and brought deep discredit upon him. Indeed, not content with abandoning Dolabella at a critical juncture, Verres deliberately subjected him to treacherous abuse. Next came his praetorship at Rome. This was one long series of thefts from temples and other public buildings, and of legal cases in which properties were awarded or given away in contravention of every conceivable proper precedent.

But the most conspicuous and numerous instances and demonstrations of his criminality come from his governorship in Sicily. For three long years he so thoroughly despoiled and pillaged the province that its restoration to its previous state is out of the question. A succession of honest governors, over a period of many years, could scarcely achieve even a partial rehabilitation. While Verres was governor the Sicilians enjoyed the benefit neither of their own laws, nor of the Roman Senate's decrees, nor even of the rights to which everyone in the world is entitled. All the property that anyone in Sicily still has for his own today is merely what happened to escape the attention of this avaricious lecher, or survived his glutted appetites.

In Sicily, during those three years, not a single lawsuit was decided without his connivance. Inheritances from a father or a grandfather, however authentic, were cancelled if Verres said the word. Under a new and immoral ruling, the properties of farmers were robbed of countless sums. Allies of unassailable loyalty were treated as enemies; Roman citizens were tortured and put to death like slaves. Criminals of the deepest dye would bribe their way to acquittal, while men of

1. The quaestor was expected to behave like a son towards his governor, but in the civil war between the Marians and Sulla, Verres deserted his governor in order to change sides to the victorious Sulla.

impeccable honesty were prosecuted in their absence, and convicted
and banished unheard. Powerfully fortified harbours, great and well-
protected cities, were left open for pirates and robbers to attack.
Sicilian soldiers and sailors, allies and friends of ours, were starved to
death. Splendid, beautifully equipped fleets were squandered and
thrown away. It was an appalling disgrace for our country.

Then again, ancient monuments given by wealthy monarchs to
adorn the cities of Sicily, or presented or restored to them by victorious Roman generals, were ravaged and stripped bare, one and all,
by this same governor. Nor was it only statues and public monuments
that he treated in this manner. Among the most sacred and revered
Sicilian sanctuaries, there was not a single one which he failed to
plunder; not one single god, if only Verres detected a good work of
art or a valuable antique, did he leave in the possession of the Sicilians.

When I turn to his adulteries and similar outrages, considerations of
decency deter me from giving details of these loathsome manifestations of his lusts. Besides, I do not want, by describing them, to worsen
the calamities of the people who have not been permitted to save their
children and their wives from Verres' sexual passions. It is, however,
incontestable that he himself did not take the slightest precaution to
prevent these abominations from becoming universally known. On
the contrary, I believe that every man alive who has heard the name
of Verres would be able to recount the atrocities which he has committed. I am more likely, therefore, to be criticized for omitting many
of his evil deeds than to be suspected of inventing non-existent ones.
This great crowd which has gathered here today to listen has not, in
my opinion, come to learn from me what happened. It has come
to go over, with my assistance, events of which it is already well
aware.

Such being the case, this degraded lunatic has to discover a new
way of fighting me. To find a clever speaker who will oppose me is
not his real aim. He places his trust in no man's popularity, or prestige, or power. He pretends otherwise; but I see what his real aim is.
Indeed he makes no great secret of it. He puts forward an empty list
of aristocratic names of arrogant persons. The nobility of these names
does not damage my case – their notoriety assists it! These are the men
upon whose protection Verres pretends to rely. Meanwhile, however,
he has long been working at quite a different scheme; and I propose

to explain to you briefly, gentlemen, what his actual hopes and designs are.

But first I must ask you to note how he handled the situation in its early stages. He returned from his province – and then, instantly, he tried to buy up the whole panel of judges! [1] The attempt cost him a large sum. All went well according to the terms and conditions then laid down, until the day when the judges were challenged. On an earlier occasion the drawing of lots by which you yourselves were appointed had constituted a defeat for his hopes and a triumph for the destiny of Rome; and now, too, in the challenging of the judges' names, my labours again frustrated the unscrupulous tactics of the opposition. Consequently, after this failure, his agents abandoned their part of the bargain altogether.

The prospects were now excellent. The lists showing your names as members of this court were published for all to see; it was evident that no marks, [2] or colours, or smudges could be superimposed to affect the verdict. Verres, who had been so lively and cheerful, suddenly displayed gloom and depression. He now appeared to share the general belief among Romans that condemnation was in store for him. But then the next year's consuls were elected, and see, the same old intrigues are promptly under way again! Behind them are even larger sums of money: against your good name, and against the well-being of the entire community, the same insidious campaign is being conducted – and by the same men.

Gentlemen, I first learnt what was going on from a minute piece of evidence that came my way. Once it had aroused suspicion, this led me unmistakably to all the most secret designs of Verres and his supporters. Quintus Hortensius [3] had just been appointed consul-elect, and a large crowd was escorting him home from the Field of Mars. Caius Scribonius Curio happened to meet them. My allusion to him here should not be regarded as derogatory – on the contrary, for if he had not intended his words during this encounter to be repeated, he would have refrained from uttering them so openly and publicly

1. i.e. promised agents a large sum to secure his acquittal by bribing the judges.

2. Such as would have indicated violation of secrecy, bribery of judges, or distrust of the bribed by the bribers.

3. Cicero's chief opponent in this case (p. 36).

in front of such a large gathering. Even so, however, my comments on what he said will be in tentative and guarded terms: I want it to be clear that considerations of our friendship and his rank are very much in my mind. Well, near the Arch of Fabius, Curio caught sight of Verres among the crowd, and shouted congratulations to him. Although Hortensius had just been elected consul, he, and his relations and friends who were also there, received not one word from Curio; it was Verres whom he accosted, with embraces and assurances that he need not worry. 'I hereby proclaim,' he declared, 'that today's elections mean your acquittal!'

This announcement was heard by a large number of reputable witnesses, and was immediately reported to me – or rather, everyone who saw me told me without delay. The statement was variously regarded as scandalous or ridiculous. It seemed ridiculous to people who believed the case to depend, not on the result of the consular elections, but on considerations such as the reliability of witnesses, the factual basis of the charges, and the powers vested in the judges. Those, on the other hand, who could see further appreciated how scandalous this congratulatory utterance was, since it implied that members of the court were corrupt.

The highly respectable people whose discussions with each other and myself led them to the latter view argued that it was now clear for all to see how impotent our courts had become. Does a man one day regard his conviction as certain, and on the next procure acquittal when his advocate has become consul? If so, it can only be assumed that the present concentration at Rome of all Sicily and all Sicilians, of the island's entire business community and whole public and private archives will be regarded as totally unimportant – if the consul-elect so desires! And the charges, the witnesses, even the good name of Rome itself – of these, presumably, the judges will take no account whatever. Instead, all power and all authority is to be vested in one single individual.

Gentlemen, I shall speak frankly: this seemed to me a deeply disturbing situation. Every decent person was saying: 'Yes, Verres will escape you, but we Senators will lose our courts: for once he is acquitted no one could have the least hesitation in transferring them out of our hands.' There was universal distress – due not so much to this rascal's sudden gaiety as to the unheard-of congratulations offered him

by so highly-placed a personage. I tried not to show how upset I felt;
I did what I could to conceal my pain by looking calm and saying
nothing.

Then, only a few days later, the praetors-elect cast lots for their
offices, and the presidency of the extortion court went to Marcus
Caecilius Metellus.[1] And behold, it was reported to me that Verres
had again received warm congratulations. He even sent people to his
home to tell his wife the news! Here, in the appointment of Metellus,
was another development which obviously could not be welcome to
me. All the same, I saw no reason to find this allotment of duties particularly frightening. But certain persons, who regularly kept me informed, brought one fact to my notice. A Senator had conveyed to a
knight a number of baskets containing Sicilian money. But about ten
other purses were retained in the Senator's house – for an object concerned with my candidature for the aedileship! And one night, the
distributing agents[2] from the tribes were summoned to Verres'
house.

One of these agents, however, always felt in duty bound to help
me in any way he could. So the very same night this man visited me
and repeated what Verres had told them. He had begun by recalling
their generous treatment at his hands on an earlier occasion, when he
had been standing for the praetorship, and also at the recent elections
of consuls and praetors. Then he had at once gone on to promise them
any sum they chose to ask if they would block my election as aedile.
On hearing this, some of his listeners answered that they dared not
make the attempt, while others declared the scheme impracticable.

1. At this period the conservative patrician clan of the Metelli gained a large
proportion of the most important offices of state – as they had formerly under
Sulla, of whose party they were the nucleus and also in the latter part of the
previous century. There was also an earlier saying (p. 47), doubtfully attributed to the poet Naevius (c. 270–201 B.C.), 'it is fated for the Metelli to become
consuls at Rome'. The consul-elect, Quintus Metellus, was later known as Creticus for his brutal reduction of Crete, a pirate base (68–66 B.C.). Lucius Metellus became consul in 68 and died during the year. (See Genealogical Table on
p. 254.)

2. Candidates in a major election formed groups of supporters in each quarter of the city, paying them sums of money through an intermediary, who employed agents to distribute the money. On the present occasion the portion of
the Sicilian plunder sent to the knight was intended for the forthcoming elections to consulships and praetorships.

However, a stout supporter turned up from his own clan – Quintus Verres of the Romilian tribe. This choice specimen of the distributing-agent tradition, a pupil and friend of Verres' father, promised to do the job for 500,000 sesterces. Then a number of the others announced that they would take part after all. In the light of these developments my informant obligingly advised me to take every possible pre-caution.

Thus within a very short space of time I was faced by a number of extremely serious anxieties. My candidature for the aedileship was impending, and in this as well as the trial vast sums of money were mobilized against me. The trial, too, was imminent; and in trial and election alike I was menaced by those baskets full of Sicilian coin. Worries concerning the election made it impossible for me to con-centrate on the trial; and, conversely, the trial prevented me from devoting adequate attention to my candidature. What is more, there was no point in threatening the distributing agents with prosecution, since I was completely tied and pinned down by this trial – as I could see they were well aware.

That was the moment when I heard for the first time how Hor-tensius had requested the Sicilians to visit him at his home, and how they, on learning the purpose of this summons, had asserted their independence by refusing to go.

And now started my election. Like all the other elections of the year, Verres believed it was under his control. Round the tribes this portentous figure circulated, with his smooth and popular son, can-vassing and seeking out all the family's friends – that is to say, the distributing agents. However, the citizens of Rome noted and under-stood what was happening, and most wholeheartedly arranged mat-ters so that the man whose riches had not availed to undermine my honesty did not succeed any better in his attempt to keep me out of office.[1]

Once relieved from the grave anxiety of standing for the aedile-ship, I felt much less distracted and preoccupied, and began to devote myself wholeheartedly to researches and plans relating to this trial. And I discovered, gentlemen, that the scheme of my opponents was this: to postpone consideration of the case, by any available means, until Marcus Caecilius Metellus becomes praetor and president of the

1. It is not known whether Verres made such an attempt.

court. They favoured this course for two reasons. First, Marcus Metellus is extremely well-disposed to Verres. Secondly, not only will Hortensius then be consul, but his colleague will be Quintus Caecilius Metellus – whose close friendship with Verres has been clearly demonstrated by substantial preliminary indications of his support. These have already made Verres feel amply rewarded for his help with those centuries [1] which voted first in Quintus's election.

You expected me to say nothing about matters as serious as this? But when our country and my honour are in peril, you would be wrong to suppose that I did not place my duty and my obligations before everything else in the whole world.

Well, the second consul-elect, Quintus Metellus, now sent for the Sicilians; and, bearing in mind that another Metellus – Lucius – had become governor in Sicily, some of them put in an appearance. Quintus spoke to them in these terms: 'I am consul, one of my brothers is governor in Sicily, the other is going to be president of the extortion court; many measures have been taken to ensure that Verres will come to no harm.' I ask you, Metellus: if that is not corruption, what is? – using your influence, and a consul's powers of intimidations, and the authority of two praetors, to browbeat witnesses: in particular, these timid, crushed Sicilians. So, in support of this degraded ruffian, who is in no way a connexion of yours, you throw duty and dignity to the winds. One may well ask what you would do to help a man who was both innocent and your kinsman! You give people every encouragement to believe what Verres was saying about you. For he was quoted as declaring that, whereas the rest of your family attained their consulships 'by act of fate', yours was the product of his efforts!

That is to say, Verres will have on his side two consuls and the president of the court. His reasoning goes like this. 'For one thing, we shall avoid having Manius Acilius Glabrio [2] as president. He is too painstaking in his inquiries, and too jealous of his high reputation. And we shall also gain another advantage. One of the present judges is Marcus Caesonius, my prosecutor's colleague as aedile-elect. He is a well-known and experienced judge, whose presence on a panel

1. See Appendix C. The centuries which voted first influenced the votes of those which followed and therefore needed particularly generous bribes.
2. In the *Brutus*, Cicero describes him as lazy and careless.

which we might want in any way to corrupt would be highly inconvenient. For on an earlier occasion, when he was judge in Gaius Julius's court[1], the corruption of the proceedings horrified him into a public denunciation. But from 1 January onwards we shall no longer have Caesonius as one of the judges.

'Nor shall we have the just and scrupulous Quintus Manlius and Quintus Cornificius,[2] since they will have taken office as tribunes of the people. Publius Sulpicius, too – another judge of strict and lofty principles – must take up his post on 5 December. Then again Marcus Crepereius, whose family of knights has so vigorous a tradition of public service; and Lucius Cassius, of a house which cherishes the most exacting standards in judicial as in all other matters; and that religious, conscientious person Gnaeus Tremellius Scrofa – these three personalities of the old stamp have been appointed to military tribuneships, and after 1 January will not be judges any longer. We shall also require a supplementary ballot to fill the place of Marcus Caecilius Metellus, since he will be presiding over this very court. That is to say, from 1 January onwards the president and almost the entire membership of the court will have changed. However imposing, therefore, may be the prosecutor's threats, however keen popular expectations of the outcome, we shall be able to frustrate them in any way we wish and choose!'

Today is 5 August. You met at one-thirty p.m.: they do not regard today as counting at all. In ten days' time are Pompey's Votive Games.[3] Those will take fifteen days; and then the Roman Games fol-

1. This court in 73 B.C. had convicted Statius Albius (or Abbius) Oppianicus, with two others, of attempting to poison his stepson Aulus Cluentius Habitus, whom in 66 B.C. Cicero was to defend against charges of poisoning Oppianicus (who had died in exile) and of bribing Gaius Junius's court – of which Cicero himself however, in the present case, has nothing good to say.

2. A 'new man', became praetor in 67 or 66. Publius Sulpicius was elected to a quaestorship for 69. Gaius Tremellius Scrofa was an agriculturist and a friend of Varro.

3. Reference is made to the following Games: *Pompey's* (last half of August, duration fifteen days), to celebrate his successful conclusion of the civil war against the ex-Marian Quintus Sertorius in Spain in 72 B.C.; *Roman* (4–19 September), annual Games originally promised to gods in event of Roman victory, gradually extended in scope: *Victory* (27–31 October), instituted by Sulla to commemorate his victory over the Samnites (Marians) in 82 B.C.; *Plebeian*, 4–17 November.

low at once. So before having to reply to my charges they count on almost forty days' grace. And even then they reckon, by making speeches and pleading other engagements, to prolong the case without difficulty until the Victory Games – which are immediately succeeded by the Plebeian Games. After all that, there will be no days, or very few, left for conducting the trial. They count on these circumstances to damp and exhaust the prosecution: and then the whole case would come up afresh before Marcus Caecilius Metellus when he becomes president of the court. As for him, if I had doubted his honesty, I should not have allowed his continuation as a judge. Nevertheless, while a decision on this case is pending, I shall feel happier to have him as a judge than as president, and to let him dispose, on oath, of his own voting-tablet rather than see him dispose, unsworn, of other people's votes.

Now, gentlemen, I must ask you what you think I ought to do. I am convinced that your unspoken advice will correspond with what my own understanding tells me is the necessary course. If I employ for my speech the whole time allotted by law, then certainly my industrious efforts will not go altogether unrewarded; for my conduct of the prosecution will at least demonstrate that no one in human memory can ever have come to court better equipped, more thoroughly prepared, and more vigilantly watchful. But there is a serious danger that amid such praises for my laborious endeavours the defendant will slip away!

What, then, can be done? The answer does not seem to me particularly complicated or obscure. I shall have to save up for another occasion the harvest of compliments which might have been earned by a continuous speech. Instead, my attack on Verres must concentrate on the evidence of records and witnesses, and the letters and other testimonies of individuals and public bodies.

Hortensius, you are the man I shall have to contend with all the time. I must speak openly. If I supposed that your opposition to me in this trial would consist of a speech refuting my charges against your client, then I too would devote all my energies to a comprehensive statement of those charges. Instead, however, you have chosen to fight me by methods more compatible with your client's critical predicament than with your own character. Consequently, I am obliged to find some way of counteracting the tactics you have adopted. Your purpose is to postpone your speech until after the two Games; mine is to reach the adjournment[1] before the first of these Games begin. And whereas the ingenuity of your plan will not fail to be appreciated, no one will question that my response has taken the only possible form.

You are the man I have to contend with, I had begun to say. What I meant was this. When the Sicilians had prevailed upon me to take on this case, I felt it a fine compliment that their experience of me as a decent, honest man should have encouraged them to put their trust in my good faith and set me this strenuous task. Later, however, after I had set to work on the brief, I formed a more ambitious purpose: namely, to demonstrate to the people of Rome how I feel for my country. To bring into a court a man already convicted by unanimous public opinion did not, in itself, commend itself to me as an achievement worth so much hard and rigorous toil. But what persuaded me, Hortensius, was your own persistence, for this utter scoundrel's support, in unendurably domineering behaviour, and in the grasping propensities that you have displayed at a number of trials during recent years.

One thing, then, that has influenced me is this gloating of yours over your tyrannical dominance in our courts; and another is the evident existence of men who feel not the slightest shame or disgust for their repulsive and outrageous behaviour. On the contrary, they seem to court, deliberately, the hatred and detestation of every Roman. For these reasons I can declare with all emphasis that the burden I have undertaken, whatever the labours and perils it may bring me, will summon up – as it should – every effort that I can command, to the utmost capacity of my strength and my manhood.

The pressure of a few unscrupulous rascals has discredited our courts and plunged the entire Senatorial Order into crisis. That is why my attack on these scoundrels will be implacable. I declare myself their ruthless, irreconcilable, unrelenting enemy! And I claim a duty – I demand it as my own. I am referring to what I propose to do in that place where the people of Rome have appointed me, from the first of next January, to collaborate with them in the affairs of our state and its defence from criminal foes. I will tell you of the grandest and most glorious spectacle which I promise the people of Rome as their aedile.

1. For at least one day – a compulsory feature of the procedure (see below, p. 57).

Regard this as my advance notice, my warning pronouncement. It is addressed to all who habitually place, or accept, or promise bribes; who act as go-betweens or intermediaries in attempting to corrupt judges; and who have offered to lend their influence or their unscrupulousness in such a cause. I proclaim to you all: in the case now being tried, keep your hands and minds clear of this detestable crime!

From January onwards, Hortensius will have a consul's rank and power. I, on the other hand, shall be an aedile, that is, little more than a private citizen. Yet the programme which I am now promising you is of such significance, and will be so welcome and agreeable to Romans, that in opposing me on an issue of this magnitude even the consul himself will seem of less importance – if this were possible – than an ordinary citizen.

For I am going to disclose to you, with full corroborating evidence, the whole story of all the abominable crimes which have been perpetrated in the courts during these ten years since they were first transferred to the Senate. Gentlemen, here are the facts which I am going to reveal to the people of Rome. While the Order of Knights controlled the courts, for nearly fifty years not one single knight who was a judge incurred the slightest suspicion of allowing his verdict to be influenced by a bribe. Yet after the courts had been transferred to the Senate – after you had escaped,[1] every one of you, from the Roman people's control – Quintus Calidius,[2] on being found guilty, was able to remark that no ex-praetor could honourably be convicted for less than three million sesterces!

Again, when the Senator Publius Septimius Scaevola was condemned by an extortion court presided over by Quintus Hortensius – then praetor – his fine had to be expressly adjusted because, while member of a court, he had accepted a bribe. The successful prosecutions of other Senators, Gaius Herennius and Gaius Popilius Laenas, for stealing public funds, and of Marcus Atilius Bulbus for high treason, likewise clearly established that they had been bribed while

1. One of the tribunes' powers removed by Sulla had been their right to arrest and bring before an Assembly or throw into prison any offender of senatorial rank.

2. Governor of Spain, condemned 77 B.C.; Publius Septimius Scaevola, condemned 72 B.C. (in his speech *For Cluentius* Cicero tries to take back the present reference); Gaius Popilius Laenas subsequently went into exile at Nuceria (Campania); Marcus Atilius Bulbus, condemned 73–71 B.C.

serving as judges. Moreover, when Gaius Verres presided as city-praetor over the drawing of lots for judgeships, certain Senators [1] actually pronounced against a defendant and convicted him without a hearing! Whereas another judge of senatorial rank accepted money from the defendant to bribe his colleagues – and simultaneously accepted a further sum from the prosecutor to secure a verdict of guilty!

A further outrage, which has had a deplorable effect on the position of our entire Order, I have no words strong enough to denounce. In the trial to which I refer, though the judges had voted under oath, their tablets proved to display markings in different colours! This happened in *our* country – and it happened under a regime of sena-torial control over the courts. From myself, I promise you, every such scandal will receive attention of the most thorough and unremitting character.

You can imagine, then, how I shall feel if I discover that the same kind of criminal irregularity has occurred in the present case! In this connexion I must record a fact which many witnesses can corro-borate. When Gaius Verres was in Sicily, a number of people heard him saying this sort of thing on various occasions: 'I have a powerful friend! Whatever I steal from the province, I am sure he will protect me. My intention is not just to make money for myself: I have mapped out the three years of my Sicilian governorship like this. I shall consider myself to be doing nicely if I can earmark one year's profits for my own use, the second year's for my protectors and coun-sel, and the whole of the third year's – the richest and most lucrative – for the judges who try me!'

This reminds me of a remark I made before Manius Acilius Glabrio recently, when the judges for this case were being challenged – and I noticed that my words made a profound impression on the Romans assembled for the occasion. I asserted my belief that, one of these days, communities from the provinces would send deputations to the people of Rome requesting that the extortion law and its court should be abolished. For if no such court existed, they suppose that each governor would only take away with him enough for himself and his

1. Gaius Fidiculanius Falcula and others were charged with this in the Oppi-anicus case (p. 48); 'another judge' is believed to have been Gaius Aelius Staienus, in the same court.

children. At present, on the other hand, with the courts as they are, a governor takes enough for himself, and his protectors, and his counsel, and the president of the court, and the judges! In other words there is no end to it. A greedy man's lust for gain they could satisfy, but they cannot afford a guilty man's acquittal. How peculiarly glorious our courts have become, how scintillating is our Order's prestige, when Rome's allies pray that the courts which our ancestors created for their benefit should be struck out of existence!

Besides, would Verres ever have been so optimistic unless he, too, had absorbed this same deplorable opinion concerning yourselves? His evident agreement with this view ought – if possible – to make you hate him even more than other Romans do: seeing that in greed, criminality, and perjury he regards you as his equals.

In God's name, gentlemen, I pray you to devote all your care and all your foresight to facing this situation. It is evident to me, and I give you solemn warning, that heaven itself has vouchsafed you this opportunity of rescuing our entire Order from its present unpopularity, disgrace, ill-fame, and scandal. People believe that strictness and good faith are not to be found in our courts – indeed, that the courts themselves no longer have any reality. So we Senators are scorned and despised by the people of Rome: long have we laboured under this painful burden of disrepute. When Romans were so eager to give the tribunes back their powers, that was the only reason. The ostensible demand was for a restitution of all their powers, but it was really the courts that the people were after.

Quintus Lutatius Catulus,[1] whose wisdom and nobility are so pre-eminent, was well aware of this. Pompey, renowned and courageous man that he is, had moved [2] that the tribunes' powers should be restored to them. Then Catulus was called upon to speak. He immediately declared, with great effect, that the Senators were exercising their control of the courts in an immoral and criminal fashion; and that if only, while acting as judges, they had seen fit to live up to

1. Consul 78 B.C., moderate conservative; for many years leader of the Senate. A relative of Quintus Hortensius.

2. Earlier this year (70 B.C.) as fellow-consul with Marcus Licinius Crassus. His first public speech was made outside Rome because he had not yet laid down his military command (after the defeat of Sertorius, p. 48, and of the slave revolt of Spartacus) and could therefore not make an electoral speech within the walls.

Rome's expectations, the tribunes' loss of their powers would have
provoked no such regrets.

Again, when Pompey himself, as consul-elect, was making his first
public speech outside Rome, he responded to the general demand by
proclaiming his intention to give the tribunes back their rights. On
hearing this, his audience duly expressed their satisfaction and grateful
approval; but only in a murmur. Later in the same speech, however,
he declared that Roman provinces had been devastated and ravaged
by their governors, that the conduct of the extortion courts was outrageous and criminal – and that he proposed to take vigorous action
to put a stop to this. At that point, the people signified its approbation
not by a murmur but by a roar.

Their eyes are upon you now. They are watching to see how far
each of you means to act in accordance with the demands of our conscience and the law. They note that since the time when the tribunes'
powers were legally restored[1] only one Senator has been found guilty:
and he was a man of negligible resources! Certainly, they do not
criticize his condemnation – but they find no great reason for high
praise. For honesty is not particularly virtuous when there is no one
with the ability or ambition to corrupt it. On the other hand your
verdict upon the present defendant will decide another verdict also:
and it is upon yourselves that this will be pronounced – by Rome. For
here is the man, and here is the case, that will provide an answer to
this question: will a court of Senators convict a guilty man if he is rich?

The defendant has only two characteristics: his appalling record,
and his exceptional wealth. If, therefore, he is acquitted, the only
reasons to which this decision can justifiably be ascribed are the worst.
For it will be inconceivable that your leniency towards his numerous
and abominable outrages could have been prompted by any personal
liking, or family tie, or any good deed he might have done on other
occasions, or even by any bad quality which he possessed in only a
mild form. And finally, gentlemen, the facts that I shall be presenting
to you in this case will be so notorious and well-attested, so glaring
and incontrovertible, that no one could possibly attempt to make you
acquit Verres as a personal favour.

1. Earlier this year by a law sponsored by the two consuls; this removed the
disabilities (other than their exclusion from the courts) which Sulla had imposed.

I have a definite and methodical plan for tracing and disposing of every scheme that he and his friends may launch. I shall handle my prosecution in such a way as to make every one of their intrigues manifest to the ears of the world, and to the eyes of the people of Rome. The shameful discredit, which for years has been so damaging to our Order, you have been granted the power to blot out of existence. Ever since these courts were allotted their present composition, it is generally agreed that they have never had such a distinguished and impressive panel of judges as is sitting today. If things go wrong with this court, any proposal to search for other and more suitable Senators as judges will be unanimously rejected as a solution, since they could not be found. Instead, the general conclusion will be that our judges must be sought from another Order altogether.

So I begin, gentlemen, by begging heaven to fulfil this hope and prayer: that, apart from the one person whose rascality has long been evident, this court shall contain not a single dishonest man. And secondly, gentlemen, I assure you, and I assure the people of Rome, that if there do prove to be other malefactors here, I will sooner lose my life itself, so help me God, than fall short in the vigour and perseverance needed to punish their wickedness.

So upon any such scandal, at the expense of whatever labour, peril, and hostility to myself, I have sworn to bring drastic retribution. That must be after its perpetration. You on the other hand, Manius Glabrio, can employ your wisdom, prestige, and industry to prevent such a scandal from happening at all. Lend your support to our courts – let justice, honesty, principle, and conscience be your cause! Stand for the interests of the Senate – help it to surmount this test, and so to win the satisfied approval of all Romans!

Think of the position you occupy; of your duty to Rome. Think also of the debt you owe your ancestors. Remember your father's Acilian Law [1] – the law which provided excellent courts and just judges to protect our people from extortion. Surrounded by splendid precedents such as these, you are in no position to forget your family's renown. Day and night, you cannot fail to remember your courageous father, your wise grandfather, the noble father of your wife. Fight these scoundrels with your father's keenness and energy; borrow the

1. 123 or 122 B.C.: made the knights judges in extortion cases. This was one of the laws which Sulla had repudiated.

foresight of your grandfather Publius Mucius Scaevola,[1] and use it to steer clear of the traps which lie in wait for all your reputations. Rival the perseverance of your father-in-law Marcus Aemilius Scaurus: let no one undermine the firmness and accuracy of your judgement. And then the people of Rome will see that a select panel of judges, under an honest and scrupulous praetor, is more likely, because of a defendant's wealth, to damn him (if he is guilty) than to set him free on that account.

I am determined to prevent a change of president or judges in this case. When the consul-elect's slaves took the unparalleled course of summoning the Sicilians collectively, they refused to go: I do not propose to allow the trial to be delayed until they can be commanded to attend – by the lictors of consuls in office. Once these unfortunate people were Rome's allies and friends, now they are its slaves and suppliants. Their enemies will use their official powers to deprive these Sicilians not only of their rights and everything that they possess, but even of the opportunity to protest against the losses that have been inflicted upon them.

Nor have I the slightest intention of permitting the other side forty days' respite [2] after I have presented my case. During that length of time, the charges would be forgotten. Crowds from all parts of Italy have assembled here and now in Rome, to attend the elections, the Games, and the census. A postponement of the decision until after they have gone I shall not tolerate.

I am convinced, gentlemen, that this trial will bring you either great popularity or great discredit. To me it will bring much toil and anxiety. But it should also provide the entire population with a chance to understand the procedure, and to memorize what each speaker will be saying.

I shall call my witnesses at once. This is no novelty; it has been done before, by men who are now among our national leaders.[3] But where

1. Consul 133 B.C., chief priest 123; Glabrio's maternal grandfather. Marcus Aemilius Scaurus was consul in 117 and 115.

2. During Pompey's Votive Games and the Roman Games (p. 48).

3. Lucius Licinius Lucullus, commander in the East and conservative enemy of Pompey, and his brother Marcus (M. Terentius Varro Lucullus) when they accused the augur Servilius (or a certain Marcus Cotta) of responsibility for their father's death. (Neither of them was a good orator, which may account for their choice of this procedure.)

you will find a certain innovation[1] is in my method of handling these witnesses. As I come to each charge in turn, I shall state it in full; I shall go on to cross-examine, argue, and plead in proof of it; and then I shall call witnesses to that particular charge. So the only deviation from customary routine will be this: generally witnesses are not produced until after the conclusion of all the speeches, whereas I am going to call those relating to each individual charge as it is dealt with.

Under this procedure, my opponents will have the same opportunities as myself for cross-examining, arguing, and discussing. Anyone who misses the usual continuous speech for the prosecution will have what he wants at the second stage. Meanwhile, he must appreciate the necessity for my present programme, which is adopted as a counter-measure to the other side's intrigues.

In the first stage of the trial, then, my charge is this. I accuse Gaius Verres of committing many acts of lechery and brutality against the citizens and allies of Rome, and many crimes against God and man. I claim that he has illegally taken from Sicily sums amounting to forty million sesterces. By the witnesses and documents, public and private, which I am going to cite, I shall convince you that these charges are true. Indeed, you will conclude that even if I had been allowed entire days, all the time I wanted, for the presentation of my case, no long speech would have been necessary. At present I have no more to say.

1. According to the normal procedure for the first part of a trial, the prosecutor opened with a long speech, which was answered by a long speech for the defence; speeches by juniors may have followed. Only then was it customary for the witnesses to give evidence – first for the prosecution, then for the defence. It is not immediately clear *how* the modification of procedure proposed by Cicero would necessarily shorten the total duration of the trial, but perhaps he foresaw that the early witnesses (to be heard, incidentally, at a time when there were many summer visitors at Rome (p. 56)) would be so damning that Verres would quit: as in fact happened, so that the second part of the trial, which normally followed after the adjournment and was again introduced by long speeches on both sides, never took place. Moreover, if there was no legal limit to the length of time which could be spent on the customary long, continuous speeches, Cicero may have believed it useful to abandon these so as to prevent the defence from spinning theirs out to an inordinate length.

CHAPTER TWO

CICERO'S LIFE AND LETTERS
(SELECTION FROM HIS CORRESPONDENCE)

It is probable that Cicero is the greatest of all letter-writers. The importance of his matter, the range of his public and private interests, the variety of his moods, his facility in expressing every shade of sense and feeling, the aptness of his quotations, above all his spontaneity, have never in combination been excelled or equalled.

J. A. K. THOMSON (1956)

From the pen or (more often) dictation of Cicero more than 800 letters, dealing with an enormous variety of subjects, have come down to us. Since nine-tenths of these letters were not intended for publication, they give an astonishingly frank and authentic picture of their writer's character: he was not only an indefatigable correspondent, but uniquely articulate about himself. 'I saw a complete picture of you in your letter,' says his brother Quintus, and Cicero's own comment is: 'a letter does not blush'. His talent for self-revelation means that we know more about him than about any other ancient personage, and almost more than about any other historical or literary figure of any date whatsoever. Furthermore, these letters are our principal – very often our only – source of knowledge for the events of this decisive period in the history of civilization.[1]

In the form in which we possess them, there are sixteen books (each containing numerous letters) addressed to Cicero's friend Atticus, sixteen containing letters to other correspondents (Ad Familiares, 'To his Friends'), three to his brother Quintus, two to Brutus; some thirty-five other books of his letters seem to have been known in antiquity but have not survived. Cicero often sent people copies of letters which he had received from others, and this fortunate habit has preserved 99 letters from his various correspondents; a few of them will be included here. But his prolonged exchange with Atticus, this 'conversation between the two of us', has come down in

1. For Cicero's epistolary style see p. 70; for his dictation, p. 75; for the significance of the epoch, p. 7; for Atticus and Quintus, pp. 68, 71; for the publication of the letters, p. 75.

one-sided shape: 'I talk to you as I do to myself,' he is assured by Cicero, who 'so as not to miss a day' would compose him a note even when there was nothing to tell, and sometimes wrote him three letters within twelve hours. Atticus, on the other hand – who survived him and by no means shared his desire for self-revelation – ensured that his own replies (other than a few tantalizing extracts and echoes) should not appear in the collection. However, he and the orator's secretary Tiro (p. 75) preserved Cicero's own letters for posterity, and at least half were published while the secretary and Atticus were still alive.

The remarkable abundance and variety of the letters that such men sent to one another bear witness to a society which, now extending unbroken over an enormous area, depended largely upon written communication. There was not yet a regular postal service, but leading Romans entrusted their letters to travellers or employed their own couriers, who could cover fifty miles a day (two letters written by Caesar in Britain to Cicero took twenty-six and twenty-eight days to arrive). Letters were normally written with reed pen and ink on papyrus; the pages were pasted together to form a roll, which was then tied with thread and sealed. But there were also many briefly scribbled notes, and these were scratched with a metal stilus on wax-covered folding tablets which the recipient could erase in order to reply on the same wax.

The earliest of our surviving letters of Cicero dates from 68 B.C., the thirty-eighth year of his life, two years after his successful prosecution of the corrupt governor of Sicily, Gaius Verres (Chapter 1). Then, in 63 B.C., he attained the climax of the Republican hierarchy, the consulship. That was an outstanding achievement, at this time, for a man from a small-town family which had never even produced any Senators, much less a consul; nobody without Senators among his ancestry had been consul for the past thirty years. Yet Cicero became consul, and while holding that office, by intense political activity, inspired amateur espionage, and brilliant speech-making, he achieved what he was always to regard as the greatest of his services to Rome,[1] the unmasking and suppression of the conspiracy which the savage, impoverished, aristocratic anarchist Catiline was about to launch against the Republican regime. The first of his Catilinarian Orations compelled the chief conspirator to flee from Rome; soon afterwards he was cornered near Pistoria, and died fighting. But before that Cicero had arrested five of Catiline's principal supporters – after they had been implicated in the plot by

1. In this selection, however, I have preferred to include one of his speeches against Verres, as dealing with a more fundamental problem – bad government.

information received from Gaulish visitors to Rome – and had caused them to be executed without trial. Now, before this was done, the Senate had agreed to the executions; they were chiefly prompted to do so by the austere, crafty, hard-drinking Stoic Cato, whose rigorous Republican principles caused the historian Sallust to regard him, with Caesar (who opposed him on this occasion), as the greatest man of his age.[1] Yet in spite of the Senate's sanction a problem which was to cloud Cicero's future was whether his action had been legally justifiable. There had, it is true, been a declaration of emergency; but did its vague terms, or any actual or threatened collapse of public order, warrant so extreme a measure as executions without trial?

It can still be argued either way. Certainly Cicero, in spite of his hesitant nature, acted with resolution in dealing, as consul, with a crisis: at least, he saved the state from fairly grave embarrassment. But as we can now see – with the unfair advantage, denied to Cicero at the time, of knowing what was going to happen next – an old-fashioned demagogic wild man like Catiline was by no means such a serious threat to the Republic and the Senate as were the great military commanders who, glorified by military victories, gathered round themselves armies and gangs of civilian dependants inspired by stronger allegiance to their leaders than to the government. At the time of Cicero's success against Catiline, one of the greatest of these commanders, Pompey, was shortly to return to Italy and to the political scene.

Arrogant, shifty, and aloof, but with no autocratic intentions, Pompey was about to come back from the East, after winning unprecedented victories. These had brought Rome vast accessions of territory in Asia Minor, Syria, and Crete, as well as a host of new dependent allies, a huge influx of treasure and revenue, and a state of peace with which the Mediterranean area was wholly unfamiliar.

Cicero, however, chose in this and other letters to dwell rather on his own services in rescuing the country from Catiline: in the words of his notorious verse:

> How fortunate a natal day was thine
> In that late consulate, O Rome, of mine!

And he requested a contemporary historian, Lucceius, to gild the lily and employ the laudatory methods of the traditional encomium in describing his achievements.[2] This emphasis was prompted not only by vanity but by the need to secure influential recognition so that his execution of Catiline's asso-

1. Sallust's estimate is quoted in *Roman Readings* (Pelican Books), pp. 123 f.
2. *Roman Readings*, p. 52.

*ciates should not be treated as illegal. Pompey had already indicated in prac-
tical fashion that this distribution of the applause failed to satisfy him, for he
had recently dispatched to Rome a representative, Quintus Metellus Nepos –
member of the dominant family of the Caecilii – who vetoed Cicero's farewell
speech as consul and introduced a critical Bill in the Assembly before being
compelled to withdraw from the capital.*

*'As a rule,' remarked a cynical young commentator Marcus Caelius
Rufus (p. 74), 'Pompey thinks one thing and says another, and yet is not
quite clever enough to conceal his wishes.' But now he was returning in
ominous silence. It is interesting to contrast Cicero's present disappointment
with his later assurance that Pompey had warmly applauded his handling of
the Catilinarian crisis (p. 108).*

TO POMPEY, IN ASIA MINOR   *Rome, summer 62 B.C.*

Like everybody else I was delighted with your official dispatch. It
held out the confident expectation of peace which I have always forecast to everyone because I rely on you so completely. I have to tell
you that your new friends,[1] who used to be your enemies, were really
shattered by what you wrote, and prostrated with disappointment at
the collapse of their high hopes.

I can only assure you that your private letter to me was also welcome – although it only contained a slender indication of your regard
for myself. However, what pleases me most in the world is feeling
that I have done the right thing by other people, and if on any occasion I do not receive the same return I am perfectly satisfied that the
balance of services rendered should be on my side. Besides, even if my
unremitting efforts on your behalf have not altogether succeeded in
attaching you to me, I am convinced that our country's needs will
bring us together and make us close associates.

All the same, I do want you to know what I missed in your letter.
I shall explain to you openly what I have in mind – my character and
our friendship being what they are, I cannot do otherwise. I have
achieved things for which I had hoped, in view of our relationship
and the national interest, to find some word of congratulation in your
letter. I expect you left it out in case you should cause someone [2]

1. Probably Caesar and his supporters.
2. Probably Quintus Caecilius Metellus Nepos (see above).

offence. But I must tell you that the reaction to what I did to save our country has been universally favourable. When you come home you will, I know, realize that what I did was brave, as well as wise; and so I am confident that you will be happy to let me join you as a political ally as well as a friend – you being so much greater than Scipio Aemilianus, and myself not much inferior to Laelius!   (*Fam.* V, 7)[1]

*

The years 60 and 59 B.C. constitute a decisive stage in the break-up of the Republic and the removal of the great families, and the Senate, from the control of events. For the three strongest men of the day, Pompey, Caesar, and Crassus, now came to an unofficial understanding, known to us as the First Triumvirate, by which they took it upon themselves to make every important decision – working together and employing their power to reduce the Republican institutions to subservience. Pompey was impelled to take this step by a series of unwise rebuffs from the senatorial leaders. Caesar, established now (in his early 40s) in Roman politics but with his military genius scarcely tested by a recent post in Spain, was prepared to do almost anything in return for two offices, which through Pompey's influence he now obtained: a consulship (59 B.C.) and the subsequent command which resulted in the conquest of Gaul and his Commentaries on the Gallic War. *He gave his daughter Julia in marriage to Pompey (and it proved an excellent match, for Pompey, like Caesar, was capable of attracting the love of women). Crassus, for whom Cicero always felt a strong distaste, was brought into the Triumvirate because of his enormous wealth: 'nobody should be called rich,' he once remarked, 'who cannot keep an army on his income.'* [2]

Cicero was told by Pompey that he, Pompey, disliked the Triumvirate – but by Caesar that he, Cicero, ought to join it: the Triumvirs could find uses for his persuasive oratory and the weight which his opinion carried in the townships of Italy. In the end, however, Cicero refused, unable to acquiesce in an arrangement which made such a mockery of his ambition to combine Senate and knights in a dominant 'Harmony between the Orders' as effective co-rulers of the empire.

1. In references to letters *Fam.* = to friends, *Att.* = to Atticus.
2. He instituted a fire-brigade at Rome, and, when there was a fire, used to buy up the threatened properties cheap.

TO ATTICUS,   *Rome, June or July 59* B.C.
ON HIS WAY TO EPIRUS

I have received several letters from you, and they gave me an idea of the anxious suspense with which you are waiting for news. Every single outlet is blocked to us. And yet far from refusing to be slaves we fear death or exile as greater evils than slavery, when they are really much smaller ones. That is how things are; everyone groans about the situation, and not a voice is raised to suggest remedies for it.

What those in charge have in mind, I suspect, is to make sure that there is nothing left which anyone else besides themselves might be able to offer as a bribe! Only one man opens his mouth and speaks against them publicly and that is young Curio.[1] Rightminded people give him tremendous applause and a highly respectful reception in the Forum as well as a great many other signs of goodwill. Fufius,[2] on the other hand, they pursue with shouts and insults and hisses. But this inspires distress rather than confidence, when you see that the people are free enough in their feelings, while their capacity for courageous action, on the other hand, is muzzled. Do not ask me to go into details, but in general things have come to this: there can be no hope of either private individuals or even state officials being free for much longer.

Yet amid all this oppression there is more free speech than ever, at any rate at social gatherings and parties. Indeed, people's indignation is beginning to outweigh their fright; though on all sides there is nothing but utter despair. The Campanian Law [3] ordains that candidates for official posts put themselves under a curse if their election speeches make any mention of land being occupied on different terms from those laid down by Caesar's legislation. Everyone else took this oath without hesitation, but Juventius Laterensis [4] abandoned his

1. For Curio, see p. 69.
2. Quintus Fufius Calenus, tribune 61 and consul 47 B.C., always a political enemy of Cicero.
3. An agrarian law passed by Caesar, consul in this year, to provide land in Campania for Pompey's ex-soldiers.
4. Marcus Juventius Laterensis, always loyal to his principles, committed suicide in 43 B.C. when he considered that his friend Lepidus was betraying the Republic.

candidature for the tribuneship rather than swear it – and he is regarded as having done a very fine thing.

I cannot bear to write any more about politics. I am disgusted with myself and find writing about it extremely painful. Considering how crushed everyone is, I manage to carry on without actual humiliation, yet without the courage I should have hoped for from myself in the light of my past achievements. Caesar very generously proposes that I should join his staff. He also offers to send me on a mission at state expense,[1] nominally to fulfil a vow. But the decent instincts of sweet Clodius[2] hardly suggest that this would be secure, and it would mean I was away from Rome when my brother[3] comes back. The other job, on Caesar's staff, is safe, and would not prevent me from being here whenever I want to – I am keeping the offer in reserve, but do not think I shall use it. I do not know what to do. I hate the idea of running away. I long to fight and have a lot of enthusiastic supporters. But I make no promises, and please say nothing about it.

I am distressed about the freeing of Statius and a number of other things, but I have become thoroughly thick-skinned by now. I wish you were here – I long for you to be. Then I should not feel so short of advice and consolation. Hold yourself ready to fly to me if I call for you.   (*Att.* II, 18)

*

After Cicero had declined to associate himself with the New Order, the Triumvirs in their turn – including, to his great disappointment, Pompey – proved unwilling or unable to save him from his enemies and from the consequences of his elimination of Catiline's supporters (p. 60). The young political gangster, Publius Clodius, of a great family with a traditional taste s'encanailler, *revenged a personal grudge against Cicero[4] by securing the*

1. A legal fiction whereby a Senator could leave Rome, and travel in greater comfort.

2. Publius Clodius: see below.

3. Quintus Cicero, who was governor of Asia. He had freed his slave Statius, thus giving (Marcus Cicero feared) offence in that province, where Statius's influence over Quintus was regarded with distaste.

4. Clodius had penetrated, in female disguise, into a ritual ceremony (rites of the Bona Dea) restricted to women (as a result Caesar had obtained a divorce with the laughter-provoking comment that his wife must be above suspicion), and Cicero had punctured his alibi (December 62 B.C.).

passage of a law punishing by exile or execution anyone who should con-
demn, or had condemned, a Roman citizen to death without trial. Cicero fled
from the capital, and was shortly afterwards sentenced to exile, his residence
to be not less than 500 miles from the city. He left for Greece; his property
at Rome was confiscated, and his house destroyed.

In the years to come Cicero's relations with his wife Terentia gradually
became colder – he found her too independent financially (accusing her of
ruining him for her own profit), and she may also have wished him to show
greater tolerance of Caesar; he therefore divorced her in 46 B.C. Though
he appreciated a literary lady-friend, Caerellia (from whom he borrowed
money), he was not very interested in sex. 'The fact is, that sort of thing
never had much attraction for me when I was a young man, much less now
that I am old.' When, after the failure of a further marriage (p. 86), the
general and writer Aulus Hirtius offered him his sister, Cicero declined on
the grounds that it was difficult to deal with a wife and philosophy at the
same time.

TO HIS WIFE TERENTIA,   *Thessalonica, November 58 B.C.*
HIS DAUGHTER TULLIA,
AND HIS SON MARCUS

Many people write to me and everybody tells me about how unbelievably brave and strong you are being, Terentia, and about how
you are refusing to allow your troubles either of mind or of body to
exhaust you. How unhappy it makes me that you with your courage,
loyalty, honesty, and kindness should have suffered all these miseries
because of me! And that our darling daughter Tullia has been plunged
into such wretchedness because of her father who used to give her so
many pleasures! And what can I say about our son, Marcus, who from
the very moment when he began to be aware of things has known the
bitterest griefs and sorrows?[1]

If I could only believe that fate alone is responsible for all that has
happened, as you say in your letter, I would bear it a little more easily.
But it is all my own fault! I thought people loved me when they were
really jealous of me, and as for those who did want me, I refused to
join them. If only I had acted upon my own judgement, and been
less influenced by the advice of friends who were misguided and

1. For Tullia and Marcus, see pp. 84, 157.

advisers who were unscrupulous, my life would now be a happy one.

As it is, since my friends tell me there is reason to hope, I will see that my health does not let your efforts down. I understand what a problem it is; also how much easier it was for you to stay at home than to go back. All the same, if we can rely on all the tribunes, and on Lentulus [1] being as friendly as he seems to be, and above all on Pompey and Caesar, there is no need to despair.

About our slaves, I shall do as you say in your letter that our friends have advised. As regards this place, the epidemic has now finished, and while it lasted I did not catch it. Plancius [2] is most helpful; he wants me to be with him and is still keeping me. I should have preferred to be somewhere less frequented – in Epirus, out of the reach of Lucius Piso [3] and his soldiers – but Plancius insists on my staying; he hopes we may be able to leave for Italy together. If I ever see that day, and come into your arms, and get you all back as well as myself, then indeed I shall really feel that our loyalty to one another has been rewarded!

Gaius Piso [4] is as kind and good and affectionate to all of us as any man possibly could be. I only hope he will derive some pleasure from it! That he will feel proud of what he has done I know. On the subject of my brother Quintus: I am not criticizing you, but I do hope you will all be as close as possible to each other, especially as there are so few of you.

I have written to thank the people you wanted me to, and I let them know that it was you who told me. My Terentia, you write that you are going to sell your block of flats. [5] But oh dear, in that case, I ask you, what is going to happen? And if our disasters continue,

1. Publius Cornelius Lentulus Spinther, a correspondent of Cicero's who was devoted to Pompey.

2. Cnaeus Plancius was later defended by Cicero in court (54 B.C.).

3. Lucius Calpurnius Piso was Caesar's father-in-law, whom Cicero later attacked in court (55 B.C.); he was consul in this year and shortly to become governor of Macedonia.

4. Gaius Calpurnius Piso Frugi was the first husband of Cicero's daughter Tullia. He died while Cicero was still abroad.

5. Cicero had earmarked the rents from these for the education of his son Marcus. When he divorced Terentia (p. 65) he had to hand back most, though probably not all, of her property.

what on earth will become of our unfortunate boy? I cannot write about the rest of it – my tears would get the better of me, and I do not want to reduce you to the same condition. I only say this: if our friends remain true to us, there will be no lack of money. If they do not, you will in any case not be able, with your own money, to achieve what we are after. Do, in the name of our unhappy fortunes, make sure that we do not ruin our already ruined boy still further. If he has enough to keep him from actual want, he only needs a fair share of good qualities and a fair share of luck, and he will be able to get the rest for himself.

Keep well, and send me messengers so that I know how things are going and how you are all getting on. In any case I do not have long to wait now. Give my love to darling Tullia and Marcus. Goodbye. (*Fam.* XIV, 1)

Dyrrhachium, 25 November

I have come to Dyrrhachium because it is a free state and very friendly to me, as well as being the nearest point to Italy. But if I find it undesirably crowded I shall go elsewhere; I will let you know.

*

Since Pompey very quickly found Clodius intolerable, he abandoned his acquiescence in the exile of Cicero, who was consequently recalled in August 57 B.C. Hoping, on his return, to play a major part in politics again, and relying on dissensions between the Triumvirs, he delivered speeches against their associates and planned to attack the legislation of Caesar's consulship. He therefore received a most unpleasant shock when Pompey, Caesar, and Crassus met in April 56 B.C. at Luca (Lucca) and patched up their differences, with mutual promises of military commands (the governorship of Spain in absentia for Pompey, a renewal of Caesar's tenure in Gaul, and an eastern expedition against Rome's Parthian enemies for Crassus). It was then intimated to Cicero that, whereas they were prepared to sugar the pill, he had better swallow it and collaborate. His next letter shows the disillusioned feelings with which he realized that the conservative Republican oligarchy (described here as the 'leaders') would not back him against the Triumvirs. Accordingly, he agreed to their requests. This 'recantation' probably took the form of a letter to Pompey – perhaps to Caesar also – and it was soon followed by a complimentary speech. But Cicero, to console himself for the restricted opportunities of political expression, now praised repose as a senior

statesman's objective – and soon began work on his constitutional treatises
On the State *and* On Laws.

*This letter, as often, refers to Cicero's houses, which Atticus was fre-
quently asked to look after in one way or another. In the course of his life
Cicero acquired an astonishing variety of house property (see map, p. 264).
He could ill afford these mansions and estates, but he loved the works of art
and other luxuries that went with them and he felt that this, like other costly
activities, was part of the price which the political 'new man' had to pay in
order to compete with the dominant clans.*

*Other tasks of Atticus, it is clear, were to help Cicero fit out his extensive
libraries, and to criticize his writings – a matter of equal professional interest
to both of them, since Atticus was not only an excellent critic but also his
publisher. A pioneer at Rome in this field, he kept a team of trained copyists
who could rapidly produce an edition of a work before anyone else had seen
it; and his services to Cicero were presumably to some extent reimbursed by
the circulation of the latter's books.*

TO ATTICUS   *Antium, May 56 B.C.*

What, do you really believe that I prefer someone other than yourself to read and approve what I have been writing? If not, then why –
you ask – did I send it to somebody else first? Because the man I sent
it to had been pressing me, and I had no second copy. Was that all?
Well: I have nibbled enough at the bitter pill, and must now swallow
it – but I felt that my recantation was just a trifle discreditable! However, to every course of action that is fair, straightforward, or honest,
we must say goodbye. One simply cannot credit the treacherous behaviour of those 'leaders' – as they claim to be, and would be if there
was any loyalty in them. I had a feeling, in fact I was in no doubt,
that they had only led me on in order to desert me and throw me
aside. Yet, in spite of that, I had decided to work with them politic-
ally. But they have turned out exactly the same as ever.

So now finally I have come to my senses – guided by you. You will
answer that your advice did not go further than suggesting that I
should refrain from speaking – you did not advise that I should write
instead! But the fact is that I *wanted* to commit myself thoroughly to
this new alignment, so that I should deprive myself of any chance
of slipping back to those other people – who even now, when

they ought to be feeling sorry for me, persist in their jealous attitude.

All the same, I have been moderate in my 'deification'.[1] Yes, you will say, but I have committed it to writing. Certainly, and I shall be free with my compliments if he takes it well, and if it causes wry faces among the men who complain that I have a house which once belonged to the great Catulus [2] (ignoring the fact that I bought it from Vettius) – and who say I ought not to have built a house, but should have sold the land. But what is the importance of that, compared to the fact that they have been revelling because the very utterances that I was making in sympathy with their views were alienating Pompey from me? It has got to stop. Since the powerless do not want to be my friends, I must make sure that the powerful are! You will say: 'I wish you had done so long ago.' I know that you wanted me to, and that I have been an utter fool. But now it is high time for me to be friends with myself and my own interests, since I cannot possibly be with the other lot.

Many thanks for going to see my house so often. Crassipes [3] is making away with all the money I could have had for travelling. As for you, turn off the main road and come straight to my gardens. You would find it more convenient for me to come to you? The next day then. It is all the same to you, isn't it? However, we can see. Your men have made my library as fine as a picture with their bindings and their title-strips; please congratulate them on my behalf.   (*Att.* IV, 5)

*

While Pompey, governor of Spain (and commander of its troops) in absentia, was uneasily resting upon his laurels in expectation of a quasi-dictatorial consulship without a colleague (52), while Caesar was completing his sensational conquest of Gaul, while Crassus was going to his death against the Parthians (53), Cicero discusses a literary matter with his friend Curio. A brilliant young man with a good knowledge of the arts but a bad

1. Of Caesar or Pompey? Cicero seems to use the Greek word *apotheosei*, but an alternative reading is *hypothesei*, which would mean 'in my treatment of the subject'.

2. One of Cicero's houses (? at Tusculum) had belonged to Quintus Lutatius Catulus (p. 53).

3. Publius Furius Crassipes, second husband of Cicero's daughter Tullia. Cicero is referring to the dowry and other expenses of the marriage.

reputation (later offensively dwelt upon by Cicero, p. 122), Curio spent vast
sums on the public spectacles needed as a bait to secure his election to office,
and was thereby impelled into dependence on Caesar, who, from the abun-
dant harvest of Gaulish spoils, paid his extensive debts.

Cicero discusses the art, or several different arts, of writing letters, even
such as his which were mostly not intended for publication. The stylistic
variety of his correspondence, ranging through every nuance from occasional
formality to more frequent colloquialism – an exceptionally valuable testi-
mony to the day-to-day speech of educated Romans – unfortunately cannot
be brought out in a translation; though certain translators have made it a
point of honour to render his numerous Greek quotations by phrases in
French or other foreign languages.

TO GAIUS SCRIBONIUS   *Rome, about the middle of 53 B.C.*
CURIO

As you know very well, there are many sorts of letter. But there is one
unmistakable sort, which actually caused letter-writing to be invented
in the first place, namely the sort intended to give people in other
places any information which for our or their sakes they ought to
know. But you certainly do not expect that sort of letter from me;
since for your personal affairs you have your own private correspondents and messengers, while my own affairs can produce absolutely nothing new to report.

There are two other sorts of letter which I like very much, one
intimate and humorous, the other serious and profound. I am not sure
which of these *genres* would be more inappropriate than the other for
me to employ in writing to you. Am I to send you letters full of jokes?
I really do not think there is a single Roman who could make jokes
in these times. And in serious vein what could Cicero possibly write
about to Curio except politics? But on this subject my situation is
that I dare not write what I feel and have no desire to write what I do
not feel.

Since, then, there is no theme left for me to write about, I shall fall
back upon my customary peroration and urge you to aim at the
highest honours. True, you are faced by a formidable rival here; by
which I mean the quite *outstandingly* optimistic expectations that
people have of you. And there is only one way in which you can

overcome this rival, and that is by deliberately developing, with continuous effort, the qualities needed for the great deeds which will achieve your purpose. I would enlarge on this theme if I were not already certain that this is precisely what you intend to do! So it is not from any idea of spurring you on that I have mentioned the matter, but only to show how affectionately I feel towards you.

(*Fam.* II, 4)

*

During these years, several important figures disappeared from the political scene. In 52 B.C. Clodius was murdered in a gang-fight – Cicero tried and failed to defend his killer Titus Annius Milo – but, before that, a tendency towards estrangement between Pompey and Caesar had become accentuated by the deaths of Crassus and of Pompey's beloved wife Julia, who was Caesar's daughter. Pompey was driven closer and closer to the conservative Republican upper class, and Cicero (as seen from the next letter) cleared the decks for an honourable move in the same direction by settling, through Atticus, a debt he owed Caesar's henchman Oppius: with his expensive tastes Cicero, in spite of inheriting enormous legacies (p. 120), was always in debt. But he now found another infuriating departure from Rome ahead of him. In 51 the Senate decreed that all qualified ex-officials who had not yet governed a province should do so. Cicero, unexpectedly called upon to cast lots for a major province, drew Cilicia, which comprised at this time a huge, mountainous area of central and southern Asia Minor.

He now describes how, on his way out of Italy, he spent an uncomfortable evening with his brother Quintus and sister-in-law Pomponia, the sister of Atticus. Quintus had seen distinguished service on Caesar's staff, but, though himself uncontrolled in temperament (and with a tendency to exaggeration), was unable to stand up to his thrifty but difficult wife. When Quintus later divorced her, he declined to marry again, observing – as Cicero reported to Atticus – that he had learnt to appreciate the blessing of going to sleep in bachelor tranquillity; and his poetry (in Gaul he once wrote four tragedies in sixteen days) includes an epigram beginning: 'entrust your ship to the winds, but not your soul to a woman'.

TO ATTICUS   *Minturnae, 5 or 6 May 51 B.C.*

Yes, I saw your feelings when we parted, and I know what mine were. That is an additional reason why you must make sure that no new decrees are passed which would extend this unhappy separation beyond the statutory year. You have taken the right steps about Annius Saturninus.[1] As to the guarantee,[2] could you please give it yourself while you are still at Rome. Certain securities in guarantee of ownership already exist, for example for the estate of Mennius or perhaps I should say Atilius. As regards Oppius you have done just what I wanted, especially in promising to credit him with 800,000 sesterces. I would rather borrow to pay this debt than keep him waiting until the last arrears due to me have come in.

Now I come to the note you wrote across the end of your letter advising me about my sister Pomponia. The situation is as follows. When I came to my house at Arpinum the first thing we did after my brother had arrived was to have a talk, largely about yourself. After that I went on to discuss the subject of the conversation you and I had about your sister at my place at Tusculum. My brother's attitude to your sister then seemed perfectly kind and conciliatory; if there had been any quarrel about expenditure there were no signs of it.

So much for that day. The next day we left Arpinum. Quintus stayed at Arcanum because of a festival, and I stopped at Aquinum, but we had lunch together at Arcanum. You know his farm there. When we got to it, Quintus said very pleasantly, 'Pomponia, you take the women, and I will have the boys.'[3] As far as I could see nothing could have been more polite, and his feelings and expression matched the words. But her reply (which we heard) was this: 'So I am evidently a stranger in my own house!' – I imagine merely because Statius[4] had gone on ahead to see to our meal. Quintus's comment to me was: 'You see? That is what I have to put up with every day!'

Surely that does not amount to very much, you will say. But it does. Indeed, she upset me too, she spoke and looked with such un-

1. Probably an ex-slave of Titus Annius Milo, whom Cicero had endeavoured to defend on the charge of murdering Publius Clodius (p. 112).

2. Cicero asks Atticus to guarantee the validity of his title to some property that he is selling. As a precedent, he seems to refer to his former sale of properties he had bought from the estate of one Mennius, who, Cicero then remembers, had previously disposed of the lands to a certain Atilius.

3. i.e., the sons of Quintus and Marcus. An alternative reading, however, is 'men'.

4. See above, p. 64.

called-for sharpness. However, I did not show my feelings, and we all took our places except her – Quintus sent her something from the table, but she refused to touch it. To sum up, my brother seemed to me thoroughly good-tempered and your sister thoroughly acrimonious; and I have refrained from mentioning a lot of things which at the time irritated me more than Quintus. Then I went on to Aquinum. Quintus stayed at Arcanum, but came to me the next morning and told me that she had refused to sleep with him and when she was leaving had been as cross as I had seen her the day before.

So, to answer your point, you could tell her yourself that in my opinion her behaviour on that day was not pleasant. I have written to you about this at perhaps rather greater length than was necessary, so that you should see that it is up to you as well to do some instructing and advising.

Now, it only remains for you to do the things I asked you to before you leave, to write to me about them all, to propel Pomptinus [1] on his way, to make sure you tell me when you have started, – and to appreciate that the affection and regard that I feel for you are quite unlimited!

At Minturnae I said a most friendly goodbye to the excellent Aulus Torquatus.[2] Please mention to him that I wrote you something about him.   (*Att.* V, 1)

*

Cicero did his best to be a good governor. He worked strenuously, fought to maintain public security, and even, unlike so many others, was in a position to claim that he had extracted no improper gains from his province – his only profit, one regarded as legitimate, being the proceeds (at famine prices) from the large amount of corn which a governor was allowed to requisition, ostensibly for his table (when the Civil War started, Pompey laid hands on this sum). In accordance with this unusual care for the interests

1. Gaius Pomptinus, a legate of Cicero in Cilicia. He was justifiably pessimistic about Cicero's chances of securing a hoped-for Triumph for his military operations against mountain tribesmen, the Pindenissitae. Cicero imagines Atticus asking 'who on earth are the Pindenissitae? I have never heard of them'.

2. Aulus Manlius Torquatus, a close friend of Atticus, had been president of the court at which Cicero defended Milo (p. 112). However, in Cilicia Cicero declined to find an appointment for a friend of his.

*of the provincials, Cicero was unwilling – as the next letter tactfully reveals –
to gratify Caelius, the fashionable Angry Young Man and brilliant public
speaker who was his political informant in the capital, with free panthers for
his electioneering show. Elsewhere, he rebukes Caelius for suggesting that
the province should support his candidature with a financial contribution.
Caelius was later to meet an unhappy end, at the age of thirty-four (47 B.C.),
stirring up revolt at Thurium in South Italy. After praising his oratory the
leading educationalist Quintilian described him as 'a man who deserved to
behave better and live longer'.*

*Cicero grudged every minute spent away from Roman politics. He em-
barked on his return journey from Side in southern Asia Minor on 3 August
50 B.C., and put into Brundisium on 24 November of the same year.*

TO MARCUS CAELIUS RUFUS   *Laodicea, 4 April 50 B.C.*

Would you ever have believed it possible that words would fail me,
and not only those words you public speakers use but even my
humble sort of language! But they do fail me, and this is why: because I am extraordinarily nervous about what is going to be decreed
concerning the provincial governorships. My longing for Rome is
quite unbounded! you could not believe how I long for my friends
and most of all for yourself.

My province, on the other hand, bores me completely. This may
be because the degree of distinction which I feel I have already attained in my career makes me not so much ambitious to add to it as
fearful of impairing it. Or perhaps it is because the whole business is
unworthy of my capacities, in comparison with the heavier burdens
which I can bear and often do bear in the service of my country. Or
it may be because we are menaced by the horror of a major war [1] in
these parts, which I seem likely to avoid if I leave the province on the
appointed day.

The matter of the panthers is being carefully attended to by my
orders through the agency of the men who make a practice of hunting them. But there are surprisingly few of the animals; and those
that there are, I am told, complain that in my province they are the

1. Cicero fears renewed war with the Parthians, who had entered Syria in 51
B.C., after killing Crassus at Carrhae (53). The last Parthian horseman did not
recross the Euphrates until July 50 B.C.

only living creatures for whom traps are laid! So rumour has it that they have decided to evacuate the province and live in Caria. Nevertheless, strenuous attempts are being made, and by nobody more than Patiscus. Anything that is caught will be yours, but what it will be I have no idea. I am deeply interested in your candidature for the aedileship, I assure you; this very day reminds me of it, because I am writing this on the actual day of the Megalensian Games.[1]

Please write me the most careful accounts of the entire political situation. For whatever information I receive from you I shall regard as more reliable than anything else.   (*Fam.* II, 11)

*

The next letter contains affectionate messages, dispatched by Cicero from the Ionian Islands on his way home, to his steward and future biographer, Tiro. This man was also his secretary: in addition to arranging dinner-parties and dealing with debtors and creditors, he took dictation from Cicero, keeping pace by a kind of shorthand which he himself had invented. He was good at correcting inaccuracies, and better than other copyists at deciphering his employer's handwriting. (One of his assistants, Spintharus, had to be dictated to syllable by syllable, but proved useful when language had to be carefully weighed.)

Cicero sent Tiro a nurse and cook to speed his convalescence. He must have made a good recovery since he is said to have lived to a hundred. Six years after the present letter, his master was to write to Atticus: 'There is no collection of my letters, but Tiro has about seventy, besides a few still to come from you.' By that date Cicero had begun to envisage publishing his letters, but only a carefully chosen and edited selection from them. But after his death Atticus and Tiro ensured that nearly twelve times the seventy letters mentioned by Cicero should survive, and in due course they were published: the Letters to Friends *by Tiro, and those* To Atticus *perhaps (though this is disputed) not for nearly a century after Cicero's death.[2]*

1. The festival of the Great Mother, 4–10 April – the touchstone of an aedile's popularity.
2. M. Jérôme Carcopino has not won general support for his theory that they were published on the instigation of Augustus as a deliberate attempt to blacken their writer's memory; see his brilliant book *Cicero: the Secrets of his Correspondence.*

FROM CICERO AND HIS
BROTHER QUINTUS AND THEIR
SONS TO TIRO
Leucas, 7 November 50 B.C.

Your letter caused me mixed feelings. I was very upset by the first page, but a little reassured by the second. As a result I am perfectly certain that until you are completely well you should not trust yourself to travel at all, whether on sea or on land. I shall see you soon enough if, when I do, you have completely recovered. As to your doctor, you write that he is well thought of and I hear the same. But I am by no means satisfied with the treatment he has been giving you. He ought not to have let you have soup when your stomach was bad. However, I have written to him in detail, and to Lyso [1] as well.

I have also written at length to that most agreeable, obliging, and kindly man, Curius. Among other things I have asked him to have you in his house – if that is what you would like. For I am afraid our friend Lyso is a little casual, first because all Greeks are, and secondly because after he had received a letter from me he did not send me any answer. But you are complimentary about him, so you will be the best judge of what ought to be done. Please, Tiro, spare no expense whatever to make yourself well. I have written to Curius telling him to give you whatever sum you ask, for I feel the doctor ought to be given something for himself, to make him more interested.

The services you have done me are beyond all number – in my home, in court, in Rome, and in the provinces; in my private and public affairs alike, as well as in my literary researches and publications. But you will have performed a greater service than any of them, if, as I hope, I am going to see you in good health. If everything goes well I think you will have a delightful sea journey home with the quaestor Mescinius. [2] He is quite a civilized person and I have reason to believe that he is very fond of you. So when you have done everything possible for your health, then, my dear Tiro, think about the

1. Cicero's host at Patrae. Manius Curius was a money-lender at Patrae who was a friend of Cicero and Atticus.

2. Lucius Mescinius Rufus is elsewhere described by Cicero as an incompetent official.

voyage. But I do not want you to hurry in the slightest respect. My one anxiety is that you should be safe and sound.

Rest assured that every friend of mine is a friend of yours too and that your well-being is of the utmost importance not only to you and myself but is a matter of concern to many others also. So far, out of your desire not to fail me in any circumstances, you have never been able to get strong. Now there is nothing to stop you. Drop everything else, and look after your own physical health. I shall measure your regard for me by the amount of care you devote to your recovery. Goodbye, my dear Tiro, goodbye and get well. Lepta[1] and all of us send you every good wish. Goodbye.   (*Fam.* XVI, 4)

*

In September 50 B.C., *Cicero first heard from Caelius his belief that Pompey and Caesar were now irreconcilable, and that civil war could not be avoided. The war began early in the following year, on the night between 10 and 11 January, when Caesar, coming from the scene of his northern triumphs, crossed the stream of the Rubicon, then the border of Italy. The rights and wrongs of the two leaders' constitutional claims and counter-claims – bearing upon the durations of commands and the dates of Caesar's eligibility for further office – were, and indeed still are, disputed (p. 113). But the plain facts were, that the Republican machinery of government had completely broken down; that, since no one could enforce (or even suggest) a practicable alternative, autocracy was inevitable; and that the state had no room for two autocrats.*

Pompey proved unable to hold Rome, but evaded pursuit and withdrew to the south-east coast of Italy. On the way, he wrote this short letter to Cicero. Flattering though the title 'general' (imperator) was to its recipient – who had been hailed by this title by his troops while governor of Cilicia – Pompey would have created a better impression upon him, crisis or no crisis, if he had attempted something a little more distinguished, both in style and substance.

1. An officer on Cicero's staff in Cilicia.

FROM POMPEY,   *Canusium (Canosa), 20 February*
PROCONSUL,   *49 B.C.*
TO CICERO, GENERAL

I was glad to read your letter. For I recognized your courage of old in the national interest. The consuls [1] have joined my army in Apulia. I urge you strongly, in the name of your exceptional and unceasing patriotism, to come to us so that we can plan together how to help and rescue our sorely afflicted country. I propose that you should travel by the Appian Way and proceed quickly to Brundisium.

(Att. VIII, 11c)

*

Cicero could not fail to prefer Pompey to Caesar, who was the less likely of the two to restore the Republic – though such was his despondency and disillusionment that he regarded Pompey also as by now inevitably committed to tyranny. Cicero was appalled both by the war itself and by Pompey's failure to hold Italy, which he skilfully evacuated on 17 March, sailing from Brundisium for Greece. Cicero was particularly distressed by the débâcle of the blue-blooded but pig-headed Republican commander Lucius Domitius Ahenobarbus, who, ignoring Pompey's orders to fall back, shut himself up in Corfinium. Domitius and his force were quickly obliged to surrender to Caesar, who then created a profound impression by releasing his distinguished prisoners.

Cicero rightly criticizes Pompey for having overestimated his ability to mobilize support in Italy, but it seems hardly fair to blame him for abandoning Domitius – or for deciding to prosecute the war from Greece, which was within reach of the wealthy eastern regions where Pompey commanded much support.

TO ATTICUS   *Formiae, 24 February 49 B.C.*

What a disgrace! – and, consequently, what misery. For my own feeling is that disgrace is the ultimate misery, or even the only one.

Pompey cherished Caesar, suddenly became afraid of him, refused all peace terms, failed to prepare for war, evacuated Rome, culpably lost Picenum, got himself tied up in Apulia, and then went off to

1. Gaius Claudius Marcellus and Lucius Cornelius Lentulus Crus.

Greece without getting in touch with us or letting us know anything about his unprecedented plan upon which so much depended. And now suddenly Domitius's letter to him, and his to the consuls.

I had almost come to believe that the Right Thing to Do had flashed before his eyes, and that Pompey – the man Pompey ought to be – had cried: 'Let them devise their uttermost to meet this occasion; let them exert their every wile against me: yet Right is on my side.'[1] But Pompey bids Right a long farewell, and is off to Brundisium. They say it was on hearing this news that Domitius and those with him surrendered. What a melancholy business! I am too deeply distressed to write you any more. I hope to hear from you. (VIII, 8)

*

Cicero now explains his dilemma in terms of principle. Of the questions that he poses here (he writes them in Greek, the language of philosophy), the last 'is a cri du cœur of Cicero's own; but the others are all familiar stations on the Via Dolorosa of modern Europe'.[2] The answers of Atticus, however, were predictable: this cautious Epicurean, 'friend to all men and ally to none' – he was to become a friend even of Cicero's killers Antony and Octavian – favoured abstention from the struggle as the best way to maintain sanity and the cultured life in an insane world, and to preserve his vast and varied banking and business interests. Though far from a Resistance type, he was a Republican by conviction and intended, by passive acquiescence, to avoid collaboration with unsavoury conquerors.

Almost exactly five years later, Cicero's problems concerning tyranny and tyrants were solved, to his immediate if not lasting satisfaction, by Brutus and Cassius. But for his own use Cicero much preferred, if possible, the weapon at which he excelled, his power of oratorical persuasion. How he wrestled with the demands of successive emergencies will be seen from the letters during the months and years to come.

TO ATTICUS   *Formiae, 12 March 49 B.C.*

Though I do not relax nowadays except while I am writing to you or reading your letters, still I feel the lack of subject-matter for a letter

---

1. A quotation from Euripides – perhaps from his lost play, the *Telephus* – which was adapted by Aristophanes in the *Acharnians*, lines 659 ff.
2. L. P. Wilkinson, *The Letters of Cicero*, p. 19.

and I believe you feel the same. The easy, intimate exchanges we are accustomed to are out of the question in these critical times; and every topic relating to the crisis we have already exhausted. However, so as not to succumb completely to morbid reflections, I have put down certain questions of principle – relating to political behaviour – which apply to the present crisis. As well as distracting me from my miserable thoughts, this has given me practice in judging the problems at issue. Here is the sort of thing:

Should one stay in one's country even if it is under totalitarian rule?

Is it justifiable to use any means to get rid of such rule, even if they endanger the whole fabric of the state? Secondly, do precautions have to be taken to prevent the liberator from becoming an autocrat himself?

If one's country is being tyrannized, what are the arguments in favour of helping it by verbal means and when occasion arises, rather than by war?

Is it statesmanlike, when one's country is under a tyranny, to retire to some other place and remain inactive there, or ought one to brave any danger in order to liberate it?

If one's country is under a tyranny, is it right to proceed to its invasion and blockade?

Ought one, even if not approving of war as a means of abolishing tyranny, to join up with the right-minded party in the struggle against it?

Ought one in matters of patriotic concern to share the dangers of one's benefactors and friends, even if their general policy seems to be unwise?

If one has done great services to one's country, and because of them has received shameful and jealous treatment, should one nevertheless voluntarily endanger oneself for one's country's sake, or is it legitimate, eventually, to take some thought for oneself and one's family, and to refrain from fighting against the people in power?

Occupying myself with such questions, and marshalling the argument on either side in Greek and Latin, I take my mind off my troubles for a little; though the problems I am here posing are far from irrelevant to them. But I am afraid I am being a trouble to you:

for if the man carrying this letter makes good speed he will bring it
to you on the day when you are due for your fever.[1]   (IX, 4)

*

*Through an intermediary Furnius (p. 98), Caesar sent Cicero a con-
ciliatory letter. But by now, as at certain other critical moments of his life,
Cicero's juristic weighings up of every side of the situation had hardened his
customary hesitancy into a more obstinate attitude; and, distressed though he
was at what he regarded as Pompey's cowardly flight, he felt increasingly re-
morseful at not having accompanied him. In the next letter, therefore, he declined to join Caesar in Rome: instead, he sent him an earnest though surely
hopeless appeal to seek an understanding with his enemy. Then, on 26
March, Cicero met Caesar at Formiae – and persevered in his refusal to go
to the capital. 'He asked me to think it over; I could not say no to that. So
we parted. I am convinced he does not like me or approve of me. But I
approve of myself, which I have not done for a long time.'*

*This was one among a relatively small number of Cicero's letters for
which he himself arranged publication. In the present case he defended his
decision to Atticus. 'I am not afraid of looking as though I am flattering him.
To save my country I should gladly have thrown myself at his feet' (a not
infrequent occurrence in the emotional turmoil of Roman public life).*

FROM CICERO, GENERAL,   *Formiae, 19 March 49 B.C.*
TO CAESAR, GENERAL

When I read your letter – passed to me by our friend Furnius – in
which you requested me to come near Rome, it did not surprise me
that you wanted to utilize my 'advice and position'. But I asked myself what you meant by also referring to my 'influence' and 'support'. However, my hopes – and I based them on your outstanding
and admirable statesmanship – made me conclude that what you
aimed at was peace, and agreement and harmony among Romans:
and for that purpose I felt that both my character and my background
suited me well.

If I am right in my interpretation, and if you are at all disposed to
protect our friend Pompey and reconcile him to yourself and the
state, you will certainly find no one better adapted to that aim than

1. Atticus suffered from a quartan fever.

myself. In speaking both to him and to the Senate I have always advocated peace ever since I first had the opportunity of doing so; and I have taken no part in the hostilities from their outset. My considered opinion was that the war involved an infringement [1] of your rights in view of the opposition by unfriendly and envious persons to a distinction the Roman people had conferred on you. But in just the same way as at that time I upheld your rightful position myself and also urged everyone else to help you, so now I am deeply concerned for the rightful position of Pompey.

A good many years have passed since I first chose you and him as the men whom, above all others, I proposed to support and have as my friends – as I do. So I ask you, indeed I pray and entreat you with all urgency, to spare some time – among your many grave cares – to consider this problem: how, by virtue of your kindness, can I best be enabled to behave decently, gratefully, and dutifully to Pompey, so as not to be oblivious of his great kindness towards myself? If this was a matter relating to myself alone, I should still hope that you would grant my request. However, I suggest that your honour and the national interest are also at stake; and what they demand is that I, who am a friend of peace and of you both, should receive every protection from you in my efforts to achieve a reconciliation between yourself and Pompey, and peace for the people of Rome.

I thanked you on another occasion for saving Lentulus,[2] as he had saved me; and now, when I read the truly thankful letter in which he told me of your generosity and kindness, I feel that in rescuing him you rescued me at the same time. If you appreciate the reasons why I am under a grateful obligation to him, I beg you to give me the opportunity of fulfilling my obligation to Pompey as well. (IX, 11a)

*

Caesar, who had in this year assumed the dictatorship for the first time (for eleven days), now left on a lightning expedition which destroyed Pompey's supporters in Spain at the battle of Ilerda. Writing on the way to Spain, perhaps from Ventimiglia, he made this further attempt, with a hint of threats, to prevent Cicero from joining Pompey in Greece – as he evidently

1. For the causes of the war, see below, p. 113.
2. Publius Cornelius Lentulus Spinther (p. 109) had been spared by Caesar after the capture of Corfinium (p. 78).

suspected was about to happen. Antony, whom Caesar had left in charge of Italy, reinforced the request with a reminder that he could allow no one to leave the country.

Caesar was not a new correspondent of Cicero's; no less than thirty-four of his letters to the orator are known in copies, digests, or allusions. He writes in a purer style than Antony, and his letter is a very much more distinguished affair than Pompey's productions (p. 78); for Caesar, in addition to his unequalled military talent, was one of the most brilliant men of letters of his age – as the consummately skilful plainness of his Commentaries reveals – and could even have rivalled Cicero in oratory if he had given the time to it. Although totally at variance in political matters, the two men greatly respected each other's talents – 'it is better,' said Caesar (as the elder Pliny tells us) of Cicero, 'to have extended the boundaries of the Roman spirit than of the Roman empire.' However, Caesar's present letter produced no result. For with himself out of the way on a hazardous campaign, Cicero at last made up his mind: on 7 June, accompanied by his brother, son, and nephew, he sailed from Formiae for Greece.

FROM CAESAR, GENERAL,   *On the march, 16 April 49 B.C.*
TO CICERO, GENERAL

Although I was convinced that you would take no rash or ill-judged action, nevertheless my anxiety about what people are saying has impelled me to write to you and urge, in the name of our friendship, that you should not make any move, now that things have gone my way, which you did not see fit to make while matters were undecided. For, everything having manifestly turned out to our advantage and the disadvantage of the other side, you will have seriously damaged the good relations between our two selves – as well as acting against your own interests – if you display resistance to the trend of events. It would then be evident that your action resulted not from support of a cause, since the cause is the same as it was when you decided to hold aloof, but from your objection to something that I have done. And that would be the severest blow you could inflict on me.

Our friendship entitles me to ask you not to do it. Besides, what could be more appropriate for a man of peace and integrity, and a good citizen, than to keep out of civil disturbance? There were many who felt that to be so, but were prevented from acting as they wished because of the dangers that would have been involved. Weigh up the evidence provided by my career and by your own assessment of our friendly relations, and you will find abstention from the quarrel the safest and most honourable course. (X, 8b)

*

The Civil War continued upon its swift and shattering course. Unable to deploy his eastern resources – or his superiority at sea – Pompey was overwhelmed at Pharsalus in Thessaly on 9 August 48 B.C., and fled to Egypt, where he was murdered on landing. Thereupon Caesar passed to a further series of victories against the remnants of the Pompeian cause in Egypt, Asia Minor, North Africa, and Spain – the landmarks of these campaigns being, respectively, Cleopatra and the battles of Zela (47), Thapsus (46), and Munda (45).

Once he reached the Balkans in 48, Cicero remained in camp on the day of Pharsalus, whether unwell (as Plutarch explains) or just unwarlike. He had disgusted everybody by grumbling incessantly, and they had disgusted him by their greedy and bloodthirsty attitude. After Pharsalus – and a quarrel with his brother and Pompey's elder son – he returned to Italy to spend eleven dismal months at Brundisium, in bad health and nerves, amid the collapse of his marriage.

Before his departure for Greece (he had delayed it until after the event), his beloved daughter Tullia had given birth to a seven months' child on 19 May. Her first child had died very young: this one, though delicate, survived. Tullia's life was tragic. Her first two marriages, resulting respectively in widowhood (at the age of about twenty-one, after eight years of marriage) and divorce, had been prompted by the endeavours of the bourgeois Cicero to raise himself to the level of the noble, plutocratic world in which a politician had to move. Next – on this occasion by her mother's choice, and perhaps her own also – she married the patrician Publius Cornelius Dolabella, who proved an outrageously bad husband: in the year following the next letter, while pregnant, she left his house for her father's and not long afterwards she died. It is painful to note that, even after that, Cicero sometimes continued to contrive, for financial, snobbish, and political reasons, to appear his friend (p. 94). But at other times he was repelled by the man, and although he could not blame himself for her disastrous third marriage his distress here includes remorse for his failure to make life happier for his daughter. He wrote of Tullia to his brother, 'I find again in her my features, my words, my soul.'

TO ATTICUS   *Brundisium, 12 or 13 June 47 B.C.*

I am giving this letter to someone else's messengers, since they are leaving urgently; that is why it is so short – also because I am about to send messengers of my own.

My Tullia came to see me on 12 June and told me all about your attentiveness and kindness to her; and she handed me three letters. But her goodness and sweet character and affection did not give me the pleasure which I ought to feel for such a wonderful daughter, because I was terribly distressed that such a person should be in so miserable a situation – which she has done nothing to deserve, since it is entirely my own lamentable fault. So I expect neither consolation from you – though I see you would like to give it me – nor advice, since there is none that can be taken. I realize you have made every possible attempt in many earlier letters as well as in these last ones.

                                                                (XI, 17)

*

While Cicero was at Brundisium, Caesar, on one of his visits to Italy, sent him a 'fairly generous letter': they met, and Cicero became ostensibly reconciled to the dictatorship. He subsequently delivered two diplomatically worded speeches requesting the dictator to pardon former enemies. But in the absence of real political activity what kept him reasonably contented was his literary work. During 46 B.C. he published two important books on oratory and the prevalent educational system which depended upon it – the Brutus *and the* Orator.

This letter is written to the greatest scholar of the day, Varro, an ex-Pompeian polymath whom Cicero treated with cautious respect but found tortuous, difficult, and over-critical.

TO MARCUS TERENTIUS VARRO   *Rome, early 46 B.C.*

From your letter to Atticus, which he read to me, I learnt of what you are doing and where you are. But I could not gather from it any hint of when we are likely to see you again. However, I am beginning to hope that you will be coming to us before long. I look forward to deriving comfort from your presence. Our problems are so vast and various that no one in his right mind should expect any relief from them. All the same, there are ways in which you can help me, and perhaps ways in which I can help you.

For let me tell you that since my arrival in Rome I have re-established friendly relations with some old friends – my books. I had ceased associating with them, not because I found them annoying but because they made me slightly ashamed. For having plunged into the middle of the most turbulent happenings in highly untrustworthy company, I felt I had not sufficiently followed the advice the books had given me. But they forgive me, and revive their old relationship with me – and say that you were wiser than I was because you never gave yours up!

Consequently, since they are reconciled with me, I feel entitled to hope that if I can see you I shall not find it hard to endure both my present troubles and those to come. So whichever of my houses you choose for our meeting – Tusculum, or Cumae, or Rome (the last would be the least satisfactory in my opinion) – provided only that we are together I will make it my business to see that wherever we meet it will be very agreeable for us both.   (*Fam.* IX, 1)

*

The death of his daughter Tullia (p. 84) at Tusculum, in February 45 B.C., inflicted on Cicero the most grievous personal sorrow he ever had to endure. At the time he had recently embarked on a second marriage, to his rich ward Publilia, so young (at seventeen) that he joked: 'she'll be a woman tomorrow!' But when Tullia died, Publilia, who had been jealous of her, showed too little sympathy, and Cicero – who had meanwhile inherited an important legacy from another source – sent her back to her parents for good.

Sadly wandering on the sea-shore at Astura, he composed a Consolation on his daughter's death.[1] Writing was now not only a partial remedy for political frustration, and a missionary endeavour to give Romans the best of Greek thought, but 'the only way I can get away from my misery'. His literary output during 45 and 44 B.C. was startling in quantity as well as in brilliance of execution; in lasting effect, it marks the climax of his life. Three of his greatest works of this period are translated in the present volume (Chapters 3, 4, and 5).

1. We also possess among his letters a very fine consolatory epistle received by him from the jurist Servius Sulpicius Rufus, which inspired St Ambrose and Byron to imitation: see *Roman Readings*, pp. 56 ff.

TO ATTICUS   *Astura, 15 May 45 B.C.*

I think I shall conquer my feelings and go from Lanuvium to my house at Tusculum. For either I must give up my property there for ever – since my grief will remain the same, though I shall become able to conceal it better – or if not it does not matter in the least whether I go there now or in ten years' time. The place will not remind me of her any more than the thoughts which consume me all the time, day and night. You will be asking me if there is no comfort to be derived from books. I am afraid that in this situation they have the contrary effect. Without them I might have been tougher; an educated man is not insensitive or impervious enough.

So do come as you wrote you would, but not if it is inconvenient. A couple of letters[1] will be enough. I will come and meet you, if necessary. Whatever you can manage, so be it.   (*Att.* XII, 46)

*

With Caesar installed as absolute ruler, Atticus's friend the high-principled though hard-hearted [2] Stoic intellectual Brutus was evidently able as late as August 45 B.C., as this next letter shows, to speak in favour of the dictator – whom certain people believed to be his father. But a month later Caesar returned to the capital for a Triumph over those whom he had crushed; so many of whom, as was painfully remarked, were distinguished Romans. The beginnings of the plot against his life cannot now have been long delayed. The matter was urgent, since in the following spring he would be off to the east to rival Alexander's conquests, retaining the title of 'perpetual dictator' (which he assumed in February 44 B.C.) and leaving a henchman to deputize for him as tyrant at Rome. Perhaps the more violent Cassius worked on the philosophical Brutus. To the classic Athenian tradition of tyrannicide, Brutus added the inspiration of semi-mythical ancestors, Lucius Brutus the first consul and Ahala, who were hymned as the ejector of Tarquin and the slayer

---

1. We do not know what business these refer to. Perhaps it related to Cicero's repayment of the dowry of his first wife Terentia, or to his divorce of his second wife Publilia.

2. While governor of Cilicia Cicero had protested against the ruthless methods Brutus favoured for collecting an exorbitant rate of interest from his debtors in Cyprus.

of a would-be autocrat Maelius in early Rome: later, Cicero was to use their names against Antony (p. 114).

Cicero's nephew Quintus, son of his brother of the same name, incurs criticism in this letter. 'Oh dear, oh dear!' says Cicero, 'it is the biggest sorrow of my life. Corrupted no doubt by our indulgent methods he has gone very far, to a point indeed which I do not venture to describe' – to the point, it was suggested, of (unsuccessfully) denouncing his own father to the dictator. In December, however, his uncle agreed to meet him: the young Quintus complained about his debts, but at this point, writes Cicero to Atticus, 'I borrowed from your style of eloquence – I held my tongue.'

TO ATTICUS   *Tusculum, 7 or 8 August, 45 B.C.*

So Brutus reports that Caesar is converted to the good party? Splendid news. But where is he going to find them? Unless he hangs himself. But how foolish of Brutus to say such a thing![1] What has happened to that masterpiece of yours which I saw in Brutus's gallery his family-tree with Ahala and Brutus the first consul? But what can he do?

I was very glad to read that even the man who started the whole criminal business has nothing good to say for my nephew, young Quintus. I was beginning to be afraid that Quintus was liked even by Brutus, who in his letter to me remarked: 'But I wish you could have had a taste of his stories.' However, when we meet, as you say. What do you advise, though? Do I fly to Rome, or stay here? Personally I am both glued to my books and unwilling to receive Quintus here. I am told his father has gone off to Red Rocks[2] to meet him – in a very bad temper indeed, so exceedingly cross that I actually remonstrated! However, I have been thoroughly inconsistent too. So much for that later.

See what you think about my coming and the whole business and let me hear first thing tomorrow morning, if you can see your way to any conclusion in the matter.   (XIII, 40)

*

In commenting on Caesar's dictatorship to Atticus, Cicero expresses a view which Atticus himself had often put forward: 'Let us give up flattery and be

1. It is not certain that this is what Cicero says; the text is corrupt.
2. On the Flaminian Way, nine miles north of Rome.

at least half free; and we can manage that by keeping quiet and out of sight.'
In the previous year Cicero had praised Caesar's arch-Republican enemy
Cato (who had committed suicide after the defeat at Thapsus), and in 45 he
drafted an open letter to the dictator about future methods of government. But
the criticisms of his friends decided him against sending this, and in May his
frustration had even moved him, in a letter to Atticus, to a bitter joke hinting
at the desirability of Caesar's death. The dictator was under no illusions:
'Can I be foolish enough to suppose,' he is quoted as saying, 'that this man,
good-natured though he be, is friendly to me when he has to sit and wait so
long for my convenience?' [1]

Yet the next letter shows how Cicero acquiesced sufficiently in the state of
affairs to have Caesar stop for dinner at one of his villas. Other prominent
men of the time are also mentioned in this letter. Gaius Marcius Philippus
(stepfather of the future Augustus) must have had a large house to hold two
thousand men. Mamurra was a nouveau riche senior officer of Caesar in
Gaul, attacked as a vulgarian in two savage epigrams by Catullus. We do
not know what news about Mamurra was broken to Caesar on this afternoon – perhaps his death. Lucius Cornelius Balbus, with whom the dictator
had a private discussion during the morning, was an enormously wealthy
Spaniard, perhaps of Levantine origin; he and Oppius (p. 71), though
holding no official posts, acted as Caesar's chief ministers. Though Balbus
had a passion for philosophy – he used to have Cicero's works copied before
they were published – Cicero's friendly relations with him had suffered since
the former's divorced wife Terentia had assigned her dowry (which Cicero
now had to repay her) to Balbus in settlement of a debt; and Balbus was in a
position to exert pressure. Caesar's gesture to Dolabella, mentioned at the
end of this letter, recalls the dictator's observation that, even if he employed
crooks and gangsters, he had to reward them.

TO ATTICUS   Puteoli, 19 December 45 B.C.

A formidable guest, yet no regrets! For everything went very pleasantly indeed. However, when he reached Philippus on the evening
of the 18th, the house was so full of soldiers that there was hardly a
room free for Caesar himself to have dinner. Two thousand men! I
was distinctly alarmed about what would happen the next day, but

1. There was some doubt about what Caesar had actually said; this is
Cicero's corrected version. For Caesar's opinion of Cicero, see above, p. 83.

Cassius Barba [1] came to my rescue with a loan of some guards. A camp was pitched on my land and the house was put under guard. On the 19th he stayed with Philippus until one o'clock and let no one in – I believe he was doing accounts with Balbus. Then he went for a walk on the shore. After two he had a bath. Then he was told about Mamurra; but there was no change in his expression. He had an oil-massage and then sat down to dinner.

He was following a course of emetics, so he ate and drank without *arrière-pensée* and at his ease. It was a sumptuous dinner and well-served, and more than that, *well-cooked and seasoned, with good talk and in a word agreeable.* [2] His entourage were very lavishly provided for in three other rooms. Even the lower-ranking ex-slaves and the slaves lacked for nothing; the more important ex-slaves I entertained in style.

In other words, we were human beings together. Still, he was not the sort of guest to whom you would say 'do please come again on your way back'. Once is enough! We talked no serious politics, but a good deal about literary matters. In short, he liked it and enjoyed himself. He said he was going to spend one day at Puteoli and the next in the neighbourhood of Baiae. There you have the story of how I entertained him – or had him billeted on me; I found it a bother, as I have said, but not disagreeable. Now I am going to stay on here for a little and then go to my place at Tusculum.

As Caesar passed Dolabella's house on horseback his whole guard paraded under arms to the right and left of him, which they did nowhere else, so I heard from Nicias.

(XIII, 52)

*

In the next letter, written to Atticus three and a half weeks after Caesar had been murdered, Cicero expresses unqualified admiration of the deed. Yet as a friend of the dictator (Gaius Matius) now remarked, 'if Caesar with all his genius could not find a solution, who is to find one now?' Cicero, too, is already painfully aware that the removal of Caesar had not automatically brought the Republic into existence again. In spite of the gradual decay of its government during the past twenty years, this came as a surprise to him, as it did to the assassins themselves. Now their lives were only safe if they

1. Not Cassius, Caesar's assassin, but a friend of Caesar and Antony.
2. A quotation from the satirist Lucilius (c. 180–102 B.C.).

stayed outside Rome. Cicero believed that he too was threatened, and moved rapidly from one to another of his country-houses, thus sacrificing, as he no doubt regretted later, his opportunity to exercise valuable influence at Rome.

In expecting no good to come from Sextus, the surviving son of Pompey, he was right, for that unstable young man, though an able naval commander, was interested in little but large-scale piracy, which he successfully maintained for eight years. He held out in Sicily until 36 B.C. and was then put to death in Asia Minor.

TO ATTICUS   *Lanuvium, 9 or 10 April 44 B.C.*

What news do you suppose I get at Lanuvium? But I suspect that in town you hear something new every day. Things are boiling up; for when Matius says so, can you not imagine what the others feel like? What distresses me is something which never happened in any other state, that the recovery of freedom did not mean the revival of free government. It is dreadful what talk and threats are going around; and I am afraid of a war in Gaul and of where Sextus will end up.

Yet come one, come all, the Ides of March are a consolation. Our heroes most splendidly and gloriously achieved everything that lay in their power. The rest requires money and men, and we have neither. That is all from me to you at the moment. But if *you* hear any news – for I am awaiting some every day – tell me it quickly, and if you hear nothing, all the same keep to our custom and do not let our exchange of notes be interrupted. I shall not.   (XIV, 4)

*

I do lack some part
Of that quick spirit that is in Antony.

So Shakespeare's Brutus admits; and Cicero too, incessantly brooding on the Ides of March and its failure due to the usurpation of Antony, feels that Brutus has been ineffective. In particular, Brutus's speech to the people on 17 March – when he attacked Caesar but promised not to interfere with grants made to ex-soldiers – had been far too academic, in Cicero's opinion, to enlist on the right side the inflammable potentialities of the Roman crowd: in which the high proportion of down-and-outs ready for hire and trouble had become, next to the army, the major factor in contemporary power politics.

Cicero's comment is professional as well as general, since Brutus was one of the leading practitioners of the austere 'Attic' style of oratory, whereas Cicero had achieved his outstanding success by a more vigorous and copious mixture of the Attic with the flamboyant Asianic style.

'If I had pleaded that cause ...' says Cicero; but he had not been there. Besides, the conspirators – though soon after the murder he had visited them on the Capitol – had not trusted him with their secret:

> O name him not:
> For he will never follow anything
> That other men begin.

In spite of all these worries, by 11 May Cicero, in the prolonged climax of his literary production, had completed and dedicated to Atticus his essay On Old Age (Chapter 5).

TO ATTICUS   *Sinuessa, 18 May 44 B.C.*

Yesterday I sent you off a letter as I was leaving my house at Puteoli; I stopped at Cumae. There I saw Pilia, who is well; indeed I saw her again before leaving Cumae. She had come for a funeral, which I attended too – our friend Gnaeus Lucullus was burying his mother. So I stayed that day at my place at Sinuessa, and am writing this letter early on the following day as I start for Arpinum.

However, I have got no news to send you or ask you for, unless you may consider that this has some significance: our friend Brutus has passed me the speech he made at the meeting on the Capitol,[1] and has requested me to correct it perfectly candidly before he publishes it. Now the sentiments of the speech are expressed with the utmost elegance, and the language could not possibly be bettered. Yet if I had pleaded that cause I should have written more fierily. You can see the potentialities of the theme – and of the speaker. So I did not feel able to suggest any corrections.

For if one bears in mind the stylistic aims of our friend Brutus and his conception of the public speaker's ideal, he has in this speech

1. Brutus made this appeal to the people while the Senate, including Cicero, were meeting in the Temple of Tellus (p. 140). Brutus and Cassius had already addressed the people in the Forum on the evening of the murder, before returning to the Capitol in which they had taken refuge.

achieved a degree of elegance that really could not be improved upon. Personally, however, I have tried to do something quite different, rightly or wrongly. But I should like you to read his speech, if you have not done so already, and let me know what you think of it yourself: though I am afraid that your name will lead you astray and that you will be hyper-Attic in your appreciation! But if you remember the thunderbolts of Demosthenes you will realize that it is possible to speak with great force and in purest Attic at the same time. But we will talk of this when we meet. At the moment what I wanted was that Metrodorus should not come to you without any letter or with a letter that had nothing in it. (XV, 1a)

*

In the next letter, Cicero reports how he attended a conference of the 'liberators' to decide on future policy, now that their cause was shattered and their lives endangered by the quasi-dictatorial regime of Antony. The meeting offers a striking testimony to the importance of leading Roman women. Servilia, the mother of Brutus (who had reputedly been Caesar's mistress), speaks as though she could control events; and perhaps she could, since her connexions were powerful and her wealth substantial. Porcia is Shakespeare's Portia, Brutus's wife; Tertia, nicknamed Tertulla, is his half-sister and the wife of Cassius, thus illustrating the marriage links with which the 'establishment' cemented their political alliances.[1] Roman matrons had long been imposing, weighty and interfering, almost like the princesses of Hellenistic courts (and far freer than respectable women of Periclean Athens). Caesar, fighting in Gaul, had found time to send presents to influential ladies at Rome.

As this discussion indicates, Antony had arranged for Brutus and Cassius to be offered minor posts overseas in order to save their faces but get them out of the way. Decimus Junius Brutus (Shakespeare's Decius), of whom the conspirators and their women here complain, was a relative of Brutus and one of their number – though, like others among them, a beneficiary and even an heir of Caesar. Showing great despondency after the Ides, Decimus had left for his allotted province of Cisalpine Gaul (North Italy), where he was now wasting his troops – in the view of Republican leaders – by stirring up local actions against Alpine tribes in the hope of being awarded a Triumph. He was executed in the proscriptions of the following year.

1. See Genealogical Table (p. 256).

The last paragraph of the letter refers to one of Cicero's hopeful plans to get away himself. As he says, the traditional expedient of a mission 'to fulfil a vow' (p. 64) looked rather feeble; he is still willing to associate himself with Dolabella (p. 84). Attachment to Dolabella's staff during his forthcoming five-year governorship of Syria would secure Cicero not only an officially sponsored post but a chance to visit Athens and see how his son's studies were progressing (p. 157). So Cicero embarked on 17 July at Pompeii: a departure which earned him the reproaches of Atticus for abandonment of his country, but which Cicero subsequently explained in retrospect as a temporary absence – approved, he had understood, by Atticus, and due to end before the New Year. His ship was driven back by contrary winds to the Italian coast. There, at Leucopetra near Rhegium, he received news that Brutus and Cassius, themselves about to leave for Macedonia and Syria,[1] had urged all senior members of the Senate to attend its meeting (after their departure) on 1 September. So he turned back, never to leave Italy again.

TO ATTICUS　　　　　　　　　　　　　　*Antium, 8 June 44 B.C.*

I came to Antium today (the eighth). Brutus was pleased I had come. Then, before a large audience – Servilia, Tertulla, Porcia – he asked me what I advised. Favonius [2] was also there. My advice, which I had been thinking out on the journey, was that he should accept the directorship of the corn-supply from Asia.[3] The only thing left for us to do, I said, was to ensure his safety, since that was equivalent to safeguarding the Republic itself. While I was talking, Cassius came in. I repeated what I had been saying. At that point Cassius, with a fierce look in his eye, and practically breathing fire and slaughter, declared that he would not go to Sicily. 'Am I to take an insult as a favour?' 'Then what will you do?' I inquired. He said he would go to Achaia. 'What about you, Brutus?' I asked. 'I will go to Rome,' he said, 'if you think that is the right thing to do.' 'On the contrary,' I replied;

1. There Cassius was to cause the suicide of Dolabella before joining Brutus and suffering with him, at the hands of Antony and Octavian, the fatal defeat of Philippi (42 B.C.).
2. Marcus Favonius, 'Cato's Sancho Panza'.
3. Early in June 44 B.C., Antony had arranged that his political enemies Brutus and Cassius should be appointed commissioners to buy corn in Asia and Sicily respectively, governorships of provinces to be assigned to them at a later date.

'you would not be safe there.' 'But if I could be safe there, would you think I should go?' 'Yes,' I said; 'I am against your going to a province either now or after your praetorship, but I do not advise you to risk going to Rome.' I gave the reasons – which no doubt occur to you – why he would not be safe there.

Then they went on talking for a long time and lamenting their lost chances, Cassius in particular, and they bitterly attacked Decimus Brutus. I offered the opinion that they ought to stop harping on the past, but I expressed agreement with what they said. When I went on to suggest what ought to have been done, saying nothing new but what everyone says every day, and not touching on the question whether anyone besides Caesar ought to have been dealt with, but observing that the Senate should have been summoned and that more should have been done to rouse the excited populace, your friend Servilia exclaimed: 'Well, I never heard anyone …!' I stopped short. However, I think Cassius will go; for Servilia has promised she will see that the appointment to the corn-supply is erased from the senatorial decree. And our friend soon dropped his foolish talk about wanting to be in Rome. So he has decided that the Games [1] shall be held in his absence but under his name. Nevertheless, I believe he intends to go to Asia, embarking from Antium.

In short, I got no satisfaction from the trip – except to my conscience. For I could not allow Brutus to leave Italy until we had met. Except for the satisfaction of fulfilling this obligation due to our friendship, I had to ask myself *'What is the point of your journey now, prophet?'* [2] I found the ship falling in pieces, or rather already in fragments. Not a sign of plan, logic, or system. So although I was certain even before, now I am even more certain that I must fly away from here at the earliest possible opportunity to *'where I shall not hear of the deeds or fame of the sons of Pelops'*.[3]

And what about this? – in case you have not heard it: on 2 June Dolabella enrolled me on his staff. I was told of it yesterday evening.

1. Brutus, owing to the political danger which had kept him and Cassius out of Rome until the second week of April, decided not to hold the Games of Apollo (6–13 July) incumbent on him as city-praetor, but to have them held by another praetor in his name. He asked Cicero to attend them, but Cicero said he 'did not understand' the request.

2. A quotation from an unknown Greek poet.

3. A quotation from the *Pelops* of the tragic dramatist, Accius (170–*c.* 85 B.C.).

Even you did not approve of the idea of a mission to fulfil a vow; for it was absurd that a vow which I had made on condition that the Republic was maintained should be fulfilled after it has been overthrown. And I fancy that these missions at state expense have a time-limit assigned to them by one of Caesar's laws, and it is not easy to get an extension. I want the sort of mission that allows you to come and go as you please, and that additional advantage is what I have now got. And the privilege of retaining the appointment on these terms for five years is very fine. Though why should I think about five years? For I believe things are coming to a head. But *absit omen*. (XV, 11)

*

While the conspirators were gathering round the dictator to murder him, one of their number, Cicero's friend Gaius Trebonius – to whom the next letter is addressed – had taken the hefty Antony aside and detained him in conversation. But though Trebonius was an admirer of Cicero (of whose bons mots he made a collection), the orator now complains to him, with a touch of pique for his own exclusion from the plot, that it would have been better for Antony to have been killed too: 'then we should have had no leavings'.

On returning to Rome on 31 August 44 B.C., Cicero had taken one of the most decisive steps of his career by launching his Philippics *against Antony (Chapter 3). On 28 November the latter, hearing that two legions had deserted him, left rapidly for the north, on the way to Cisalpine Gaul of which he had made himself governor (in place of Decimus Brutus). The Senate then declared war upon Antony, perhaps on the very day on which Cicero wrote this letter. He dispatched it to Asia, of which Trebonius had been appointed governor. But the letter never reached its recipient, for in January Trebonius had been murdered in Smyrna by Dolabella (soon to die himself, p. 94).*

Cicero's hopes, alluded to here, that the cold young adoptive son of Caesar, Octavian (the future Augustus), was interested in restoring the Republic or in respectfully allowing himself to be patronized, were to prove within the year to have been pathetically misguided. Probably Cicero, who could never resist an epigram, was unwise to have suggested – as Octavian discovered – that the young man should be 'lauded, applauded, and dropped'.

It is astonishing evidence of Cicero's energy that the great Second Philippic *was ready by October 44 B.C., and the completion of his treatise*

On Duties (*Chapter 4*) *is announced in a letter of 5 December. The speech of 20 December to which Cicero refers in this letter was the* Third Philippic.

TO GAIUS TREBONIUS   *Rome, about 2 February 43 B.C.*

How I wish you had invited me to that superb banquet on the Ides of March! Then we should have had no leavings. As it is, on the other hand, they are giving us so much bother that the superhuman service you people did for the Republic is liable to some qualification. Indeed the fact that this pestilential character was taken aside by you, excellent man that you are, and consequently owes his survival to your generosity, makes me feel just a little indignant with you (though I am hardly entitled to do so): since you left me with more trouble to be dealt with by my single self than by all the rest of the world beside me. For as soon as meetings of the Senate could be held in free conditions – after Antony's thoroughly discreditable withdrawal – I reassumed that old spirit of mine which you and your patriotic father were always approving and praising.

For when the tribunes summoned the Senate on 20 December and put another question to the House, I rose and reviewed the entire political situation. Using forceful rather than intellectual methods – for I was speaking with intense urgency – I brought the drooping and weary Senate back to its old, traditional courage. That day, and my energetic pleading, gave the Roman people its first hopes of becoming free again. And from that time onwards I have given every moment not only to thinking about national affairs but to participating actively in them.

If I were not under the impression that you already receive reports about everything that happens in Rome, I should give you full details myself, in spite of all the important business that is taking up my time. But you will get that from others; so this is only a brief summary. We have a firm Senate – though some of the ex-consuls are timid and others unsound. Servius [1] is a grave loss. Lucius Caesar is completely loyal; but being Antony's uncle he does not express himself very vigorously. The consuls are first-class; Decimus Brutus is admirable;

---

1. The jurist, Servius Sulpicius Rufus, who had sent Cicero a fine consolation for the death of his daughter Tullia (p. 86), had died while on a mission to Antony.

Octavian is an excellent boy, of whom I personally have high hopes for the future. And you can take this as certain, that if Octavian had not quickly mobilized the ex-service men, and if two legions of Antony's army had not transferred themselves to his command – thus frightening Antony – Antony would have committed every sort of crime and cruelty. Though I expect you have heard all this, all the same I want you to know more about it. I will write at greater length if I get more free time.

(*Fam.* X, 28)

*

Cicero tried to stiffen the resolution of the military commanders in the neighbourhood of Antony. One of them was Plancus, governor of Gallia Comata (northern and central France), later described as 'pathologically treacherous'[1] – a watchful and obsequious time-server who, by frequent changes of side, was to outlive this whole period of civil war into a successful old age under Augustus. Cicero's present sermon must have exerted a temporary effect, since Plancus wrote back placing himself under the orders of the Senate – an elegant letter, since he is the best stylist of Cicero's correspondents. Nevertheless, he went over to Antony soon afterwards. Plancus's brother Gaius (not the 'excellent brother' mentioned here) was less skilful at survival, since during the proscriptions later this year his executioners located his hiding-place by the smell of his favourite scent.

Marcus Aemilius Lepidus, referred to by Cicero here, was another political weathercock – a 'barren-spirited fellow' who, although Brutus's brother-in-law, owed too much to Antony, and deserted to him three months later. He, like Plancus, survived, but in disgrace (from 36 B.C.): though Chief Priest, he was kept by Augustus in enforced seclusion at Circeii for nearly a quarter of a century.

Gaius Furnius, who figures here as an intermediary, was a moderate anti-Caesarian – and an honest man. He was said to be the ablest speaker in Rome. Augustus honoured him, but it is recorded that on one occasion Furnius failed to hold the attention of Antony who, catching sight of Cleopatra crossing the square outside, jumped up and ran out.

1. By the historian Velleius Paterculus.

TO LUCIUS MUNATIUS PLANCUS   *Rome, 20 March 43 B.C.*

The report by our friend Gaius Furnius about your attitude to the Republic pleased the Senate and satisfied the Assembly very greatly. But your letter which was read out in the Senate seemed by no means to agree with what Furnius had said. For you spoke in favour of peace at a time when your distinguished colleague Decimus Brutus was under siege from a gang of repulsive brigands. It is imperative that they should lay down their arms and beg for peace. Alternatively, if they are determined to fight in order to secure this peace, then victory, not negotiation, is the only way for us to win it.

As to the reception given to your letters or those from Lepidus, you will be able to obtain news from your excellent brother and from Furnius. Nevertheless, in spite of my conviction of your own sound sense and accessibility to the loyal, friendly wisdom of your brother and Furnius, I am eager that some advice from myself also should reach you, carrying with it such influence as the very numerous bonds between us warrant.

Believe me then, Plancus: all the public distinctions that you have received – and you have received the most glorious distinctions that exist – will be universally regarded not as indications of merit but as mere honorific titles, if you do not now identify yourself with the cause of Roman freedom and senatorial authority. I entreat you to dissociate yourself, finally, from the men you have joined [1] – joined through the compelling force of circumstances, and not from your own free decision.

Amid our political confusion a good many men have come to be called ex-consuls, but not one of them has been regarded as of truly consular rank unless in national affairs he showed a consul's spirit. Consequently, your foremost duty is to break away from bad Romans with whom you have nothing in common. Secondly, you should offer the Senate and all right-thinking persons your services as counsellor, chief, and leader. And lastly, you must make up your mind that peace will not be achieved by laying down your arms: abolition of the general terror of arms and of enslavement is what will bring peace. If you act along those lines, and associate yourself with people of that

1. Probably Cicero is referring principally to Lepidus.

calibre, then you will not only be a consul and a consular, but a great one. Otherwise, those resplendent official distinctions of yours will bring you no dignity but utter disgrace.

It is only because I am your friend that I have written you these rather harsh words. Put them to the test in the only way which is worthy of you, and you will find that they are true.   (X, 6)

*

In April 43 B.C., Antony was defeated by the armies of the Republic beneath the walls of Mutina. But their victory was marred by the deaths of both consuls (Hirtius and Pansa). And then disaster followed. Just as seventeen years earlier the first Triumvirs had leagued together to suppress the Republican government, so now the twenty-year-old Octavian, though he had fought on the Republican side at Mutina, felt himself rebuffed by the Senate (as Pompey had on that previous occasion), and joined Antony. With Lepidus as their associate, in November 43 B.C., they announced the formation of the Second Triumvirate – this time on a formal basis, as a committee of joint dictators.

In the following year the Triumvirs overwhelmed the Republican cause at Philippi in Macedonia, and Brutus and Cassius met their deaths. But first the Triumvirate had arranged the 'proscriptions': the many leading Romans who opposed them, or might oppose them, were to die. Cicero and his brother and nephew were on the list. They decided to escape across the Adriatic to Brutus and Cassius. But the two Quintuses were betrayed by their servants and killed. Cicero himself, after many changes of mind, put back to shore and went to his villa at Astura. Urged by his slaves to depart he set out again for the coast in a litter on 7 December 43 B.C., but while he was on the way two officers of the Triumvirs came upon him. They cut off his head, and the hands which had written the Philippics.

*

The letters which have been translated here are the following (*Fam.* = *To Friends, Att.* = *To Atticus*): *Fam.* V, 7 (p. 61); *Att.* II, 18 (p. 63); *Fam.* XIV, 1 (p. 65); *Att.* IV, 5 (p. 68); *Fam.* II, 4 (p. 70); *Att.* V, 1 (p. 71); *Fam.* II, 11 (p. 74), XVI, 4 (p. 76); *Att.* VIII, 11C and 8 (p. 78), IX, 4 (p. 79), 11A (p. 81), X, 8B (p. 83), XI, 17 (p. 85); *Fam.* IX, 1 (p. 85); *Att.* XII, 46 (p. 87), XIII, 40 (p. 88), 52 (p. 89), XIV, 4 (p. 91), XV, 1A (p. 92), 11 (p. 94); *Fam.* X, 28 (p. 97), 6 (p. 99).

CHAPTER THREE

ATTACK ON AN ENEMY OF FREEDOM

(THE SECOND PHILIPPIC AGAINST ANTONY)

These Republicans [of the French Revolution] were mostly
young people who, brought up on readings of Cicero at school,
were fired by them with the passion for freedom.

CAMILLE DESMOULINS (1793)

*After the murder of Caesar, it had proved impossible to restore the Republic,
since Antony showed his intention of grasping dictatorial power for himself.
Within a month of the threatening popular manifestations at Caesar's
funeral, Brutus and Cassius had found it prudent to leave Rome, and never
returned, sailing east from Italy in August 44 B.C. With the field apparently to himself (the young Octavian, soon to become Augustus, not yet being
regarded as a serious threat), Antony had quickly made unscrupulous use of
Caesar's papers, recruited armed supporters for himself, and irregularly
passed a law giving himself north and central and Cisalpine Gaul for five
years. When Cicero, who had stayed away from the capital, finally returned
on 31 August from his despairing, abortive journey towards Greece, Antony
criticized him in the Senate on the following day for absenting himself from
the meeting; he threatened to send men to pull his house about his ears. On
2 September Cicero attended the Senate and delivered the First Philippic.*[1]
*This was couched in fairly moderate terms, but earned a savage reply from
Antony, 'who as usual', says Cicero, 'seemed to be spewing rather than
speaking'. In October Cicero withdrew to the country, and composed and
circulated the present scathing defamation including invective which, in spite
of his comment to his brother that abuse was unscholarly and ungentlemanly,
would rapidly provoke many a libel action today. The speech was never delivered, but in its present form (incorporating two out of three corrections suggested by Atticus) is the most famous and effective of all political pamphlets.
No reconciliation took place: twelve further Philippics followed within the*

---

1. So called – first by Cicero himself, as a joke – in imitation of the speeches
which, in the fourth century B.C., the Athenian orator Demosthenes had delivered against King Philip II of Macedon. For Cicero's motives in attacking
Antony, see above, p. 10.

*next few months, and when, after withdrawal from Rome and defeat, Antony
– by allying himself with Caesar's young grandnephew Octavian – confirmed his possession of the upper hand, it was decided that Cicero should pay
for his political courage with his life.*

> 'O happy Rome! that happen'd to be sav'd
> By me, her consul, sole.' –
> Such had his pleadings been, no haughty lord
> Had deem'd the jingle worthy of his sword:
> Yet such would I prefer, the scorn of Rome,
> To that *Philippic* which provok'd his doom,
> That second burst, where eloquence divine
> Pour'd on the ear from every nervous line.[1]

*Antony's biographer Plutarch offers this comment on Cicero's dashing,
impulsive enemy; it is given in the translation of Thomas North, of which
Shakespeare shows knowledge in* Julius Caesar *and* Antony and Cleopatra: *'When he [Antony] was grown to great credit, then was his authority
and power also very great ... on the other side, the noblemen (as Cicero
saith) did not only mislike him, but also hate him for his naughty life: for they
did abhor his banquets and drunken feasts he made at unseasonable times, and
his extreme wasteful expenses upon vain light huswives.'*

The Second Philippic *gives, from Cicero's point of view, a vivid and
invaluable, though prejudiced, résumé of much recent history: this speech is
his political testament. Strangely enough, while he was at work on it, he was
also completing his treatise* On Friendship!

MEMBERS OF THE SENATE: Why is this my fate? I am
obliged to record that, for twenty years past, our country has never
had an enemy who has not, simultaneously, made himself an enemy
of mine as well. I need mention no names. You remember the men
for yourselves. They have paid me graver penalties than I could have
wished.[2]

---

1. Juvenal, translated by William Gifford (1802). For another version of
Cicero's much ridiculed line, see p. 60.
2. Catiline fell in battle as a rebel in 62 B.C., and Cicero may also refer to his
other enemy Publius Clodius, who was murdered in 52: he mentions both in
the next paragraph.

Antony, you are modelling your actions on theirs. So what happened to them ought to frighten you; I am amazed that it does not. When those others were against me as well as against Rome I was less surprised. For they did not seek me out as an enemy. No, it was I who, for patriotic reasons, took the initiative against every one of them. But you I have never injured, even in words. And yet, without provocation, you have assailed me with gross insults. Catiline himself could not have been so outrageous, nor Publius Clodius so hysterical. Evidently you felt that the way to make friends, in disreputable circles, was by breaking off relations with me.

Did you take this step in a spirit of contempt? I should not have thought that my life, and my reputation, and my qualities – such as they are – provide suitable material for Antony's contempt. Nor can he have believed, surely, that he could successfully disparage me before the Senate. Accustomed though it is to complimenting distinguished Romans for good service to the state, the Senate has praised only one man for actually rescuing it from annihilation: and that is myself. But perhaps Antony's ambition was to compete with me as a speaker? If so, how extremely generous of him to present me with such a subject – justification of myself, criticism of him: the richest and most promising theme imaginable! No, the truth is clearly this. He saw no chance of proving to people like himself that he was Rome's enemy, unless he became mine too.

Before I reply to his other accusations, I should like to say a few words in answer to one particular complaint, namely that it was I who broke our friendship. Because I regard this as a very serious charge. He has protested that I once spoke against him in a lawsuit. But surely I was obliged to support my close friend [1] against someone with whom I had no connexion. Besides, the backer of my friend's opponent was only interested in him from a discreditable interest in his youthfulness, and not because the young man was really promising. Since his supporter had procured an unfair result through a scandalous exercise of the veto, I had no choice but to intervene. However, I think I know why you brought the matter up. You wanted to ingratiate yourself with the underworld, by reminding everybody that

---

1. A certain Sicca, with whom Cicero sometimes stayed at Vibo Valentia. Against Sicca, Antony had put up a tribune to interpose his veto.

you are the son-in-law of an ex-slave, Quintus Fadius;[1] in other words, a former slave is the grandfather of your children.

Yet you allege that you constantly visited my house, in order to receive my tuition. If you had, your reputation and your morals would have benefited. But you did not! Even if you had wanted to, Gaius Scribonius Curio[2] would never have let you. Then you claim that you retired from the election to the augurship[3] in my favour. That is sheer effrontery: monstrous, shameless, and unbelievable. In those days, when the entire Board of Augurs was pressing me to become a member, and my nominators (only two being allowed) were Pompey and Quintus Hortensius, you were completely destitute. There was only one hope of safety which you could see, and that was revolution. At that juncture you stood no chance whatever of becoming an augur; for Curio was out of Italy. Later, when you came up for election, you could not have secured the votes of a single tribe without Curio. So energetic, indeed, was the canvassing of his friends on your behalf, that they were condemned in the courts for the use of violence!

You did me a favour, you object. Certainly; I have always admitted the instance that you quote. It seemed to me less undesirable to admit my obligation to you than to let ignorant people think me ungrateful. However, the favour was this, was it not? – that you did not kill me at Brundisium.[4] But I do not see how you could have killed me. For I had been ordered to Italy by the conqueror himself – the very man whose chief gangster you were congratulating yourself on having become.

Nevertheless, let us imagine that you could have killed me. That, Senators, is what a favour from gangsters amounts to. They refrain from murdering someone; then they boast that they have spared him! If that is a true favour, then those who killed Caesar, after he had

1. His daughter Fadia had been Antony's first wife, but Fadius's connexion with this obscure business is unknown.

2. This sneer alleging Curio's undue influence over Antony is explained later (p. 122).

3. For this office and the tribes see Appendix C. Cicero became an augur in 53 B.C., Antony in 50, while his friend Curio was quaestor in Asia (western Asia Minor).

4. When Cicero arrived there in October 48 B.C., after the defeat of the Pompeians at the battle of Pharsalus.

spared them,[1] would never have been regarded as so glorious – and they are men whom you yourself habitually describe as noble. But the mere abstention from a dreadful crime is surely no sort of favour. In the situation in which this 'favour' placed me, my dominant feelings ought not to have been pleasure because you did not kill me, but sorrow because you could have done so with impunity.

However, let us even assume that it was a favour; at any rate the best favour that a gangster could confer. Still, in what respect can you call me ungrateful? Were my protests against the downfall of our country wrong, because you might think they showed ingratitude? I admit that there was no lack of grief and misery in my complaints.[2] But a man in my position, the position conferred on me by the Senate and people of Rome, could not help that. And my words were restrained and friendly, never insulting. Surely that is real moderation – to protest about Antony and yet refrain from abuse!

For what was left of Rome, Antony, owed its final annihilation to yourself. In your home everything had a price: and a truly sordid series of deals it was. Laws you passed,[3] laws you caused to be put through in your interests, had never even been formally proposed. You admitted this yourself. You were an augur, yet you never took the auspices. You were a consul, yet you blocked the legal right of other officials to exercise the veto. Your armed escort was shocking. You are a drink-sodden, sex-ridden wreck. Never a day passes in that ill-reputed house of yours without orgies of the most repulsive kind.

In spite of all that, I restricted myself in my speech to solemn complaints concerning the state of our nation. I said nothing personal about the man. I might have been conducting a case against Marcus Licinius Crassus [4] (as I often have, on grave issues) instead of against this utterly loathsome gladiator.

Today, therefore, I am going to ensure that he understands what a favour I, on that occasion, conferred upon himself. He read out a

1. Caesar spared Brutus and Cassius after Pharsalus.

2. In the *First Philippic* against Antony (p. 101).

3. Antony had established a land commission which, contrary to the Licinian (c. 145 B.C.) and other laws, included among its members his own relatives.

4. The triumvir (killed at Carrhae, 53 B.C.): Crassus had believed that Cicero suspected him of complicity in the Catilinarian plot, and Cicero had suspected Crassus, perhaps of intriguing for his exile, certainly of obstructing his recall.

letter,[1] this creature, which he said I had sent him. But he has absolutely no idea how to behave – how other people behave. Who, with
the slightest knowledge of decent people's habits, could conceivably
produce letters sent him by a friend, and read them in public, merely
because some quarrel has arisen between him and the other? Such conduct strikes at the roots of human relations; it means that absent
friends are excluded from communicating with each other. For
men fill their letters with flippancies which appear tasteless if they
are published – and with serious matters which are quite un-
suitable for wide circulation. Antony's action proves he is totally
uncivilized.

But just see how unbelievably stupid he is as well. Try to answer
my next point, you marvel of eloquence! (At least that is what you
seem to Seius Mustela and Numisius Tiro, who stand here in full view
of the Senate at this very moment, sword in hand: and even I shall
admit that you are an eloquent orator after you explain to me how,
when they were charged with assassination, you could get them acquitted.) However, to resume – what if I denied that I had ever sent
you that letter? You would be left without an answer: you could not
find a shred of evidence to convict me. By the handwriting? It is true
that you have found your knowledge of handwriting very lucrative.[2]
All the same, your efforts would be pointless, because the letter was
written by a secretary. What a lucky man your teacher of oratory
was! You paid him very handsomely (as I shall remind you later), and
yet when you left his hands you were still a complete fool. To charge
one's opponent with something which, in the face of a blank denial,
he cannot press home to the slightest effect is of no service whatever to
any speaker; indeed to anyone with any sense at all. Nevertheless I do
not deny authorship. And when I say that, I am also saying that you
are not ill-behaved but a lunatic. For my whole letter was replete
with dutiful kindness – it was a veritable model of how to behave.
Your criticism concerning its contents merely amounts to this: that I
do not express a bad opinion of you; and that I address you as a

1. Antony had brought back from exile Sextus Cloelius, an ex-slave of the
late Publius Clodius, and had first sought and received from Cicero a letter
indicating his agreement.
2. A reference to Antony's production of forged decrees purporting to have
been drawn up by Caesar.

Roman citizen and a decent man, instead of as a bandit and a criminal.

Now I do not propose to produce *your* letter, though under this provocation I should be entitled to: the letter in which you begged me to consent to someone's return from exile, and promised that you would not bring him back unless I agreed. And I did agree. For it was not for me to stand in the way of your outrageous behaviour, seeing that this is uncontrollable even by the authority of this Senatorial Order, and universal public opinion, and the whole body of the law. But what was the point of making me such a plea, when Caesar had actually passed a law authorizing the return of the very man with whom your letter was concerned? No doubt Antony was eager that I should get the credit! – seeing that even he was not going to win any credit, since the matter had already been settled by legislation.

Senators: in self-defence, and in denunciation of Antony, I have no lack of material. But as regards the former of those themes, I have an appeal to make: while I speak in my own defence I urge you to be indulgent. The second matter I shall look after on my own account – I shall ensure that what I am going to say against Antony impresses itself upon your attention. At the same time I beg this of you. My whole career as a speaker, indeed my whole life, has, I believe, demonstrated to you that I am a moderate man and not an extremist. So do not suppose that I have forgotten myself when I reply to this man in the spirit in which he has challenged me. I am not going to treat him as a consul, for he did not treat me as a former consul, as a man of consular rank. Besides, he is no true consul at all. He does not live like one; he does not work like one; and he was never elected to be one. Whereas a former consul I unquestionably am.

You can see what sort of a consul he claims to be by the way in which he criticizes my tenure of that office. Yet my consulship, Senators, though it can be called mine, was in plain fact yours. For everything I decided, every policy I carried out, every action I took, derived from this Senatorial Order – from its deliberations, its authority, and its rulings. What a strange kind of wisdom you show, Antony – eloquence is evidently not your only quality – when you abuse me before the very men whose corporate judgement inspired those actions of mine! The only people who have ever abused my consulship are Publius Clodius and yourself. And his fate – the fate

which also overtook Curio – will be yours: for what brought death
to both of them is now in your home![1]

So Antony disapproves of my consulship.[2] But – to name first the
most recently deceased of the ex-consuls of that time – Publius Servilius Vatia Isauricus thought well of it. Quintus Lutatius Catulus,
who will always carry weight among our countrymen, likewise be-
stowed upon me his approval. So did Lucius Licinius Lucullus and his
brother Marcus, and Marcus Licinius Crassus, Quintus Hortensius,[3]
Gaius Scribonius Curio the elder, Gaius Calpurnius Piso, Manius
Acilius Glabrio, Manius Aemilius Lepidus, Lucius Volcacius Tullus,
Gaius Marcius Figulus, and the two consuls designate at the time,
Decimus Junius Silanus and Lucius Licinius Murena. And Marcus
Porcius Cato felt the same as those of consular rank: he too praised
my activities as consul. *Your* consulship, on the other hand, was the
worst of the many things which death spared Cato. Another very
strong supporter of mine was Pompey. When we first met after his
return from Syria, he embraced me, offered his congratulations, and
declared that it was through my services that there was still a Rome
for him to see. But why do I mention individuals? A very full house
of the Senate [4] so warmly applauded my consulship that there was not
a man there who did not thank me as if I had been his father. Their
possessions, their lives, their children's lives, their country – they owed
all these, said every one of them, to me.

However, since Rome has lost all the great men whom I have mentioned, let us pass to the two ex-consuls of that time who are still with
us. For those very actions which you denounce, that brilliant statesman Lucius Aurelius Cotta [5] proposed that I should be accorded a most

1. Fulvia, successively the wife of Publius Clodius, Curio, and Antony.
2. Because of Cicero's action against the supporters of Catiline in 63 B.C.
3. Cicero's opponent in the case against Verres (Chapter I); Manius Acilius
Glabrio presided over the judges in the same case. Decimus Junius Silanus, consul-elect, had declared himself in favour of the death-penalty for Catiline's supporters, but after hearing a speech by Caesar urging moderation he had changed
his mind. As regards Pompey, at the time Cicero had complained of his wound-
ing failure to praise (p. 61).
4. The meeting of 3 December 63 B.C., at which the Senate approved the
arrest of the conspirators.
5. Related to Caesar's mother. Author of the law of 70 B.C. depriving the
Senate of their monopoly of the courts. In 57 he expressed the view that, since
Cicero had not been legally banished, no law was necessary for his recall.

generous vote of thanks. And this proposal was adopted – by those very ex-consuls whose names I have just recorded, and indeed by the whole Senate. This was an honour which, ever since the city's foundation, had been awarded to no civilian before me. On that occasion your uncle Lucius Julius Caesar attacked his sister's husband, your stepfather; [1] and he spoke with great eloquence, solemnity, and firmness. In all your activities throughout your whole life, your inspiration, your teacher, ought to have been Lucius Caesar. But instead of your uncle, the man on whom you preferred to model yourself was your stepfather. When I was consul I consulted Lucius Caesar, though we were not related. You are his sister's son: but when did you ever consult him on state affairs?

Who, indeed, are Antony's advisers? Evidently people whose birthdays have not come to our attention. Antony is not attending the Senate today. Why? He is giving a birthday-party on his estate. For whom? I shall name no names. No doubt it is some comic Phormio or other, some Gnatho or Ballio.[2] What a disgusting, intolerable sensualist the man is, as well as a vicious, unsavoury crook! How is it possible, Antony, that you should consistently fail to consult that admirable leading Senator Lucius Caesar, who is your close relation, while instead you prefer to rely on the advice of this collection of down-and-out spongers?

I see; *your* consulship is beneficent, *mine* was destructive. Your impudence must be equal to your debauchery if you dare make that assertion in the very place where, as consul, I consulted the Senate, which once, in its glory, presided over the whole world: namely, in this temple of Concord, now crammed – by your agency – with delinquents bristling with weapons. And yet you had the effrontery, the unlimited effrontery, to claim that, when I was consul, the road up the Capitoline Hill was packed with armed slaves! Do you really mean to suggest that I was applying violent pressure upon the Senate in order to force through those decrees of mine – in other words, that they were discreditable? You poor fool, to utter such impertinences

1. Publius Cornelius Lentulus Sura, one of the Catilinarians who was subsequently put to death.

2. Phormio and Gnatho were parasites in the *Phormio* and *Eunuch* respectively, comedies by Terence (c. 195–159 B.C.). Ballio was the pimp in *The Cheat* by Plautus (c. 254–184 B.C.).

before men of this calibre! – if the facts are known to you: or perhaps they are not, since all that is good is completely foreign to your mind.

When the Senate met in this temple, every single Roman knight, every young man of aristocratic birth – except yourself – every man (of whatever class) who was conscious of his Roman citizenship, gathered together on the road to the Capitol; each of them gave in his name. So many were they that no number of secretaries or writing tablets could have been enough for the registration of the entire multitude of them.

For that was the very moment when evil men were confessing that they had planned to assassinate their country. The revelations of their own accomplices had forced them to this admission. So had their own handwriting, and the almost audible testimony of their own letters. To murder the citizens of Rome – that was the intention which emerged; to ravage Italy; revolution! At such a time, no one could fail to hear the call to defend the common cause – especially as the Senate and Roman people, in those days, possessed a leader. If they had his like as a leader now, the fate that descended upon those anarchists would be yours also.

Antony protests that I refused to give up his stepfather's body for burial. But even Publius Clodius never brought that charge. I was the enemy of Clodius – justifiably: but your faults, I regret to see, are blacker even than his. Why did it occur to you, I wonder, to remind us of your upbringing in your stepfather's home? I suppose you were afraid that we should be sceptical of nature's unaided effects; that we should need this evidence of upbringing before we could understand why you had turned out so criminally.

Really, your speech was demented, it was so full of inconsistencies. From beginning to end, you were not merely incoherent but glaringly self-contradictory: indeed you contradicted yourself more often than you contradicted me. You admitted that your stepfather was involved in that terrible crime, and yet you complained because he had been punished for what he did. But the effect of that argument was to praise my part in the matter, and to blame what was wholly the Senate's part. For whereas it was I who arrested the guilty men, it was the Senate which punished them. So our masterly speaker here does not realize he is praising the man he is trying to attack, and is abusing those who sit here listening to him!

I will not call this effrontery – which is in any case a quality he proudly claims. But Antony has no desire to be stupid, and he must be the most stupid man alive to talk of the Capitoline road at this moment – when armed men are actually standing here among our benches, are stationed with their swords in that same temple of Concord, heaven bear me witness, where my consulship saw decisions which saved our nation and brought us in safety to this day.

Go on, criticize the Senate, criticize the knights who were at that time its partners. Assail every class and every citizen with your accusations, provided you admit that at the present moment this meeting of ours here is picketed by your Ituraean police.[1] Unscrupulousness is not what prompts these shameless statements of yours; you make them because you entirely fail to grasp how you are contradicting yourself. In fact, you must be an imbecile. How could a sane person first take up arms to destroy his country, and then protest because someone else had armed himself to save it?

At one point you tried to be witty. Heaven knows this did not suit you. And your failure is particularly blameworthy, since you could have acquired some wit from that professional actress [2] known as your wife. 'Let gown be mightier than sword' [3] were the words of mine that you mocked. Well, that was so in those days, was it not? But since then your swords have won. Let us consider which was the better: the time when gangsters' weapons were overcome by men defending Roman freedom, or now, when your weapons have struck that freedom down. As far as my poem is concerned that is the only answer I have to give. I will merely add briefly that you understand neither this poem nor any other literature. I, on the other hand, though I have not neglected my duty to our country or to my friends, have nevertheless employed my leisure hours in literary productions of many kinds. All that I have written, the whole of my effort, has been intended for the benefit of young people and for the greater glory of Rome. However, that is another matter. Let us turn to questions of more importance.

1. Archers from the region north-east of the Sea of Galilee, conquered by Pompey in 63 B.C.

2. A reference to Antony's mistress, Volumnia (ex-slave of Volumnius Eutrapelus); her stage-name was Cytheris.

3. A quotation from Cicero's much maligned poem *On his Consulate*. The verse went on: 'let laurel yield to honest worth.'

It was upon my initiative, you said, that Publius Clodius was killed by Titus Annius Milo.[1] But what would people have thought if he had been killed when, sword in hand, *you* chased him into the Forum, with the whole of Rome looking on? If he had not stopped you by hiding under the stairs of a bookshop and barricading them, you would have finished him off. Now I admit that I viewed your attempt with favour; yet even you do not claim that I prompted you. But as for Milo, I did not have an opportunity even to favour his attempt, since he had completed the job before anyone suspected what he was going to do. You say I prompted him. So presumably Milo was not the sort of man who could perform a patriotic action without a prompter! I celebrated the deed when it was done, you point out. But when the whole nation was rejoicing, why should I be the only mourner? Certainly, the inquiry into Clodius's death was not very judiciously designed. For when an established legal procedure for murder was available, the creation of a new law [2] to deal with the case was pointless. Anyway, that is what was done, and the inquiry took its course. At the time, when the matter was under active consideration, no one brought this charge against me. It remained for you to perpetrate the fabrication after all these years!

Your next impudent accusation – made at considerable length – is that I was responsible for alienating Pompey from Caesar, and that by so doing I caused the Civil War. Your mistake in saying this is not wholly factual, but chronological; and this is a significant point. It is true that, during the consulship of the admirable Marcus Calpurnius Bibulus,[3] I made every possible attempt to separate Pompey from Caesar. But Caesar was more successful: for he alienated Pompey from me. And when Pompey had wholeheartedly joined Caesar, how could I endeavour to set them apart? I should have been foolish to hope for such a thing – and impertinent to attempt persuasion. Yet there were two occasions on which I advised Pompey against Caesar.

1. 52 B.C., in a brawl on the Appian Way. Cicero defended Milo (with less vigour than he had intended, owing to threats of force), but he was condemned and went into exile at Massilia (thanking Cicero for thus allowing him to enjoy the mullets there). In 48 he was executed at Cosa for creating disorders with Marcus Caelius Rufus.

2. The Pompeian Law concerning violence.

3. Caesar's conservative fellow-consul and ineffective political opponent in 59 B.C.

Blame me for them, if you can. First, I advised him not to renew Caesar's five-year term in Gaul; [1] secondly, I urged him not to allow Caesar's candidature for the consulship *in absentia*.[2] If I had been successful on either occasion, our present miseries would never have befallen us.

But instead Pompey made a present to Caesar of all his own resources,[3] and all the resources of Rome. Only then did he belatedly begin to understand what I had foreseen long before. But by that time I had also come to realize that a criminal attack on our country was imminent. That is why, from then onward, I never ceased to urge peace, harmony, and arrangement. Many people knew what I was saying: 'If only, Pompey, you had either avoided joining Caesar or avoided breaking with him! Your strength of character demanded the former course, and your wisdom the latter!' That, Antony, was the advice I consistently gave in regard to Pompey and the crisis of our Republic. If this advice had prevailed, the Republic would still be flourishing: but you would not be, for your scandalous, down-at-heels, infamous behaviour would have brought you down.

However, these are old stories. Your new story is this: I was responsible for the killing of Caesar. Now, Senators, I am afraid I may look guilty, at this point, of a deplorable offence: namely the production, in a case against myself, of a sham prosecutor – a man who will load me with compliments whether I am entitled to them or not.[4] For among the company who did that most glorious of deeds, my name was never once heard. Yet not a name among them

1. Caesar's five-year command in Gaul and Illyricum, due to terminate in 54 B.C., was renewed by the Pompeian–Licinian Law of 55 (sponsored by his fellow-triumvirs): the date which the law fixed for the termination of this command – a question on which (constitutionally speaking) the responsibility for the subsequent Civil War largely hinges – was, and still is, highly controversial.

2. It was necessary for Caesar to stand *in absentia* in 49 B.C., since otherwise in order to become consul again (which he regarded as a necessity) he would have had to come to Rome as an unprivileged private individual and run the risk of prosecution by his political enemies. Cicero may to some extent be misrepresenting his own part in these events, on which he had written in different terms to Caesar himself (p. 82).

3. Perhaps Cicero is referring, with exaggeration, to a legion which Pompey had lent Caesar during the winter of 54/53 B.C.

4. A feature of the tactics of Cicero's opponents in the case against Verres (p. 36).

remained secret. Secret, do I say? Every one of them was instantly known far and wide! It was much more likely, believe me, that men should have boasted of complicity, though they had nothing to do with the deed, than that having been accomplices they should have desired to conceal the fact. There were quite a number of them; some obscure, some youthful – not the sort of people who would keep anyone's identity quiet. So, if I had been involved, how on earth could my participation have remained unknown?

Besides – if we really need to assume that the prime movers in that operation needed prompting to free their country! – was it for me to inspire the two Brutuses? Every day, in their own homes, each of them had the statue of Lucius Junius Brutus [1] to gaze upon – and one of them had Gaius Servilius Ahala as well. These living Brutuses, with these ancestors, needed no outside advisers from other houses: they had advisers ready to hand within their own homes. Gaius Cassius Longinus,[2] too, belongs to a clan incapable of tolerating not only autocracy but even excessive power in any single individual. Yet apparently he needed me as his instigator! On the contrary, even before his present distinguished associates were available, Cassius had proposed to perform this same task in Cilicia at the mouth of the Cydnus, if only Caesar, after deciding to moor his ships on one bank of the river, had not moored them on the other instead. And then again, when the recovery of freedom was at stake, what need had Gnaeus Domitius Ahenobarbus [3] of me to inspire him? Inspiration enough for Domitius was the memory of how his noble father and his uncle had died – and how he himself had been deprived of his rights as a citizen. As for Gaius Trebonius, far from persuading him, I should not even have ventured to advise him – so close were his ties with Caesar. The

1. The (? mythical) expeller of King Tarquin the Proud and founder of the Roman Republic, allegedly consul in 509 B.C. Gaius Servilius Ahala was said to have saved the Republic in 439 B.C. by killing the usurper Spurius Maelius.

2. Cassius, the assassin of Caesar. The reference is to Spurius Cassius Vecellinus, believed to have been consul in 503, 492, and 486 B.C., and to have been put to death at his own father's instance for aiming at tyranny. The alleged incident on the Cydnus should probably be dated to 47 B.C., when Caesar had pardoned Cassius for fighting on Pompey's side.

3. Son of Lucius who had capitulated at Corfinium (p. 78) and been killed by Antony in the pursuit after Pharsalus; nephew of Cato on his mother's side, Gnaeus had, in fact, been pardoned by Caesar, but did not re-enter public life.

existence of those ties increases the debt of gratitude which our country owes Trebonius: for one man's friendship seemed to him of less importance than the freedom of the Roman people – he could have shared autocracy, but he preferred to strike it down. Or was I Lucius Tillius Cimber's counsellor? No, my admiration for him after he had done the deed was a great deal stronger than my confidence, beforehand, that he would do it; I admired him all the more because he disregarded the personal favours he had received: he thought only of Rome. And then the two Serviliuses – whether to call them Cascas [1] or Ahalas I do not know. Do you suppose they needed my advice to urge them on? They had their love for their country. To enumerate all the rest would take too long; it reflects great credit on themselves, and great glory on Rome, that they were so many!

But remember, please, how this astute man demonstrated my complicity. 'When Caesar had been killed,' said he, 'Brutus immediately brandished aloft his bloodstained dagger and called out Cicero's name, congratulating him on the recovery of national freedom.' But this choice of myself, above all others – why must it indicate my foreknowledge? Consider instead whether the reason why Brutus called upon me was not this. The deed which he had done resembled the deeds which I had done myself: that is why he singled me out – to proclaim that he had modelled himself on me.

What a fool you are, Antony. Do you not understand this? If wanting Caesar to be killed (as you complain that I did) is a crime, then it is also criminal to have rejoiced when he was dead. For between the man who advises an action and the man who approves when it is done there is not the slightest difference. Whether I wished the deed to be performed or am glad after its performance, is wholly immaterial. Yet, with the exception of the men who wanted to make an autocratic monarch of him, all were willing for this to happen – or were glad when it had happened. So everyone is guilty! For every decent person, in so far as he had any say in the matter, killed Caesar! Plans, courage, opportunities were in some cases lacking; but the desire nobody lacked.

Just listen to the fatuity of this man – this sheep, rather. Here were his words: 'Brutus, whose name I mention with all respect, called out

1. Publius Servilius Casca, who struck the first blow against Caesar, and his brother Gaius. For Ahala see above, p. 114.

Cicero's name while he was holding the bloodstained dagger: from which you must understand that Cicero was an accomplice.' So, just because you suspect that I suspected something you call me a criminal, yet the man who brandished a dripping dagger is mentioned by you 'with all respect'! Very well, use this imbecile language if you must; and your actions and opinions are even more brainless. In the end, Consul, you will have to make up your mind! You must pronounce your final judgement on the cause of the Brutuses, Cassius, Gnaeus Domitius Ahenobarbus, Gaius Trebonius, and the rest. Sleep off your hangover – breathe it out. Perhaps a torch might be administered, to sting you out of your snoring over this far from unimportant matter. Will you never understand that you *must* decide which description to apply to the men who did that deed: are they murderers or are they the restorers of national freedom?

Concentrate, please – just for a little. Try to make your brain work for a moment as if you were sober. I confess I am their friend – you prefer to call me their associate. And yet even I refuse to see any compromise solution. If these men are not liberators of the Roman people and saviours of the state, then even I assert that they are worse than assassins, worse than murderers. Indeed, on the assumption that even the murder of one's own father is less horrible than to kill the father of one's country,[1] even parricides are better than they are.

Well, then, you wise and thoughtful man, what do you say to this: if they are parricides, why, in the Senate and Assembly, do you refer to them with respect? You will also have to explain why you yourself proposed Marcus Brutus's exemption from the laws [2] when he remained outside the city for more than ten days; why, at the Games of Apollo,[3] he received such a complimentary reception; and why he and Cassius were given provincial commands,[4] and supernumerary quaestors and legates were assigned to them for the purpose. This was

1. Caesar was hailed as this (as Cicero himself had been, less formally, after the Catilinarian conspiracy).

2. As city-praetor he was not allowed to be away from Rome for more than ten nights.

3. For the Games of Apollo, see above, p. 95.

4. After being assigned corn-commissionerships in June 44 B.C. (p. 94), in August Brutus was made governor of Crete and Cassius of Cyrene. But they left instead for Macedonia and Syria respectively, and collected the armies which were defeated in 42 B.C. at Philippi by Antony and Octavian.

all your doing! So evidently you do not regard them as murderers. It follows – since no compromise is possible – that you must regard them as liberators. What is the matter? I am not embarrassing you, am I? For I doubt if you are quite competent to grasp the sort of dilemma in which this places you. Anyway, what my conclusion amounts to is this: by not regarding Brutus and the rest as criminals, you have automatically proclaimed that they deserve the most glorious rewards.

So I must re-design my speech. I shall write to these men and say that, if anyone asks whether your charge against me is true, they must offer no denials. For, if I was their accomplice and they conceal the fact, I am afraid this may discredit them; whereas if I was invited to join them and refused, this will reflect the gravest discredit on me. For heaven will bear witness that Rome – that any nation throughout the whole world – has never seen a greater act than theirs! There has never been an achievement more glorious – more greatly deserving of renown for all eternity. So if you pen me in a Trojan horse of complicity with the chief partners in that deed, I do not protest. Thank you, I say – whatever your motives. For where so outstanding an action is concerned, I account the unpopularity, which you hope to unload upon me, as nothing beside the glory.

You have driven these men away and expelled them, you boast. Yet they are blessed beyond measure. There is no place in the world too deserted and too barbarous to welcome them and delight in their presence. All people on earth, however uncivilized, are capable of understanding that life could offer no more outstanding happiness than a sight of these men. Writers will continue, for generation after generation throughout time everlasting, to immortalize the glory of their achievement.

Enrol me among such heroes, I beg of you! Though I am afraid that one thing may not be to your liking. If I had been among their number I should have freed our country not only from the autocrat but from the autocracy. For if, as you assert, I had been the author of the work, believe me, I should not have been satisfied to finish only one act: I should have completed the play! [1]

If it is a crime to have wanted Caesar to be put to death, consider

1. i.e. killed Antony too. Cicero expressed a similar sentiment in a letter to Trebonius (p. 96).

your own situation, Antony. Everyone knows that at Narbo [1] you formed a similar plan with Gaius Trebonius: it was because of this plot, while Caesar was being killed, that we saw Trebonius taking you aside. You see – my intentions to you are friendly. I am praising you for the good intention you once had! For not having reported the plot, I thank you; for not having carried it out, I excuse you. That task needed a man.

But suppose that someone prosecutes you; that he applies the test of the jurist Lucius Cassius Longinus: 'who benefited thereby?'. Then you will have to take care, for you might be implicated. True, you used to observe, once upon a time, that such an act would benefit all who were unwilling to be slaves. Nevertheless, whom did its performance benefit most of all? Yourself! You, who, far from being a slave, are an autocratic ruler: you, who employed the treasure in the Temple of Ops [2] to wipe off your gigantic debts, who after manipulating these same account-books squandered countless sums, who transferred enormous possessions from Caesar's house to your own. What an immensely profitable output of fake memoranda and forged handwritings your home produces! The place is a forger's workshop, a black market: whole properties and cities, mass exemptions from tribute and taxation are the wares of its truly scandalous trade.

Nothing short of Caesar's death could have rescued you from your debtor's ruin. You look rather worried. Are you secretly nervous that you may be implicated? No, I can set your fears at rest: no one will ever believe such a thing of you. You are not the man to perform a patriotic act. Our country has great men, and they did that noble deed. I do not say you took part. I only say you were glad.

Now I have answered your most serious accusations. Well, I must reply to the others. You have complained about my presence in Pompey's camp, [3] and about my conduct throughout that period. True, at that time – and I have said this before – if my advice and authority had prevailed, you would be a poor man today, and we should be free; and our country would not have lost so many armies and com-

1. Apparently during Caesar's return march from Spain in 45 B.C. Plutarch records that Antony did not respond to the suggestion but omitted to inform Caesar.

2. Antony had gradually made use of Caesar's funds deposited in this temple on the Capitoline Hill.

3. See above, p. 84.

manders. For when I foresaw what has now happened, I confess that I mourned as sadly as all other good citizens, if they had possessed my foresight, would likewise have mourned. I grieved, Senators, I grieved that our Republic, which your and my counsels had once preserved, was moving towards rapid annihilation. In such circumstances I was not uneducated and ignorant enough to be overcome by fears whether I personally should survive. For my life, while it was still mine, was full of anguish; whereas its loss would mean an end of all troubles. But I wanted life to remain for the magnificent men who were Rome's glory – all those who have served as consul and praetor, the fine Senators, the flower and promise of our nobility, the armies of good Romans. So for me any peace that could unite our citizens seemed preferable to a war that tore them apart. And indeed, however hard the circumstances of peace, if those men were only living today, at least the Republic would still be with us.

If this view of mine had prevailed, and if the very men whose lives I sought to preserve had not, in their military over-optimism, set themselves against me, one of many results would certainly be this: you would never still be in the Senate. You would not even be at Rome!

You object that my speech alienated Pompey from me. That is absurd. He had more affection for me than for anyone. There was no one in the world whom he talked to and consulted more often. Indeed it was a splendid thing that two men with so widely differing views on government policy should remain such close friends. Each of us knew, equally well, the thoughts and opinions of the other. My first concern was to keep our fellow-Romans alive: by so doing, we could give ourselves time to think later on about their civic rights. Pompey, on the other hand, was preoccupied with their rights in the immediate present. Nevertheless, our disagreement was tolerable – the more so because we both concentrated on our own specific objectives.

But what Pompey, with his outstanding and almost superhuman gifts, thought about myself is well known to those who accompanied him on his retreat from Pharsalus to Paphos.[1] He never mentioned my name except in complimentary terms and with an abundance of

1. In Cyprus; Pompey's last port of call after the battle of Pharsalus on his way to Egypt, where he was murdered (48 B.C.).

friendly regrets that we were not together. He also admitted that, whereas his had been the higher hopes, the more accurate prophet had been myself. But how can you have the effrontery to taunt me with Pompey, when you have to admit that I was his friend: whereas you, on the other hand, were the purchaser of his confiscated property!

However, let us say no more about that war – in which you fared only too well. Nor have I any answer to give you about the jokes which you say I made while I was in camp. Life was certainly anxious there. Yet however grim circumstances are, human beings, if they really are human, occasionally relax. Antony criticizes my gloom, and he criticizes my jokes! Which proves that I showed moderation in both.

No one left me any legacies,[1] you said. I only wish that the charge were justified, for then more of my friends and relations would be alive today. But I wonder how that idea came into your mind. For men have made me bequests amounting to more than twenty million sesterces. True, I admit that in this respect you have been more fortunate than I have. For all who have made me their heirs have been my friends. That has been their way of soothing my grief with some mitigating benefit – if it could be regarded as such. But you inherited from Lucius Rubrius Casinas: whom you had never seen! He must indeed have loved you dearly, seeing that you do not even know whether he was black or white. He passed over in your favour the sons of that very worthy knight, his friend Quintus Fufius. Rubrius had constantly announced, in public, that Fufius's son was to be his heir. And yet he did not even mention him in his will! Instead, you were the man he made his heir – you whom he had never seen or, at any rate, had never spoken to. And tell me this, please, if it is not too much trouble: what did your other benefactor Lucius Turselius look like? How tall was he, where did he come from, what was his tribe? 'I know nothing,' you will answer, 'except what properties he owned.' Was that sufficient cause for him to disinherit his brother and make you his heir? But there were many others too, equally remote from any connexion with him, from whom Antony grabbed huge sums of money, ejecting the true heirs, and behaving as if he himself were the inheritor.

1. It was regarded as a slight not to be mentioned in a friend's will. Lawyers, who were not allowed to accept fees, particularly expected this sort of reward.

And there is another reason too why I am surprised, particularly surprised, that you should have had the impudence even to mention matters of inheritance. For you did not come into your own father's property! [1]

Fool! Were these the arguments you were trying to hunt out when you spent day after day in another man's country house, practising oratory? Though your oratorical practice, as your closest friends point out, is intended to work off your hangovers rather than to sharpen your brain, you have facetiously appointed a teacher of oratory – the appointment carried by the supporting votes of your fellow-drinkers – and you have allowed the man to speak against you in any way he likes. He is certainly an amusing enough fellow. But, since you and your friends are his targets, he cannot complain of any lack of material!

Note the contrast between yourself and your grandfather. [2] He, with deliberation, produced arguments relevant to his case; you just pour out irrelevancies. And yet what a salary your teacher of rhetoric has drawn from you. Listen to this, Senators: take note of the wounds inflicted upon our nation. To this elocution trainer – Sextus Clodius – he handed over 1,250 acres of land, tax-free. You made the people of Rome defray this enormous charge, Antony, with no other result than to make you learn to be the idiot that you are. You unprincipled rogue! Was this one of the directions you found in Caesar's notebooks? However, about this estate at Leontini I will say something later; also about other properties in Campania – all of them lands which Antony has wrenched from Rome, and polluted by the utterly degraded characters of the men to whom he has given them.

I have said enough in answer to his charges. Now some attention must be given to our moralist and reformer himself. However, I do not propose to tell the whole story at once: so that if I have to return to the fray, I shall not need to repeat myself. In view of the extraordinary quantity of his crimes and vices, that presents no difficulty.

1. Probably the meaning is that Antony's father Marcus Antonius Creticus left an estate too heavily encumbered with debt for the guardians of Antony (who was eleven at the time) to accept it on his behalf. Non-acceptance of an inheritance cast a slur on the family name.

2. Marcus Antonius the Orator, consul 99 B.C., killed in 87. He and Lucius Licinius Crassus, the principal spokesmen in Cicero's On the Orator, had been the foremost speakers of their generation.

Would you like us to consider your behaviour from boyhood onwards, Antony? I think so. Let us begin then at the beginning. Your
bankruptcy, in early adolescence – do you remember that? Your
father's fault, you will say. Certainly; and what a truly filial self-
defence! But it was typical of your impudence to go to the theatre and
sit in one of the fourteen rows reserved for knights, when the Roscian
Law [1] assigned special seats for bankrupts – and meant this to apply
whether it was bad luck or bad conduct had caused the bankruptcy.
Then you graduated to man's clothing – or rather it was woman's as
far as you were concerned. At first you were just a public prostitute,
with a fixed price: quite a high one, too. But very soon Curio inter-
vened and took you off the streets, promoting you, one might say, to
wifely status, and making a sound, steady, married woman of you.
No boy bought for sensual purposes was ever so completely in his
master's power as you were in Curio's. On countless occasions his
father threw you out of the house. He even stationed guards to keep
you out! Nevertheless, helped by nocturnal darkness, urged on by
sensuality, compelled by the promised fee – in, through the roof, you
climbed.

The household found these repulsive goings on completely unendurable. I wonder if you realize that I have a very thorough knowledge of what I am speaking about. Cast your mind back to the time
when Curio's father lay weeping in his bed. The son, likewise in tears,
threw himself at my feet and begged me to help you – and to defend
himself against a demand, which he expected from his own father, for
six million sesterces. The young man loved you so passionately that
he swore he would leave the country because he could not bear to be
kept apart from you. In those days, within that renowned family,
there were troubles without number which I helped to mitigate – or
rather, brought to an end altogether. I persuaded the father to pay his
son's debts. I persuaded him to sacrifice part of his property to restore
the position of this young man, whose promise of brain and character
was so brilliant. But I also persuaded him to use all his legal authority
as a father to prevent Curio from associating with you or even meeting you. When you remembered all these interventions of mine, only

1. This law assigned the fourteen front rows in the theatre to the knights (67
B.C.). There is no other evidence that it also made special provision for bankrupts.

one thing can have given you the nerve to provoke and abuse me in the way you have, and that is your reliance on the brute force of arms: the weapons which we see in the Senate today.

But about Antony's degradations and sex-crimes that is as far as I will go. For there are some things which it would be indecent for me to describe. As far as free speaking goes you have the advantage of me! – since you have done things which a respectable opponent cannot even mention. So instead I will now turn briefly to the remaining portion of this man's life. For our thoughts will naturally run on to what he did during the national miseries of the Civil War – and what he is doing today. You know those things, Senators, as well as I do, and indeed much better. Yet continue, I beg of you, to listen to them carefully. For in such cases knowledge about events is not enough. There is also need to be reminded of them: only thus will they be fully felt.

However, since I must allow myself time to reach the end of these happenings, I must cut short the middle part of the story. Well, Antony now recounts his kindnesses towards me. All the same, when Publius Clodius was tribune, the two men were intimate friends. Antony was the firebrand who started all Clodius's fires. Indeed, one of his projects – he knows very well which one I mean – was actually located in Clodius's home.[1] Then Antony went to Alexandria:[2] in defiance of the Senate, and of patriotism, and of the will of heaven. But he was under a man with whom he could do no wrong – Aulus Gabinius. Then consider the nature and circumstances of Antony's return. Before he came home, he went from Egypt to farthest Gaul. Home, did I say? At that time, other men still possessed homes: but you, Antony, had none at all. Home? You had no piece of ground of your own in the whole world, except at Misenum; and that you only shared with partners, as though it were a company affair like the Sisapo mines.[3]

From Gaul you came to stand for the quaestorship. On that occasion, I dare you to claim that you went to your father before you came

1. Probably Cicero refers to the fact that Fulvia was Clodius's wife before she was Antony's.
2. On a mission (in defiance of the Sibylline Books as well as the Senate) to restore King Ptolemy XII 'the Flute-Player' to the Egyptian throne (55 B.C.).
3. Vermilion (cinnabar) mines in southern Spain.

to me! I had already received a letter from Caesar asking me to accept your excuses; so I did not even allow you to thank me. After that, you treated me with respect, and I helped you in your candidature for the quaestorship. That was the time when, with the approval of Rome, you tried to kill Publius Clodius. Now, though this was entirely your own idea, and owed nothing to my initiative, nevertheless you proclaimed the conviction that only his murder could ever repay me for the injuries I had suffered from you.[1] This makes me wonder why you say Titus Annius Milo killed Clodius on my instigation. For, when you spontaneously proposed to me that you should perform the same action, I had given you no encouragement. If you went through with the deed, I wanted you yourself, and not my influence upon you, to have the glory.

Well, you became quaestor;[2] and instantly – without benefit of Senate's decree, drawing of lots, or legal sanction – you ran off to Caesar. For that seemed to you the only place on earth where destitution, debt, and crime could find shelter: the only refuge for ruined men. There, through Caesar's generosity and your own looting, you reimbursed your losses – if you can call it reimbursement when you immediately squander what you have embezzled! So then, beggared again, you hastened to apply for a tribuneship. Your aim in acquiring it, presumably, was to model yourself on your lover.[3]

Now listen, I beg you, Senators, I do not mean to the personal and domestic scandals created by Antony's disgusting improprieties, but to the evil, godless way in which he has undermined us all, and our fortunes, and our whole country. At the root of all our disasters you will find his wickedness. When Lucius Cornelius Lentulus Crus and Gaius Claudius Marcellus became consuls on the first of January,[4] the Republican government was tottering and on the verge of collapse. You, members of the Senate, wanted to support the government; you also desired to meet the wishes of Caesar himself, if he was in his right mind. Yet Antony had sold and subjected his tribuneship to another man, and he exploited the office for your obstruction. That is to say, to the axe which had struck down many men for lesser crimes

---

1. Probably the reference is to Antony's friendship with Publius Clodius.
2. Antony's quaestorship was in 52 or 51 B.C.
3. Curio who, while tribune in 50 B.C., had strongly supported Caesar.
4. 49 B.C. On 1 January Curio handed the Senate Caesar's ultimatum.

he had the audacity to expose his own neck. In those days the Senate was still its own master; those honourable members who are now dead were still among its number. That Senate, Antony, employed for your censure the decree [1] reserved, by ancestral custom, for Roman citizens who are the enemies of Rome. And yet, as audience for your criticisms of me, you have the impertinence to select the Senate – that very body which pronounced me to be its saviour, and you the enemy of the state!

Your criminal action at that time has not been mentioned lately; but what you did has not been forgotten. So long as there are human beings in the world, so long as the name of Rome remains upon the earth – and that means everlastingly, barring destructive action by yourself – that pestilential veto [2] of yours will be remembered. In the Senate's proceedings there had not been the slightest sign of bias or impetuosity. Yet you, a single young man, imposed your veto, and thus prevented the entire Senatorial Order from passing a measure on which the safety of our nation depended. And this you did not once, but repeatedly. Furthermore, you rejected all efforts to open negotiations with you about upholding the authority of this House. Yet the matter at stake was nothing less than your itch to plunge the whole country into anarchy and desolation. The pleas of the nation's leaders, the warnings of your elders, a crowded Senate, none of them sufficed to deter you from this measure you had been bribed and bought into proposing.

Next, therefore, after many attempts to dissuade you, there was no alternative; you had to be dealt the blow which few had received before – and which none had survived. So this Senatorial Order directed the consuls, and other powers and authorities, to take up arms against you. You only escaped those arms by sheltering behind Caesar's.

Caesar's intentions were wholly revolutionary. But the man who gave him his principal excuse for attacking his country was yourself. For that was the only pretext he claimed, the only reason he put forward for his maniacal decision and action: he quoted the Senate's

1. 'Let the consuls [and other officials] ensure that the state suffers no harm', an emergency conferment of dictatorial powers.

2. On 2 January 49 B.C., Antony and another tribune had vetoed a proposal in the Senate that unless Caesar disbanded his army before a named date he should be declared a public enemy. Caesar crossed the Rubicon eight days later.

disregard of a veto, its abolition of a tribune's entitlement, its encroachment on Antony's rights. I say nothing of the falsity and frivolity of these charges – though no man can possibly be justified in taking up arms against his own nation. But I am not speaking of Caesar. You, Antony, were the man who provided the pretext for this most catastrophic of wars: you cannot deny it.

If what I am now going to say is known to you already, then your fate is sad indeed: and sadder still if it is not. Now, there exist written records, to be recollected without possibility of oblivion by remotest posterity until the end of time, proving that these things happened. That the consuls were expelled from Italy; that they were accompanied by the man whose glory illuminated our nation – Pompey; that all former consuls whose health enabled them to share in that disastrous retreat, all praetors and ex-praetors, tribunes of the people, a great part of the Senate, the flower of our young manhood, in a word all the components of the entire Roman state, were uprooted and driven from their homes.

Just as seeds are the origins of trees and plants, so, with equal certainty, you were the seed of that most grievous war. Senators, you are mourning three armies [1] of Roman soldiers slain in battle: Antony killed them. You are sorrowing for great men of Rome: Antony robbed you of them. The authority of your Order has been destroyed: Antony destroyed it. For every evil which we have seen since that time – and what evils have we not seen? – he is responsible. There can be no other conclusion. He has been our Helen of Troy! He has brought upon our country war, and pestilence, and annihilation.

The rest of his tribuneship resembled the beginning. Of all the misdeeds which the Senate, while the Republic was still with us, had rendered impossible there was not one which he left undone. And note the crimes within his crime. Though he rehabilitated many who were in trouble, there was no mention of his uncle [2] among them. But if he was severe, why was he not severe to everyone? and if merciful, why not merciful to his own kinsmen?

Among those whose civil rights he restored I will only mention

1. At Pharsalus (48 B.C.), Thapsus (46), and Munda (45).
2. The spendthrift Gaius Antonius Hybrida, expelled from the Senate in 70 B.C., Cicero's fellow-consul in 63, exiled for extortion after governing Macedonia (62–60), censor in 42.

Licinius Lenticula, his fellow-dicer – a man convicted for gambling. I can only suppose Antony protested that his partner at the tables must not be a convict! But his real aim was to utilize the law cancelling Lenticula's sentence as a cloak for the cancellation of his own gaming debts. Now, Antony, what reasons justifying his reinstatement did you quote to the people of Rome? The normal sort of argument would run like this: that Lenticula had been absent when the prosecution was instituted against him; that the case went undefended, that the law provided no judicial procedure to deal with dicing, that armed violence had been used to procure his downfall, or as a final objection what was said in your uncle's case – that the court's decision had been influenced by bribery. But not at all. Those were not your excuses. What you urged was that Lenticula was a good man, useful to his country. Well, that was irrelevant. All the same, I should excuse you on that count if your plea were only true, for the mere fact of having been convicted is of no great importance. But there is not a word of truth in it. Lenticula has been condemned under the law which relates to dicing: he is the sort of person who would not hesitate to throw dice in the Forum itself – a thoroughly criminal type. The man who can restore the rights of such a ruffian reveals a great deal about his own character.

Then consider another aspect of Antony's tribuneship. When Caesar, on his way to Spain, had given him Italy to trample upon, the journeys Antony made and the towns he visited are well worth looking into. I realize I am speaking of matters which are thoroughly well known and widely talked about. I am also aware that the events of which I am, and shall be, speaking are better known to anyone who was in Italy at that time than to myself who was absent.[1] Nevertheless, although what I tell you will undoubtedly fall short of what you know already, allow me to recall certain particulars.

For never, anywhere in the world, have there been stories of such depraved and discreditable misconduct. He travelled about in a lady's carriage, did this tribune of the people. In front of him marched attendants crowned with laurel-wreaths. Among them, carried in an open litter, went an actress. The respectable citizens of the country towns, compelled to come and meet him, greeted her, not by her

1. Cicero left Italy on 7 June 49 B.C.; Caesar had left Rome for Spain on 7 April.

well-known stage name, but as Volumnia.[1] Next followed a repulsive collection of his friends: a four-wheeler full of procurers. Only then came his neglected mother, following, like a mother-in-law, her debauched son's mistress. Poor woman! Her capacity for child-bearing has indeed been catastrophic. In such fashion a wide variety of country towns, indeed the whole of Italy, was branded by Antony with the marks of his degraded behaviour.

To censure his other actions, Senators, is difficult and delicate. He fought in the war. He wallowed in the blood of Romans who were in every way his opposites. He was fortunate, if there can ever be good fortune in criminality. But since we do not want to offend the old soldiers – though the soldiers' case and yours, Antony, are wholly unlike (they followed their leader, you went to seek him out) – nevertheless I shall give you no opportunity to incite them against me. For concerning the character of the war I shall say nothing.

From Thessaly to Brundisium you returned as conqueror with your legions. At Brundisium you refrained from killing me. How very kind of you! For you could have killed me, I admit. Though the men who were with you at that time unanimously maintained I must be spared. For even your own legionaries revered me: so great is man's love for their country, which they remembered that I had saved. However, let us concede that you gave me as a present what you did not take away from me; you did not deprive me of my life, which I therefore retain as a gift from yourself. After hearing all your insults I nearly forgot my gratitude, though not quite. And there was something particularly impudent about your abuse, because you knew how I would be able to retaliate!

Arrival at Brundisium for you meant envelopment in the embraces of your little actress. Well, is that a lie? It is distressing, is it not, to be unable to deny something that is disreputable to admit. But if the townsmen caused you to feel no shame, did not your own veteran army? For every single soldier who was at Brundisium saw her. Every one of them knew she had come all those days' journey to congratulate you: every man grieved to have found out so late in the day the worthlessness of the leader he had followed.

Again you toured Italy, with this actress by your side. In the communities through which you passed, amid scenes of brutality and

1. See above, p. 111.

misery, you planted your soldiers as settlers. At Rome you cut a deplorable figure as a robber of gold and silver – and of wine. As a climax, unknown to Caesar (who was at Alexandria), Caesar's friends were kind enough to make Antony his Master of Horse. At that juncture he felt entitled to live with Hippias; [1] and to hand over race-horses, intended for the national games, to another actor Sergius. At that time Antony had chosen to live, not in the house which he so discreditably retains now, but in Marcus Pupius Piso's home. His decrees, his looting, his legacies inherited and grabbed I will pass over in silence. Need compelled him: he did not know which way to turn. Those substantial inheritances from Lucius Rubrius Casinas and Lucius Turselius had not yet come to him; not yet had he become the unexpected 'heir' to Pompey, and many more. He had nothing except what he could plunder; he was obliged to live like a bandit.

But about these examples of the tougher sorts of rascality, I shall speak no more. Let us turn instead to meaner kinds of misbehaviour. With those jaws of yours, and those lungs, and that gladiatorial strength, you drank so much wine at Hippias's wedding, Antony, that on the next day you had to be sick in full view of the people of Rome. It was a disgusting sight; even to hear what happened is disgusting. If you had behaved like that at a private dinner party, among those outsize drinking cups of yours, everyone would have regarded it as disgraceful enough. But here, in the Assembly of the Roman People, was a man holding public office, a Master of the Horse – from whom even a belch would have been unseemly – flooding his own lap and the whole platform with the gobbets of wine-reeking food he had vomited up. He admits that this was one of his filthier actions: let us now return to his grander misdeeds.

Well, Caesar returned from Alexandria, a fortunate man – as he seemed to himself at least: though in my view no one who brings misfortune upon his country can be called fortunate. The spear [2] was set up before the temple of Jupiter Stator; and Pompey's property – the very thought brings unhappiness! for even when the tears no

1. There is an uncommunicable pun on the derivation of the name Hippias (Greek *hippos* – horse), presumably with some reference to Antony's office of Master of the Horse (deputy to the dictator). The exiled tyrant of Athens, son of Pisistratus, had been called Hippias (527–510 B.C.). The meaning of the subsequent reference to race-horses is obscure.

2. At Roman auctions a spear was fastened in the ground.

longer flow the sorrow remains deeply fixed in my heart – Pompey's property, I say, was subjected to the pitiless voice of the auctioneer.

On that single occasion the nation forgot its slavery, and mourned. Men felt slaves, because fear gripped them all, yet, even so, the people of Rome lamented freely enough. Every man waited to see if there would be some depraved madman, repulsive to heaven and humanity, who would dare to take part in that criminal auction. Though some of the men round that spear would have stopped at nothing else, no one had audacity enough for this – no one except Antony alone! One person, only one, was shameless enough to perpetrate the act which all others, however great their effrontery, had shunned in horror. But, Antony, were you too totally witless – or is not insanity the appropriate word? – to realize this: that in your station of life to become a purchaser of confiscated property, and of Pompey's property at that, would earn you the curses and loathing of the Roman people, the detestation of all gods and all human beings, now and for evermore? And then, think of the arrogance with which this debauchee took instant possession of the estate! The estate of a man who through his valour had made Rome more greatly feared, and by his justice had made her more greatly loved, by all the other nations upon earth.

So, abruptly seizing that great man's property, Antony wallowed in its midst. In his mighty satisfaction he gloated, like the character in a play who was poor and has suddenly become rich. But as some poet[1] wrote, 'ill-gotten gains will soon be squandered'. And the unbelievable – almost miraculous – fact is that he squandered Pompey's substantial fortune, not in a few months, but in a few days! In that house there were large quantities of wine, heavy pieces of the finest silver-ware, costly robes, ample and elegant furniture – all the splendid and abundant property of a man who, though not luxurious, had none the less been nobly endowed with possessions. Of these, within a few days, nothing was left! Charybdis,[2] if she ever existed, was but a single animal. I swear that such a number of objects so widely scattered in so great a variety of places could hardly have been swallowed up, at such a speed, by the Ocean itself.

Nothing was locked up, nothing sealed, nothing listed. Whole

1. Naevius.
2. Whirlpool or maelstrom (later identified with Straits of Messina), personified as voracious daughter of Earth and Poseidon.

store-rooms were disposed of as gifts, to unmitigated scoundrels. Actors and actresses grabbed everything they wanted. The place was packed with gamblers, crammed with inebriates. For days on end, in many parts of the house, the orgies of drinking went on and on. Gaming losses piled up; Antony's good luck did not always hold. On view were the richly worked counterpanes which had belonged to Pompey – now they were in the garrets of slaves, and on their beds!

So let it not surprise you that these riches were consumed with such speed. A profligacy so boundless as Antony's could have rapidly devoured not just a single man's patrimony, even one so abundant as Pompey's, but whole cities and whole kingdoms. And then the mansion and the parks that he took over! Your impudence, Antony, was preposterous. How could you have the effrontery to enter that house, to pass its most sacred threshold, to let the household gods of such an abode see you flaunting your degraded features? This was a home which no one, for many days and months, could gaze upon or pass by without weeping. As you linger on within its rooms, are you not overcome with shame?

You are brainless, I know: yet surely, even so, none of the things that are there can bring you enjoyment. When you look at those beaks of ships [1] in the hall, you cannot possibly imagine that the house you are entering is your own! That would be out of the question. For all your lack of sense and sensibility, still you are aware of what you yourself are, you know your own people and possessions. So I do not believe that, waking or sleeping, you can ever feel easy in your mind. Drink-sodden and demented though you are, the appearance in your dreams of that great man must surely rouse you in terror; and when you are awake, too, his recurring image must unhinge your mind still further.

I pity the very walls and roof of that house. For never before had the place witnessed anything but strict propriety – fine, high-minded tradition and virtue. As you know very well, Senators, Pompey was as praiseworthy in his domestic as in his international dealings; as admirable in his home life as in public affairs he was renowned. Yet nowadays, in his home, every dining-room is a taproom, every bedroom a brothel. Antony may deny this nowadays. Be tactful; do not

1. Captured by Pompey in his campaign against the pirates in 67 B.C.

investigate! For he has become economical. He has told that actress of his to gather up her own property and hand back his keys, as the Twelve Tables ordain – and he has driven her out. What a reputable citizen! What solid respectability! Here is the most honourable action of his whole life; he has divorced his actress.

How he harps on the phrase: 'I, the consul Antony.' That amounts to saying, 'I, the consul, debauchee', or 'I, the consul, criminal'. For that is the significance of 'Antony'. If there were any dignity in the name, I presume that your grandfather, too, would sometimes have called himself 'the consul, Antony'. But he never did. So would your uncle, who was my colleague. Or has there been no Antony but yourself?

However, I pass over these offences, for they had no direct connexion with the part you played in ruining our country. I return to the latter – to the Civil War, which owed its birth, its rise, and its performance to yourself. True, your role in the war was insignificant. That was because you were frightened, or rather preoccupied with your sexual interests. But you had tasted Roman blood; indeed you had drunk deeply of it. At Pharsalus you were in the front rank. It was you who killed that fine nobleman, Lucius Domitius Ahenobarbus – as well as many others, fugitives from the battle-field. Caesar would perhaps have spared them, as he spared others. But you, on the other hand, hunted them down for your slaughter.

However, after these grand and glorious achievements, the war was still by no means ended. So why did you not follow Caesar to Africa?[1] And then, when Caesar had returned from Africa, let us note the position and rank which he assigned to you. As general he had made you quaestor, when he was dictator you had become his Master of the Horse. You had begun the war. Every atrocity had been instigated by yourself; in each successive robbery you had been his associate. We have it on your own authority that his will adopted you as his son.[2] Yet what did he now do? He took action against you – the sums you owed for the house, and for its parks and the other property you acquired in the auction, were all demanded back from you by Caesar.

1. For the campaign of Thapsus (46 B.C.).
2. It had been a blow for Antony when Caesar's published will reserved this distinction for Octavian, appointing Antony as one of the secondary heirs only.

Your initial reply was vigorous enough: and, I admit – for I do not want to seem prejudiced against you – reasonably fair and just. 'So Caesar claims money from me? Could I not just as reasonably claim money from him – or did he win the war without my help? No: nor could he have. It was I who provided him with the pretext for the Civil War, I who proposed those subversive laws, who forcibly resisted not merely the Roman people's consuls and generals, but the entire Senate and Roman people and the gods and altars and homes of our fathers – indeed Rome itself. Caesar did not conquer for himself alone; why should those who shared the work not share the plunder too?' Reasonable enough. But reason was beside the point, for Caesar was the stronger. So he silenced you, and you and your guarantors received a visit from his soldiers.

And then, suddenly, out came that spectacular list of yours. Everyone laughed at the size of the list – at the varied and extensive catalogue of possessions, none of which (except a part of the Misenum property) the seller could call his own. But the auction itself was a melancholy sight. Few of Pompey's robes were now to be seen, and even they were covered with stains; a certain amount of his silver plate appeared in battered condition; and there were some seedy-looking slaves. So the remains were meagre enough. If nothing at all had survived, our grief would have been less.

However, the heirs of Lucius Rubrius Casinas prevented the auction, and they were backed by a decree from Caesar. Antony, the wild spender, was embarrassed – he had nowhere to turn. And that was the precise moment of the arrest in Caesar's house (so the report went) of an assassin, dagger in hand – sent by you, Antony: and Caesar charged you openly with this in the Senate. Next, however, after allowing you a few days for payment – since you were so poor – he departed for Spain.[1] Even then you did not follow him. So early a retirement, for so good a gladiator? A man who showed such timidity in standing up for his party (and that means standing up for himself) need surely inspire no fear in others!

In the end, some time afterwards, Antony did leave for Spain. But he proved unable to reach that country safely, he maintains. Then how did Publius Cornelius Dolabella get there? Either you ought not to have backed the cause you did, Antony, or, having done so, you

1. For the campaign of Munda.

ought to have stood up for your side to the end. Three times Caesar fought against his fellow-citizens: in Thessaly, in Africa, and in Spain. Dolabella took part in all these campaigns; in the Spanish war he was wounded. If you want to know my view, I wish he had not been there. Yet however blameworthy his initial decision, at least he deserves praise for consistent adherence thereafter. But what about yourself? That was the time when Pompey's sons [1] were fighting to make their way home – a matter, surely, which concerned all Caesar's partisans. In other words, Pompey's sons were struggling to recover the shrines of their household gods, their sacred hearth and home, and the guardian spirits of their family – all of which you had seized. When, in order to recover what was theirs by law, they were obliged to use force, who would most justly (though indeed among such grievous wrongs to speak of justice is impossible) – who, I say, would be their principal target? The answer is, yourself, the taker of their property. So it was your battle, was it not, that Dolabella had to fight in Spain: while you stayed at Narbo, vomiting over your hosts' tables.

And your return from Narbo! Antony actually wanted to know why *I* returned from my journey [2] so suddenly. Now I have recently explained to the Senate the reasons for my return. I wanted, if I could, to be of service to the state even before the New Year. You ask how I returned. First, I arrived by daylight, not after dark. Secondly, I came in my boots and toga, not in Gallic sandals and a cloak.[3] I see your eyes fixed upon me: in anger, it appears. But you ought, instead, to harbour friendly feelings if only you knew how ashamed I am – unlike yourself – of the depths to which you have fallen. Of all the offences that I have seen or heard of as committed by any single person this is the most deplorable. You, who claimed to have been Master of the Horse, who were standing for one of next year's consulships – or rather begging for one of them as a personal favour – off you went, in your Gallic sandals and mantle, speeding through the towns of Cisalpine Gaul: the towns in which, when we were candi-

1. Gnaeus the younger, killed after Munda, and Sextus (p. 91).
2. i.e. in summer 44 (p. 94).
3. Even much later it was a solecism to wear sandals in the street. Cloaks were probably a novelty in Rome at this time; Augustus forbade their use in the Forum.

dates for consulships, we used to seek votes – in the days when these appointments went by votes and not by personal favour.

Note the frivolity of the man. When, at about three o'clock, he approached Rome and came to Red Rocks,[1] he dived into a wretched little wine-shop, and, hiding there, drank and drank until evening. Then a two-wheeler took him rapidly into the city and he arrived at his house with his head veiled. 'Who are you?' said the porter. 'A messenger from Antony,' he replied. He was immediately taken to the lady [2] for whose sake he had come, and he handed her a letter. As she read the contents, she wept; for it was amorously written – and the gist was that he had given up the actress and transferred all his love to this other lady. And as her weeping increased, this soft-hearted fellow could bear the sight no longer, but uncovered his head and threw his arms round her neck. Depraved character! No other epithet is adequate for this creature who plunged the city into terror by night, plunged Italy into a series of nerve-racking days, merely in order to make his sudden appearance before this woman. What a surprise this must have been to her: to see such behaviour from a male prostitute.

At home, then, you could lay claim to a love affair. But elsewhere there was an even nastier affair for you: to prevent Lucius Munatius Plancus [3] from selling up your sureties. A tribune brought you before a public meeting, and you replied: 'I have come here on a matter concerning my private property.' This was regarded by everyone as an excellent joke.[4]

However, that is enough about trivialities; let us turn to more significant matters. When Caesar came back from Spain, you travelled a long way to meet him. You went quickly, and you returned quickly: Caesar could therefore note that, if not brave, you were at least energetic. Somehow or other you got on friendly terms with him again. Caesar was like that. He was extremely ready to offer his intimate friendship to anyone whom he knew to be corrupt and

1. See above, p. 88.

2. Fulvia. She was his wife, but Romans found this urgency frivolous.

3. See p. 98; one of six (or eight) Prefects to whom Caesar officially entrusted Rome during his absence in Spain.

4. The joke was that Antony was notoriously impoverished, a disgrace according to Roman ideas.

unbalanced, penniless, and hopelessly in debt. In these respects your credentials were excellent. So he gave orders that you should be made consul – with himself, moreover, as your colleague. One can only feel sympathy with Publius Cornelius Dolabella, who had been urged to stand, brought forward, and then fobbed off. Everyone knows how deceitfully both of you treated Dolabella in this matter. Caesar induced him to be a candidate for the consulship, and then, after promising and virtually granting him election, blocked the proceedings and transferred the post to himself. And you supported this treachery.

The first of January arrived. We were made to attend the Senate. Dolabella attacked Antony – with much greater fullness and preparation than I do now. And heavens, the things that Antony himself said in his rage! Caesar indicated his intention, before his forthcoming departure for the east, of ordering that Dolabella should become consul in his own place. And yet they deny that the man who was always acting and speaking like that was a totalitarian monarch! Well, after Caesar had said that, this splendid augur Antony announced that his priesthood empowered him to employ the auspices in order to obstruct or invalidate the proceedings of the Assembly. And he declared that this is what he would do. But first note the man's unbelievable stupidity. For your priestly office of augur, Antony, was what you relied upon for entitlement to perform those actions. Yet, as consul alone, without the added possession of your augurship, your entitlement would still have been just as good. Indeed, was your consulship not actually a better qualification? For we augurs are only empowered to report omens, whereas the consuls and other state officials have the right actually to watch the heavens.

Very well, you bungled the matter through inexperience. We cannot expect good judgement from someone who is never sober. But just observe the man's impudence. Many months earlier he had declared in the Senate that he would either use the auspices to prevent the Assembly from meeting to elect Dolabella, or alternatively would act as he finally did. Now, who on earth can divine what flaws there are going to be in the auspices, except the man who has already formally set about watching the heavens? Which cannot legally be done during an election [1] – and if anyone has been watching the heavens

1. ? correct text: the right of a magistrate to prohibit business in this way had been abolished in 58 B.C., at least for legislative Assemblies. Here Cicero accepts

previously, he is obliged to make his report not after but before the election has begun. But Antony is as ignorant as he is shameless: the insolence his actions display is as unbounded as his ignorance of what an augur ought to do. And yet cast your minds back to his consulship, from that day onwards until the fifteenth of March. No servant was ever so humble and abject. He could do nothing himself; everything had to be begged for. You could see him poking his head into the back of his litter asking his colleague [1] for the favours Antony wanted to market.

So the day of Dolabella's election arrived. The right of the first vote is settled by lot; Antony said nothing. The result of this ballot was announced. He remained silent. The first class was called to vote, its vote announced; then the six centuries which voted next, then the second class – all this in a shorter time than it takes to tell the story. Then, when the proceedings were over, came our brilliant augur's announcement – you would say he was Gaius Laelius [2] himself: 'the meeting is adjourned until another day'. What monstrous impudence! You had neither seen, nor understood, nor heard, any omen whatever. You did not even claim to have watched the heavens; you do not today. So the flaw in question was the one which you had foreseen and foretold as long ago as the first of January! In other words, you undoubtedly falsified the auspices. You employed religion to constrain an Assembly of the Roman People. You announced unfavourable omens, augur to augur, consul to consul: and you did so fraudulently. May the calamitous consequences fall not upon Rome, but upon your own head.

That is all I shall say, in case I should seem to be invalidating the actions of Dolabella – which must, at some time, be referred to our Board of Augurs. But mark the man's audacious arrogance. As long as it is your pleasure, Antony, the election of Dolabella as consul was

the abolition for electoral Assemblies also (though elsewhere he takes a different view – just as his own attitude towards omens and auspices varies from intellectual disbelief to acceptance as a national institution). Antony's preference here for acting as an augur was probably due to the greater acceptability of this procedure to public opinion. The meeting was then declared to be adjourned on the grounds that the omens were unfavourable. For the Assembly and its centuries and tribes, and for the augurs and auspices, see Appendix C.

1. Caesar, his fellow-consul.
2. Known as 'the wise' (p. 211).

irregular. Then you change your mind: the procedure in regard to the auspices had nothing wrong with it after all! If an augur's report in the terms you employed has no meaning, then admit that when you demanded an adjournment you were drunk. If, on the other hand, the words have any meaning at all, then I request you, as my fellow-augur, to tell me what their meaning is.

But I must make sure that this survey of Antony's numerous exploits does not by accident omit one outstandingly brilliant action. So let us turn to the festival of the Lupercalia.[1] Look, Senators! He cannot hide his anxiety. Do you see how upset he looks – pale, and sweating? Never mind, so long as he is not sick, as he was in the Minucian Colonnade. How does he defend his scandalous behaviour at the Lupercalia? I should like to hear – and thereby learn the results of that generous fee and those lands at Leontini,[2] which he gave his teacher of oratory.

Upon the dais on a golden chair, wearing a purple robe and a wreath, was seated your colleague. You mounted the dais. You went up to Caesar's chair – Lupercus though you were, you should have remembered you were consul too – and you displayed a diadem. From all over the Forum there were groans. Where did the diadem come from? You had not just found one on the ground and picked it up. No, you had brought it from your own house! This was crime, deliberate and premeditated. Then you placed the diadem on his head: the people groaned. He took it off – and they applauded.

So, criminal, you were ready, alone among all that gathering, to propose that there should be a king and autocrat at Rome; to transform your fellow-consul into your lord and master; and to inflict upon the Roman people this ultimate test of its capacity to suffer and endure. You even tried to move him to pity – when you hurled yourself at his feet as a suppliant. What were you begging for? To become his slave? For yourself alone that would be a fitting plea, seeing that from boyhood onwards there was nothing which you had not

1. 15 February 44 B.C. At this ancient pastoral and propitiatory festival, young men called Luperci – wearing the skins of sacrificed goats, with whose blood their foreheads were smeared – ran round the foot of the Palatine striking any women they met with strips of these skins, as a fertility charm. Antony was one of these Luperci.

2. See above, p. 121.

allowed to be done to you. For your own person, adjustment to slavery was easy. But from ourselves, and from the people of Rome, you had no such mandate.

What glorious eloquence that was – when you made that speech with no clothes on! Offensive misbehaviour could go no further. Nothing could have been more thoroughly deserving of the severest possible punishment. Are you a slave, cowering in expectation of the lash? If you have any feelings at all, you must be feeling the lash now: and my account of these events must surely be drawing blood. Far be it from me to detract from the glory of our noble liberators. Yet such is my grief that I must speak out. Seeing that the man who rejected the diadem was killed, and was, by general consent, killed justly, it is appalling that the man who made him the offer should still be alive. In the public records, what is more, under the heading of the Lupercalia, he even caused the following entry to be made: 'At the bidding of the people, Antony, consul, offered Caesar, perpetual dictator, the kingship: Caesar refused.'

So I feel no surprise when you disturb the peace, when you shun Rome and the very daylight itself, when you drink with thieving riff-raff from early in one day until dawn of the next. For you, no refuge can be safe. Where could you possibly find a place in any community owning laws and lawcourts – since these are precisely what you have done your utmost to abolish and to replace by tyranny? Was this why Tarquin was expelled, why Spurius Cassius Vecellinus and Spurius Maelius[1] and Marcus Manlius Capitolinus were slain: to allow Antony, centuries after they were dead, to commit the forbidden evil of setting up a king at Rome?

Let us return to the auspices, the subject on which Caesar intended to address the Senate on the fifteenth of March. Antony, I must ask you this: what would you then have said?[2] You came here today (or so I heard) primed to rebut my assertion that the auspices – which unless declared invalid require scrupulous obedience – were employed by you in a fraudulent manner. However, that day's business was

1. See above, p. 114. Marcus Manlius Capitolinus saved the Capitol from the invading Gauls (c. 390 B.C.), but later, after accusing the Senate of embezzlement, was imprisoned and executed.

2. i.e., would Antony have opposed Caesar, or would he have declared Dolabella duly elected?

eliminated – by our national destiny. Did Caesar's death also eliminate your opinion concerning the auspices? [1]

But now I have come to that time which I must discuss before the subject upon which I had embarked. On that glorious day, you fled panic-stricken – your criminal conscience certain of impending death. You slunk surreptitiously home. Men interested in your survival looked after you; for they hoped you would behave sanely. My prophecies of the future have always fallen upon deaf ears. Yet how completely right they have proved! On the Capitol, when our noble liberators desired me to go to you and urge you to uphold the Republican government, I told them this: that as long as you were still frightened you would promise anything, but as soon as your fears ceased you would be yourself again. When, therefore, the other former consuls were continually in and out of your house, I held to my opinion. And I did not see you on that day or the next. For I believed that good Romans could come to no understanding, could have no association, with a totally unprincipled enemy.

After two days had passed, I came to the Temple of Tellus [2] – reluctantly enough even then, since armed men locked all its approaches. What a day that was for you, Antony! Even though you have abruptly turned against me, yet I am sorry for you – because you have subsequently done so little justice to your own good fame. If only you had been able to maintain the attitude you showed on that day, heaven knows, you would have been a hero! And the peace, which was pledged on that occasion by the cession of an aristocratic hostage – the young grandson of Marcus Fulvius Bambalio [3] – would be ours.

Fear made you a good citizen. However, as an instructor of good behaviour, fear lacks permanency; and your unscrupulousness – which never leaves you unless you are afraid – soon perverted you into evil ways again. And indeed even at that time, when people (other than myself) had an excellent opinion of you, your manner of presiding over the tyrant's funeral – if funeral that ceremony can be

1. On 17 March 44 B.C., Antony withdrew his opposition to Dolabella's consulship.

2. Earth: on the Esquiline Hill. Meeting here on 17 March the Senate adopted a compromise, granting an amnesty to Caesar's murderers but confirming his official acts (including 'those which could be found among his papers').

3. The father of Antony's wife Fulvia. Bambalio means 'stammerer'.

called – was outrageous. For you were the man who pronounced that grandiose eulogy,[1] that lachrymose appeal to morality. You lit the torches which charred the very body of Caesar, which burnt down the house of Lucius Bellienus. You, Antony, unleashed against our homes those ruffians, slaves most of them, whose ferocity we had to repel with our own hands.

And yet you seemed to have wiped off the soot. For upon the Capitol, in the days that followed, the resolutions that you proposed before the Senate were excellent. I mean those declaring that, from the fifteenth of March onwards, there should be no publication of any announcement conferring exemptions from taxes, or similar favours. As regards these exemptions, and the men in exile, you yourself remember what you said. But the finest thing of all was that you abolished from the constitution, for ever, the title of dictator. On account of men's recent fears of dictators you decided to abolish, once and for all, the whole institution: so tremendous was the hatred of this tyranny which had apparently taken hold of you.

So to other men the government seemed securely established – though to me things looked differently, for with you at the helm I expected all manner of shipwreck. Was I wrong? Could a man, for very long, remain unlike himself? Members of the Senate, what happened next you saw for yourselves. Announcements were posted up all over the Capitol: tax exemptions were put on sale, not merely to individuals but to whole peoples. Citizenship was granted not to single persons only but to entire provinces. If these decisions are going to stand, it means the downfall of our state. Senators, you have lost complete provinces. In his own domestic market, this man has slashed the revenues of Rome. He has slashed the Roman empire itself.

Those seven hundred million sesterces, recorded in the account-books of the Temple of Ops [2] – where are they now? The origins of that treasure store were tragic enough. Nevertheless, if the money was not going to be returned to its rightful owners, it could be used to

1. The earliest contemporary evidence does not suggest, with Shakespeare, that Antony – who was still attempting to be conciliatory – delivered a passionate and provocative speech. However, the crowd broke loose and burned Caesar's body in the Forum; and the Liberators barricaded themselves in their houses.

2. See above, p. 118.

save us from property-tax. But how do you account for the fact, Antony, that whereas on the fifteenth of March you owed four million sesterces, you had ceased to owe this sum by the first of April?

Your people sold countless concessions: and you were well aware of them. Nevertheless, the decrees posted up on the Capitol did include one excellent measure. This concerned a very good friend of Rome, King Deiotarus.[1] Yet all who saw the document could not help laughing, in spite of their grief. For no man has ever hated another so much as Caesar hated Deiotarus. He felt quite as much hatred for Deiotarus as he felt for this Senate, and the Roman knights, and the citizens of Massilia,[2] and every other person in whom he discerned a love for the Roman nation and its people. In his lifetime Caesar never treated Deiotarus fairly or kindly, either to his face or in his absence. Yet we are invited to believe that, when Caesar was dead, Deiotarus gained his favours! When they were together, and Deiotarus was his host, Caesar had summoned him, demanded an account of his resources, planted a Greek agent in his principality, and deprived him of Armenia, which the Roman Senate had added to his kingdom. And now we are asked to believe that what the living Caesar had confiscated, the dead Caesar gave back.

And the way in which he is stated to have expressed himself! At one point, apparently, he described this restoration as 'fair'; at another as 'not unfair'. A peculiar way of putting the matter! I was not with Deiotarus, but I always supported him; whereas Caesar never once said that anything we asked for on his behalf seemed to him fair.

A bond for ten million sesterces was negotiated at Antony's house in the women's suite – where a lot of selling went on, and goes on still. The negotiators were the envoys of Deiotarus. They were good men, but timid and inexperienced. I and the king's other friends were not asked for our views. About this bond, I suggest that you should consider carefully what you are to do. For, when he heard of Caesar's death, the king himself – with no thought for any memorandum Caesar might have left – recovered what belonged to him of his own accord, by the strength of his own hand. Deiotarus was wise. He

1. A monarch in Galatia who had been defended by Cicero on charges of acting against Caesar.

2. One of the most powerful city-states of the day until, having sided with Pompey, it had been compelled to surrender to Caesar in 49 B.C.

knew that this had always been the law: that when tyrants who had stolen things were killed, the men whose property they had stolen take them back. So no jurist, not even the man whose only client is yourself [1] and who is now representing you, will say that there is a debt on that bond for what Deiotarus had recovered before the bond was executed. For he did not buy these possessions from you: before you could sell him his own property, he took it himself. He was a man! How contemptible, on the other hand, are we, who uphold the actions of someone whose memory we hate.[2]

Of the countless memoranda, the innumerable alleged examples of Caesar's handwriting which have been brought forward, I shall say nothing. We can view their forgers, selling their efforts as openly as though these were programmes of gladiatorial shows. Today, as a result, the house where Antony lives is piled high with such enormous heaps of money that they have to be weighed out instead of counted. But this greed has its blind spots. For example one of the recently displayed notices exempts from taxation the wealthiest communities of Crete. This notice decrees that Crete shall cease to be a province 'when the governorship of Marcus Junius Brutus [3] comes to an end'. But where is your sanity, Antony? Are you fit to be at large? How could there possibly be a decree by Caesar exempting Crete 'when the tenure of Brutus comes to an end', seeing that in Caesar's lifetime Brutus had not yet even formed this connexion with Crete at all? However, do not suppose, Senators, that this consideration prevented the decree from being put on sale – indeed it has resulted in your losing your Cretan province! There was never a thing, provided a buyer was available, that Antony was not ready to sell.

And this law, Antony, which you posted up about recalling exiles – I suppose Caesar composed that too? Far be it from me to persecute anyone who is in trouble. My only complaints are these. First, that the men recalled from exile because Caesar had singled them out as especially deserving have been discredited by this new batch. Secondly, I cannot see why you do not treat everyone alike. Not

1. Perhaps the Sicilian rhetorician Sextus Clodius (p. 121) – or Sextus Cloelius, restored from exile (p. 106).

2. Caesar's acts had been officially confirmed on 17 March (p. 91).

3. See above, p. 116.

more than three or four are now left unrecalled, and I do not understand why men whose plight is the same do not qualify for the same
degree of your indulgence: I refer to your uncle and those whom
you have treated like him. When you legislated about the others, you
refused to include him. Yet at the same time you encouraged him to
stand for election as censor![1] Indeed, you even encouraged his election
campaign – thus arousing universal ridicule and protest. But, having
done so, why did you refrain from holding his election? Was it because a tribune had announced an ill-omened flash of lightning?
When you personally are involved, the auspices are immaterial. Your
scruples are reserved for when your friends are concerned. And then,
while your uncle was standing for membership of the Board of Seven,
you deserted him again. Do not tell us that this was because of objections by some formidable member to whom you could not say no,
for fear of your life! If you had any family loyalty, you ought to have
respected Gaius Antonius like a father. Instead, you loaded him with
insults.

What is more, you threw his daughter out of the house – Antonia [2]
your cousin. You had looked around and made an alternative
arrangement. And not content with that, though no woman could
have been more blameless, you even charged her with adultery! You
could hardly have sunk further. Yet you were still not satisfied. On
January the first, at a full meeting of the Senate at which your uncle
was present, you had the audacity to declare that this was why you
regarded Publius Cornelius Dolabella as an enemy: because you had
learnt of his adultery with your wife and cousin. It would be difficult
to say which was the most outrageous – your audacity in making such
allegations before the Senate; your unscrupulousness in directing
them against Dolabella; your indecency in speaking in such terms
before her father; or your brutality in employing against that poor
woman such filthy, god-forsaken language.

But let us return to the documents supposed to be in Caesar's handwriting. How did you verify them, Antony? To preserve the peace,
the Senate had confirmed Caesar's acts – the acts which were truly his,

1. C. Antonius Hybrida finally became censor in 42 (p. 126).
2. Antony's second wife (his wives were (1) Fadia, (2) Antonia, (3) Fulvia,
(4) Octavia (40 B.C.), and ?(5) (if married according to Egyptian – though certainly not Roman – law) Cleopatra). See Appendix B.

not those which Antony alleged were his. Now, where do all these memoranda spring from? On whose authority are they produced? If they are forgeries, why are they approved? If genuine, why does money have to be paid for them? The decision had been taken that, from the first of June onwards, you should examine Caesar's acts, with the assistance of an advisory board. What was this board, and which of its members did you ever convene? And as for your await-ing the first of June, no doubt that was the day when you returned from your tour of the ex-soldiers' settlements: for you brought an armed guard to surround you.

That trip of yours in April and May, when you have even tried to found a settlement at Capua, what a splendid affair it was! We all know how you escaped from that town – or rather very nearly did not escape.[1] And you are still uttering threats against Capua. I wish you would try to put them into practice: then that 'very nearly' could be struck out. Your progress was truly magnificent. Of your elaborate banquets and frantic drinking I say nothing; all that only damaged yourself. But we were damaged too. Even when, at an earlier date, the Campanian territory had been exempted from taxa-tion,[2] we regarded this as a grave blow to our national interests – although, on that occasion, soldiers were its recipients. But when *you* distributed land there, the beneficiaries were your fellow-diners and fellow-gamblers. Members of the Senate, these latest settlers in Cam-pania were nothing but actors and actresses. Equally objectionable was the settlement at Leontini; seeing that at one time the crops in that area, like those of Campania, were renowned for their fertile and abundant contribution to the Roman domains of which they formed an integral part. You gave your doctor 1,875 acres. Whatever vast sum, one may ask, would you have given him if he had cured your mind? Your oratorical trainer received 1,250: what on earth would the total have been if he had succeeded in making a speaker of you?

But let us return to your journey, and to its effects on Italy. You founded a settlement of ex-soldiers at Casilinum, where Caesar had founded one before. About Capua, you had written asking for my

1. The arrival of the new colonists was resented by the inhabitants, and An-tony was roughly handled.

2. During Caesar's consulship in 59 B.C.

advice; but I should have sent the same reply about Casilinum. You inquired whether it was legal to plant a new settlement where there was one already. I replied that the establishment of a new settlement, where there existed an earlier one duly founded in accordance with the auspices, was not legitimate – though I also pointed out that new settlers could be added to the old foundation. In spite of this, you had the arrogance to upset all the provisions of the auspices and plant a settlement at Casilinum, even though another settlement had been established there only a few years previously. You raised your standard; you marked out the boundaries with a plough. Indeed, your ploughshare nearly grazed the very gate of Capua, and the territory of that most flourishing settlement suffered grievous encroachment at your hands.

Fresh from this violation of religious observance, you rushed elsewhere: for you had designs on the property of the devout and high-principled Marcus Terentius Varro [1] at Casinum. But what was the legal or moral sanction for this project? The same, you will say, as had enabled you to displace from their estates the heirs of Lucius Rubrius Casinas and Lucius Turselius – and countless others too. Now, if you had occupied these properties as a result of an auction, we may allow auctions their proper rights. We may concede rights also to written instructions, provided that they were Caesar's and not yours – and provided that they recorded you as a debtor, instead of releasing you from your debts!

As for Varro's farm at Casinum, who claims that this was ever sold at all? Did anyone ever see the auctioneer's spear or hear his voice? You sent someone to Alexandria, you say, to buy the place from Caesar. It was too much to expect that you should await his return! But no one ever heard that any part of Varro's property had been confiscated; and yet there was no man whose welfare was of more general concern. Now, if the truth is that Caesar wrote ordering you to hand the estate back, no words are fit to describe the outrage that you perpetrated. Just call off, for a spell, those armed men whom we see all round us. Do that, and you will very soon learn this lesson: whatever the justification for Caesar's auctions, your own deplorable conduct is on quite another level – for, once the armed men are gone, you will find yourself thrown outside Varro's gates. And it will not

1. See above, p. 85.

be the owner alone who expels you. Not one of his friends, his neighbours, his visitors, or his agents will fail to take a hand.

Day after day, at Varro's mansion, you continued your disgusting orgies. From seven in the morning onwards, there was incessant drinking, gambling, and vomiting. What a tragic fate for that house; and 'what an ill-matched master'![1]

Though how could Antony be described as its master? Let us call him occupant. Well then, he was an occupant who matched it ill. For Marcus Varro had chosen this place not for indulgence, but for retirement and study. Those walls had witnessed noble discussions, noble thoughts, noble writings; laws for the Roman people, the history of our ancestors, the principles of all wisdom and all learning. When, you, on the other hand, became the lodger – for householder I will not call you – the house rang with the din of drunkards, the pavements swam with wine, the walls dripped with it. On view were young free-born Roman youths consorting with paid boys; Roman matrons with prostitutes.

From Casinum, from Aquinum, from Interamna, came men to greet Antony. But no one was allowed in. And that was entirely proper, for in his degradation the emblems of office were a complete anomaly. When he left for Rome and approached Aquinum, quite a large crowd came to meet him, since the town has a considerable population. But he was carried through the streets in a covered litter, like a dead man. The people of Aquinum had no doubt been foolish to come; yet they did live beside the road on which he was passing by. What about the men of Anagnia? They, on the other hand, lived away from his path. But they too came down to greet him, on the supposition that he was consul. The incredible fact is – though I as a neighbour can vouch that everyone noticed it at the time – he did not return a single greeting. This was especially remarkable since he had with him two men of Anagnia, Mustela to look after his swords and Laco in charge of his drinking cups.

There is no need to recall to you the threats and insults with which he assailed the population of Teanum Sidicinum and harassed the inhabitants of Puteoli. This was because they had adopted Cassius and the Brutuses as their patrons. Their choice had been dictated by enthusiastic approval, sound judgement, friendly feelings, and personal

1. From an unknown tragedy.

affection – not by force and violence, which compelled others to choose you and Minucius Basilus, and others like you, whom no one could voluntarily choose as their patrons. Even as dependants you would be undesirable.

Meantime, while you were away, your colleague [1] had a great day when he overturned, in the Forum, the funeral monument which you had persistently treated with reverence. When you were told of this, you fainted: everyone who was with you agrees that this is so. What happened afterwards I do not know. I suppose terror and armed violence had the final word. For you pulled your colleague down from heaven; you made him quite unlike himself – to say you made him your own replica would be going too far.

And that return of yours to Rome! The whole city was in an uproar. Lucius Cornelius Cinna's [2] excess of power, Sulla's domination we remembered; Caesar's autocratic monarchy was fresh in our memories. In those days there had been swords perhaps, but they had stayed in their sheaths, and there were not many of them. Your procession, on the other hand, was totally barbaric. Your followers were in battle order, with drawn swords, and whole litter-loads of shields. And yet, Senators, familiarity with such spectacles has inured us to the shock.

The decision had been taken that the Senate should meet on the first of June, and we did our best to attend. But we encountered intimidation and were abruptly forced to retire. Antony, however, feeling no need of a Senate, missed none of us; on the contrary, our departure pleased him. Without delay he embarked on his extraordinary exploits. He, who had defended Caesar's memoranda for his own personal profit, suppressed Caesar's laws – good laws, too – in

1. Dolabella, now consul. After the construction, in honour of Caesar, of this altar and column (by a demagogue of shady origins known as Herophilus or Amatius), participants in the accompanying demonstrations were executed by Dolabella without trial (Amatius himself was executed on about 13 April). Cicero's attitude to Dolabella, who had gravely maltreated his daughter (p. 84) and was suspected by him of embezzling from the Temple of Ops, was strangely ambivalent: the *Eleventh Philippic* in mid-March 43 contains a violent attack on him for the murder of Trebonius.

2. In control of Rome while Sulla was in the east (87–84 B.C.), Cinna was killed in a mutiny at Brundisium. His daughter was Caesar's first wife (see Genealogical Table, p. 255).

order to upset the constitution. He lengthened the tenures of provincial governorships. Instead of protecting Caesar's acts, as he should have, he annulled them: those relating to national and private affairs alike. Now in the national sphere nothing has greater weight than a law; while in private affairs the most valid of all things is a will. Antony abolished both – laws, with or without notice; wills, although even the humblest citizens have always respected them. The statues, the pictures, which Caesar, along with his gardens, had bequeathed to the people of Rome as his heirs – now they all went to Pompey's gardens, or Scipio's mansion: removed by Antony.

And yet, Antony, you are so attentive to Caesar's memory; you love the dead man, do you not? Now, the greatest honours he ever received were the sacred couch,[1] the image, the gable, the priest for his worship. Because of these honours, on the analogy of the priesthoods of Jupiter, Mars, and Quirinus, Antony is the priest of the divine Julius. Yet you delay, Antony, to assume these duties: you have not been inducted. Why? Choose a day, choose someone to induct you. We are colleagues; no one will refuse. Loathsome man! – equally loathsome as priest of a tyrant, or priest of a dead human being!

And now I have to ask you a question: *Do you not know what day this is?* Yesterday, in case it escaped your notice, was the fourth day of the Roman Games in the Circus. Now you yourself moved in the Assembly a proposal that a fifth day also should be added to these Games in Caesar's honour. Why, then, are we not in our official robes? Why do we allow the honour which your law conferred on Caesar to be neglected? You were prepared to concede, apparently, that this holy day should be polluted by the addition of a thanksgiving, but not by a sacred couch ceremony. But you should either disregard religious observances altogether, or maintain them invariably.

You ask whether I like this couch, gable, priest of the divinity. I

1. At the rite of the *lectisternium*, borrowed from Greece (399 B.C.), images of the gods were placed on cushioned couches and tables of food were set before them. 'The image' perhaps refers in general terms to statues implying that Caesar was superhuman (he was not 'deified' by the state until 42 B.C. and the extent to which, according to Hellenistic custom, he was treated as a god during his lifetime is disputed). 'The gable' – characteristic mark of a temple. 'The priest' – Plutarch says that Antony assumed this office in 40 B.C.

like none of them. But you, who defend the acts of Caesar, cannot possibly justify the maintenance of some of them and the neglect of others. Unless, that is, you are prepared to admit that your own profit, rather than Caesar's honour, is your guide. Come, answer these arguments! I look forward to your eloquence. I knew your grandfather; he was a very fine orator. And you certainly speak with even greater freedom than he did. For he never made a public speech naked! – whereas you, straightforward fellow that you are, have let us all have a look at your torso. Are you going to let me have a reply? Are you even going to venture to open your mouth? Indeed, I wonder whether in the whole of my long speech you will find anything at all which you can pluck up the courage to answer.

But let us leave the past. Your behaviour today, at the present day and moment at which I am speaking – defend that if you can! Explain why the Senate is surrounded by a ring of men with arms; why my listeners include gangsters of yours, sword in hand; why the doors of the temple of Concord are closed; why you bring into the Forum the world's most savage people, Ituraeans, with their bows and arrows. I do these things in self-defence, says Antony. But surely a thousand deaths are better than the inability to live in one's own community without an armed guard. A guard is no protection, I can tell you! The protection you need is not weapons, but the affection and goodwill of your fellow-citizens. The people of Rome will seize your weapons and wrench them from you. I pray that we shall not perish before that is done! But however you behave towards ourselves, believe me, these are methods which cannot preserve you for long. Your wife – she is no miser, and this reference implies no disrespect – is already taking too long to pay the Roman people her third instalment.[1]

Our country does not lack men to place in charge of its affairs. Wherever they are, they are our national defence, indeed our very nation. Rome has avenged itself: but it has not yet recovered. However, that there are young noblemen ready to leap to its defence is beyond doubt. They may choose to retire for a spell, seeking quiet, but Rome will call them back.

The name of peace is beautiful – and peace itself is a blessing. Yet peace and slavery are very different things. Peace is freedom tranquilly enjoyed, slavery is the worst of all evils, to be repelled, if need be, at

1. Her three instalments were her three husbands (p. 108).

the cost of war and even of death. Even if those liberators of ours have withdrawn from our sight, they have left behind them the example of their deeds. They achieved what no one had ever achieved before. Lucius Junius Brutus [1] made war against Tarquin, who was king at a time when kingship was lawful at Rome. Spurius Cassius Vecellinus, Spurius Maelius, and Marcus Manlius Capitolinus were killed because of the suspicion that they aimed at autocratic monarchy. But here, for the first time, are men raising their swords to kill one who was not merely aiming at monarchy, but actually reigning as monarch. Their action was superhumanly noble in itself, and it is set before us for our imitation: all the more conspicuously, because heaven itself is scarcely immense enough to hold the glory which this deeds has made theirs. The consciousness of a noble achievement was reward enough; yet no one, I believe, should spurn that further reward which they have also won – immortality.

The day you ought to remember, Antony, is that day on which you abolished the dictatorship for ever. Let your memory dwell on the rejoicing of the Senate and people of Rome on that occasion. Contrast it with the haggling with which you and your friends busy yourselves now. Then you will realize that gain is a different thing from glory. Just as there are diseases, or dullnesses of the senses, which prevent certain people from being able to taste food: so, by the same token, debauchees, misers, and criminals are unattracted by glory.

However, if the hope of being praised cannot entice you to behave decently, is fear equally incapable of scaring you out of your repulsive behaviour? I know the lawcourts cause you no alarm. If that is due to innocence, you are to be commended. But if the reason is your reliance upon force, do you not understand this: that the man whose imperviousness to judicial processes is due to such a cause has pressing reason to feel terrors of quite another kind? For if you are not afraid of brave men and good Romans – seeing that armed satellites keep them away from your person – believe me, your own supporters will not stand you for very much longer. To be afraid of danger from one's own people night and day is no sort of a life; and you can hardly have men who owe you more, in terms of benefactions, than some of Caesar's killers owed to him.

1. See above, pp. 114, 139.

However, you and he are not in any way comparable! His character was an amalgamation of genius, method, memory, culture, thoroughness, intellect, and industry. His achievements in war, though disastrous for our country, were none the less mighty. After working for many years to become king and autocrat, he surmounted tremendous efforts and perils and achieved his purpose. By entertainments, public works, food-distributions, and banquets, he seduced the ignorant populace; his friends he bound to his allegiance by rewarding them, his enemies by what looked like mercy. By a mixture of intimidation and indulgence, he inculcated in a free community the habit of servitude.

Your ambition to reign, Antony, certainly deserves to be compared with Caesar's. But in not a single other respect are you entitled to the same comparison. For the many evils which Caesar inflicted upon our country have at least yielded certain benefits. To take a single example, the people of Rome have now discovered what degrees of confidence they can repose in this or that person. They have discovered who are fit to be entrusted with their fortunes, and who, on the other hand, need to be shunned. Do these facts never occur to you? Do you never understand the significance of this: that brave men have now learnt to appreciate the noble achievement, the wonderful benefaction, the glorious renown, of killing a tyrant? When men could not endure Caesar, will they endure you? Mark my words, this time there will be crowds competing to do the deed. They will not wait for a suitable opportunity – they will be too impatient.

Antony: some time, at long last, think of your country. Think of the people from whom you come – not the people with whom you associate. Let your relationship with myself be as you please: but your country I pray you to make your friend once again. However, your behaviour is a matter for yourself to decide. As for mine, I will declare how I shall conduct myself. When I was a young man I defended our state: in my old age I shall not abandon it. Having scorned the swords of Catiline, I shall not be intimidated by yours. On the contrary, I would gladly offer my own body, if my death could redeem the freedom of our nation – if it could cause the long-suffering people of Rome to find final relief from its labours. For if, nearly twenty years ago, I declared in this very temple that death could not come prematurely to a man who had been consul, how much greater will be my reason to say this again now that I am old. After the honours that I have been awarded, Senators, after the deeds that I have done, death actually seems to me desirable. Two things only I pray for. One, that in dying I may leave the Roman people free – the immortal gods could grant me no greater gift. My other prayer is this: that no man's fortunes may fail to correspond with his services to our country!

PART TWO

HOW TO LIVE

CHAPTER FOUR

A PRACTICAL CODE OF BEHAVIOUR

(ON DUTIES · III)

No one will ever write anything more wise, more true, or more useful. From now on, those whose ambition it is to give men instruction, to provide them with precepts, will be charlatans if they want to rise above you, or will all be your imitators.

VOLTAIRE (1771)

This work, which exercised so unparalleled an influence from the early Fathers until the nineteenth century (pp. 25 ff.), is a manual of right behaviour and civics, ostensibly addressed to the writer's son Marcus who was studying at Athens (and who had the instincts not of a philosopher but of a hard-drinking soldier). In the first two of its three Books Cicero has drawn heavily upon the eminent Greek Stoic, Panaetius of Cos (c. 185–109 B.C.),[1] the writer of a book with a similar title in which he endeavoured to relate the austere Stoic morality to the practical needs of contemporary public and commercial life. The first Book of Cicero's work discusses Moral Right, the second Advantage, and this third Book deals with a problem with which life confronts us every day: namely, what is to be done when right and advantage seem to clash. He concludes by pointing out that such clashes can only be apparent, never real, and this gives him occasion to reassert the supremacy of moral considerations over all others. In this part of the treatise Cicero shows many signs of drawing away from Panaetius, who had never carried out his declared intention of tackling this branch of the subject. Cicero calls upon other Stoics, including a contemporary – Athenodorus Calvus, who summarized for him, as we know from a letter, a relevant work by the Stoic polymath Posidonius of Apamea in Syria. But on the whole, as Cicero himself states and as his wealth of Roman illustrations and anecdotes (not to speak of the unphilosophical structure of the book) confirms, he is now writing independently and in accordance with his own experience and his own interpretation of what he has read. The result is a remarkable discussion of how a

1. For Panaetius, Posidonius, and other Hellenistic philosophers, see above p. 18.

Roman citizen ought to meet the various problems of his life. Cicero, interpreting life as a complex of obligations to others as well as oneself, offers a splendid testimony to the beliefs in human cooperation which he so enthusiastically confirmed from his readings of the Stoics, and yet tempered with his own undogmatic good sense.

Such a study follows naturally enough after the works on cosmology and theology which he had recently completed.[1] Yet On Duties also had a topical significance: for, although perhaps not published until after Cicero's death (this may account for some textual uncertainties), the book was for the most part written between September and November 44 B.C., during that very same astonishingly productive period of Cicero's life which produced the Philippics and so much else. This accounts for its bitter incidental allusions to the suppression of Roman public life by the autocracies of Caesar and Antony. One of Cicero's letters indicates that Atticus (though he helped him to choose the title of the present work) sought to divert him to history as a safe subject. For although the illustrations are mostly derived from early rather than contemporary events – a device later used by the satirist Juvenal – the whole spirit of this analysis of a Roman's duty to his Commonwealth was fundamentally, if for the most part obliquely, as hostile to tyranny as the Second Philippic (Chapter 3). On Duties represents an attempt to provide a moral code for an aristocracy liberated from one tyranny and in danger of being enslaved by another – the loss of political rights being clearly recognized as a corrupter of moral values. Cicero himself seems to have regarded this treatise as his spiritual testament and masterpiece.

1. For a list of Cicero's writings, see below, p. 251.

I

PERSONAL STATEMENT TO CICERO'S SON

PUBLIUS CORNELIUS SCIPIO,[1] the first of that family to be called Africanus, used to remark that he was never less idle than when he had nothing to do, and never less lonely than when he was by himself. We have this on the authority of Marcus Porcius Cato the Censor,[2] who was almost his contemporary. It is a fine sentiment – as you would expect from so great and wise a man. Scipio means that even when he was working his thoughts were occupied with public affairs; and that even when he was alone he did not stop taking counsel – with himself. That is to say, he was never unoccupied; and often the only company he needed was his own. Other men are enervated by leisure and seclusion, but he derived stimulation from them.

I wish I could truthfully say the same of myself. Of course, however hard I try to imitate Scipio I cannot give myself a remarkable character like his. Nevertheless, if aspiration counts for anything, I do come as near to him as I can. At present, seeing that criminal, armed violence excludes me both from politics and from my legal practice, I have no work to do. For that reason I have left Rome, and I am travelling from one place in the country to another – and I am often alone.

But I must not compare this leisure and solitude of mine with Scipio's. He, when he felt the need to rest from his splendid services to

1. The conqueror of Hannibal at Zama (202 B.C.). In his treatise *On the State* Cicero had interpreted his remark differently, i.e. as meaning that Scipio had found philosophy in solitude the highest intellectual activity.
2. See below, p. 211.

his country, used occasionally to take a holiday: he would leave the massed gatherings of men, and withdraw into the haven of his own company. My leisure, on the other hand, is not prompted by any desire for retirement: it is forced upon me because I have nothing to do. For now that the Senate has been abolished and the courts annihilated, what work in keeping with my position is there for me to do, either in the Senate or in the Forum? Once I lived with great crowds around me, in the forefront of Roman publicity. But now I shun the sight of the scoundrels who swarm on every side. I withdraw as completely as I can; and I am often alone.

However, as the philosophers instruct, one must not only choose the least among evils, one must also extract from them any good that they may contain. That being so, I am making use of my rest – though it is scarcely the kind of rest deserved by the man whose services gave Rome itself rest from its troubles! Nevertheless, dictated though my solitude is by necessity rather than choice, I am refusing to let it make me idle.

Scipio deserves a higher compliment, I admit. For we have inherited no literary record of his talents, no products of his leisure hours, no fruits of his seclusion. From this one may infer that he was never idle or lonely, because he was incessantly engaged in contemplating the problems which he had selected for study. Whereas I have not enough strength of character to relieve my solitude by silent meditation. I have therefore concentrated my whole attention and will-power upon literary work; and this is one of its products. Indeed, my output during the brief period since the destruction of the government has exceeded the total of many years while the Republic was still intact.

My son: every part of philosophy is fruitful and rewarding, none barren or desolate. But the most luxuriantly fertile field of all is that of our moral obligations – since, if we clearly understand these, we have mastered the rules for leading a good and consistent life. No doubt you are conscientiously attending and absorbing the lectures on this subject by my friend Cratippus,[1] and he is our leading contemporary philosopher. Nevertheless, I hope to make your ears ring with this kind of moralizing from every quarter! Indeed, if it were only possible, I should like them to hear nothing else.

1. The Peripatetic philosopher with whom Cicero's son Marcus was studying in Athens.

To everyone who proposes to have a good career, moral philosophy is indispensable. And I am inclined to think that this applies particularly to yourself. For upon your shoulders rests a special responsibility. People have high expectations that you will work hard, as I have. They also trust that you will have a career like mine; and perhaps they look to you to win the same sort of reputation. Athens and Cratippus add to your responsibilities. You went to them in order to take on board, if one may put it in this way, a cargo of education. It would be discreditable, then, if you came back empty; for in that case you would not have lived up either to the city or to your professor. So make every effort you can. Work as hard as possible (if study comes under the heading of work and not of pleasure!) and do your very best. I have supplied you with all you need, so do not let people say that the failure is on your side.

But enough of this! I have sent you similar exhortations times without number. Let us now return to the subject we proposed for discussion, and deal with its outstanding subdivision.

II

A PRACTICAL CODE

The most thorough analysis of moral obligations is unquestionably that of Panaetius, and on the whole, with certain modifications, I have followed him. The questions relating to this topic which arouse most discussion and inquiry are classified by Panaetius under three headings:

1. Is a thing morally right or wrong?
2. Is it advantageous or disadvantageous?
3. If apparent right and apparent advantage clash, what is to be the basis for our choice between them?

Panaetius wrote a three-part treatise about the first two of these questions; the third question he said he would deal with in its proper turn. But he never fulfilled his promise. This seems to me all the more surprising because he was still alive thirty years after the publication of the first three parts of his work – his pupil Posidonius records this.

Posidonius himself briefly refers to the subject in certain notes,[1] but it seems to me strange that he, too, did not deal with it at greater length. For he expressed the opinion that there is no more vital theme in the whole range of philosophy.

Now one theory is that Panaetius did not overlook this problem but that his omission was deliberate – indeed that no discussion on the subject was required, since the possibility of a clash between right and advantage does not exist. Personally I cannot agree with such a view. Or rather, this last point *could* raise legitimate doubts: had Panaetius been right to include this third heading in his classification – should he not instead have omitted it altogether? But the other fact is incontrovertible; the subject was included in his classification, and yet he never dealt with it. If someone draws up a triple classification and completes two parts of his threefold task, he obviously still has the third ahead of him. Besides, at the end of his third part Panaetius actually promises that he will deal with this third topic at the proper time.

On this point Posidonius is a reliable witness. In one of his letters he quotes a favourite remark of Publius Rutilius Rufus,[2] himself a pupil of Panaetius, about the painting of the Venus of Cos. No painter, said Rutilius, had ever been able to complete that part of the picture which Apelles had left unfinished, since the beauty of Venus's face made the adequate representation of the rest of her a hopeless task. Similarly, the quality of what Panaetius had written was so outstanding that nobody was able to supply his omissions.

What Panaetius intended, then, is not in doubt. But whether he had been justified when, at the outset, he included this third heading in his programme for the study of moral obligations may well be, as I have said, a matter for discussion. The Stoics believe that right is the only good. Your Peripatetics, on the other hand, hold that right is the *highest* good – to the degree that all other things collected together scarcely begin to weigh down the balance on the other side. Now, according to either doctrine, there can be no doubt whatever about one point: *advantage can never conflict with right.* That is why Socrates, as the tradition goes, used to curse the men who had first begun to

---

1. Summarized for Cicero by Athenodorus Calvus, see above, p. 157.

2. Consul 105 B.C., statesman, orator, and man of letters. Apelles of Colophon (fourth century B.C.) painted Alexander the Great.

differentiate between these things which nature had made inseparable. The Stoics agreed with him; for their view is that everything which is morally right is advantageous, and there can be no advantage in anything which is not right.

Those, on the other hand, whose yardstick of desirability is pleasure[1] or absence of pain say that right is only worth cultivating as a source of advantage. If Panaetius were the kind of man to hold the same opinion he might argue that clashes between right and advantage are conceivable. However, he is not that sort of thinker at all. On the contrary, he interprets right as the only good, and judges that things which conflict with this, however advantageous they may look, can in fact make life neither better by their presence nor worse by their absence. So we reach the conclusion, after all, that there was no need for Panaetius to deal with the comparison between what is right and what appears (falsely) to be advantageous.

Besides, the Stoics' ideal is *to live consistently with nature*.[2] I suppose what they mean is this: throughout our lives we ought invariably to aim at morally right courses of action, and, in so far as we have other aims also, we must select only those which do not clash with such courses. That is another reason why, according to the school of thought that I have mentioned, there ought never to have been any question of weighing advantage against right, and the whole topic ought to have been excluded from any philosophical discussion.

*

However, there is more to the matter than that. For moral goodness, in the truest and fullest sense of the word – goodness and right being wholly synonymous – could only be found among those hypothetical people who are endowed with ideal wisdom. Nobody who falls short of this perfect wisdom can possibly claim perfect goodness: its semblance is the most he can acquire. And these are the men, the ordinary men falling short of the ideal, whose moral obligations form the sub-

1. Aristippus and the Cyrenaics (cf. the Epicureans). Hieronymus of Rhodes (c. 290–230 B.C.) preferred to define the criterion as mere 'absence of pain'.

2. i.e. 'not merely with the visible creation, but the thoughts, observances, and aspirations of mankind, the moral phenomena of society' (Sir H. Maine). Chrysippus, the third head of the Stoic school, had added 'with nature' to Zeno's original formula 'to live consistently'.

ject of my present work. The Stoics call these 'second-class' obligations.[1] They are incumbent upon everybody in the world – so their
application could not be wider! And what is more, natural decency
and progress in understanding enable many people to live up to these
obligations.

On the one hand, then, there is that ideal, unlimited obligation – the
perfect obligation, as the Stoics put it, 'satisfying all the numbers'[2] –
which none but the ideally wise man can fulfil. And then there are
also these other actions in which we see the working of a 'second-
class' obligation. When the latter situation arises, there is often a very
general impression that here, too, an ideal action has been performed;
most people fail to understand that, in fact, the deed falls short of the
ideal – their intelligence is insufficient to appreciate what is lacking.
Judgements of poems, paintings, and much else reveal the same fault:
uninformed readers and viewers admire and praise things that do not
deserve to be praised. For evidently ignorant people can grasp such
merits as these poems and pictures and so on may possess without
being capable of detecting their deficiencies. What they need is expert
instruction, and then they quickly revise their opinions.

The obligations, then, which I am discussing in this book are those
related by the Stoics to this 'second-class' kind of goodness, which is
not the exclusive possession of the hypothetical man of ideal wisdom,
but is relevant to the whole of mankind. That is to say, everyone who
is not devoid of good is prompted by obligations of this sort. Take for
example the two Deciuses,[3] or the two Scipios.[4] We call them 'brave
men'; and we describe Gaius Fabricius Luscinus[5] as 'just'. But this
does not mean that they are perfect models of bravery or justice as the
truly wise man would be. For none of them were 'wise' in the ideal

1. 'Middle' duties, i.e. admitting of degrees and improvement.
2. Fulfilling all the requirements of perfection – perhaps a reference to the
Pythagorean belief that specific numbers stand for perfection of specific kinds,
so that when all the numbers are satisfied there is absolute perfection.
3. Each named Publius Decius Mus. The father was believed to have sacrificed himself in the perhaps apocryphal First Samnite War (c. 343 B.C.), the son
fell at the battle of Sentinum (295 B.C.) against the Gauls, Samnites, and Etruscans.
4. The elder Africanus and his younger namesake (Aemilianus). See Genealogical Table (p. 257).
5. Gaius Fabricius Luscinus was consul in 280 and 278 and censor in 275 B.C.

sense we are here attributing to that word. Nor was Cato the Censor, nor was Gaius Laelius,[1] although they received names indicating that they were so regarded. Even the Seven Wise Men [2] were not wise in this sense – they merely bore a certain resemblance to wise men, because of their consistent performance of 'second-class' obligations.

Now it is mistaken, we know, to weigh what is ideally right against apparent advantage when the two things are in conflict. And apparent advantage should equally not be weighed against this 'second-class' sort of right which is cultivated by everyone who aspires to a reputation for goodness. For we are morally bound to cherish and observe the degree of right which comes within our comprehension just as carefully as the ideally wise man is obliged to cherish what is right in the full and ideal sense of the word. Because that is the only way in which we can maintain whatever progress we have made towards achieving goodness.

So much then for people who fulfil their moral obligations sufficiently well to be regarded as good. But those who habitually weigh the right course against what they regard as advantageous are in quite a different category. Unlike good men, they judge everything by profits and gains, which seem to them just as valuable as what is right. Panaetius observed that people *often doubtingly weigh those two things against one another*. I am sure he meant just what he said: that they *often* do this, not that they ought to. For preferring advantage to right is not the only crime. It is also sinful even to attempt a comparison between the two things – even to hesitate between them.

But can there be any sort of contingency warranting doubts and special consideration? I believe that there can; certain situations are perplexingly difficult to assess. On occasion, a course of action generally regarded as wrong turns out not to be wrong after all. Let me quote a particular instance, which admits of a wider application. There could be no more terrible crime than to kill someone who is not merely a fellow human being but a close friend. Yet surely someone who kills a tyrant, however close friends the two men have been, has not committed a crime. At any rate the people of Rome do not think so, since they regard that deed [3] which was done as the most

1. See below, p. 211.
2. Bias, Chilo, Cleobulus, Pittacus, Periander (or Myson), Solon, Thales.
3. i.e. the recent murder of Julius Caesar.

splendid of all noble actions. Has advantage then, in this case, prevailed over right? No; advantage has *come from* right.

All the same, there are occasions on which advantage, as we understand the term, will give the impression of clashing with what we interpret as right. In order to avoid mistaken conclusions when this happens, we must establish some rule to guide us in comparing the two things, and to keep us true to our obligations. That rule will be in accordance with the teaching and system of the Stoics. They are my models in this work; and I will tell you why. It is true that the earlier members of the Academy and your Peripatetics (who were once indistinguishable[1] from them) regard right as *preferable* to apparent advantage. But the Stoics go further, and actually identify advantage with right, insisting that a thing must be right before it can be advantageous. This treatment of the subject is more impressive than the Peripatetic and earlier Academic belief that some particular good actions may not be advantageous and some advantageous actions may not be good. I, however, belong to the New Academy, which allows wide latitude to adopt any theory supported by probability.

III

THE UNNATURALNESS OF DOING WRONG

But to return to my rule.

Well, then, to take something away from someone else – to profit by another's loss – is more unnatural than death, or destitution, or pain, or any other physical or external blow. To begin with, this strikes at the roots of human society and fellowship. For if we each of us propose to rob or injure one another for our personal gain, then we are clearly going to demolish what is more emphatically nature's creation than anything else in the whole world: namely, the link that unites every human being with every other. Just imagine if each of our limbs had its own consciousness and saw advantage for itself in appropriating the nearest limb's strength! Of course the whole body would inevitably collapse and die. In precisely the same way, a general

1. In that Plato, founder of the Academy, and Aristotle, founder of the Peripatetic School, both drew many of their beliefs from Socrates.

seizure and appropriation of other people's property would cause the collapse of the human community, the brotherhood of man. Granted that there is nothing unnatural in a man preferring to earn a living for himself rather than for someone else, what nature forbids is that we should increase our own means, property, and resources by plundering others.

Indeed this idea – that one must not injure anybody else for one's own profit – is not only natural law, an international valid principle: the same idea is also incorporated in the statutes which individual communities have framed for their national purposes. The whole point and intention of these statutes is that one citizen shall live safely with another; anyone who attempts to undermine that association is punished with fines, imprisonment, exile, or death.

The same conclusion follows even more forcibly from nature's *rational principle*, the law that governs gods and men alike. Whoever obeys this principle – and everyone who wants to live according to nature's laws must obey it – will never be guilty of coveting another man's goods or taking things from someone else and appropriating them for himself. For great-heartedness and heroism, and courtesy, and justice, and generosity, are far more in conformity with nature than self-indulgence, or wealth, or even life itself. But to despise this latter category of things, to attach no importance to them in comparison with the common good, really does need a heroic and lofty heart.

In the same way, it is more truly natural to model oneself on Hercules and undergo the most terrible labours and troubles in order to help and save all the nations of the earth than (however superior you are in looks or strength) to live a secluded, untroubled life with plenty of money and pleasures. And mankind was grateful to Hercules for his services; popular belief gave him a place among the gods. That is to say, the finest and noblest characters prefer a life of dedication to a life of self-indulgence: and one may conclude that such men conform with nature and are therefore incapable of doing harm to their fellow-men.

A man who wrongs another for his own benefit can be explained in two different ways. Either he does not see that what he is doing is unnatural, or he refuses to agree that death, destitution, pain, the loss of children, relations, and friends are less deplorable than doing wrong to another person. But if he sees nothing unnatural in wronging a fellow-man, is he not beyond the reach of argument? – he is taking away from human beings all that makes them human. If, however, he concedes that this ought to be avoided, yet still regards death, destitution, and pain as even more undesirable, he is mistaken. He ought not to concede that *any* damage, either to his person or to his property, is worse than a moral failure.

So everyone ought to have the same purpose: to identify the interest of each with the interest of all. Once men grab for themselves, human society will completely collapse. But if nature prescribes (as she does) that every human being must help every other human being, whoever he is, just precisely because they are all human beings, then – by the same authority – all men have identical interests. Having identical interests means that we are all subject to one and the same law of nature: and, that being so, the very least that such a law enjoins is that we must not wrong one another. This conclusion follows inevitably from the truth of the initial assumption.

If people claim (as they sometimes do) that they have no intention of robbing their parents or brothers for their own gain, but that robbing their other compatriots is a different matter, they are not talking sense. For that is the same as denying their common interest with their fellow-countrymen, and all the legal or social obligations that follow therefrom: a denial which shatters the whole fabric of national life. Another objection urges that one ought to take account of compatriots but not of foreigners. But people who put forward these arguments subvert the whole foundation of the human community – and its removal means the annihilation of all kindness, generosity, goodness, and justice: which is a sin against the immortal gods, since they were the creators of the society which such men are seeking to undermine. And the tightest of the bonds uniting that society is the belief that robbery from another man for the sake of one's personal gain is more unnatural than the endurance of any loss whatsoever to one's person or property – or even to one's very soul. That is, provided that no violation of justice is involved: seeing that of all the virtues justice is the sovereign and queen.

IV

DIFFICULT MORAL DECISIONS

Let us consider possible objections.

1. Suppose a man of great wisdom were starving to death: would he not be justified in taking food belonging to someone who was completely useless? 2. Suppose an honest man had the chance to steal the clothes of a cruel and inhuman tyrant like Phalaris,[1] and needed them to avoid freezing to death, should he not do so?

These questions are very easy to answer. For to rob even a completely useless man for your own advantage is an unnatural, inhuman action. If, however, your qualities were such that, provided you stayed alive, you could render great services to your country and to mankind, then there would be nothing blameworthy .in taking something from another person *for that reason*. But, apart from such cases, every man must bear his own misfortunes rather than remedy them by damaging someone else. The possible exception I have quoted does not mean that stealing and covetousness in general are any less unnatural than illness, want, and the rest. The point is rather that neglect of the common interest is unnatural, because it is unjust; that nature's law promotes and coincides with the common interest; and therefore that this law must surely ordain that the means of subsistence may, if necessary, be transferred from the feeble, useless person to the wise, honest, brave man, whose death would be a grave loss to society. But in that case the wise man must guard against any excessive self-regard and conceit, since that could only lead to a wrongful course of action. If he avoids these pitfalls, he will be doing his duty – working for the interests of his fellow-men, and, I repeat yet again, of the human community.

An answer to the query about Phalaris can very easily be given. With autocrats we have nothing in common; in fact we and they are totally at variance. There is nothing unnatural about robbing – if you can – a man whom it is morally right even to kill. Indeed, the whole sinful and pestilential gang of dictatorial rulers ought to be cast out

1. Tyrant of Acragas (Agrigentum) in Sicily (c. 570–544 B.C.), believed to have roasted his victims alive in a brazen bull.

from human society. For when limbs have lost their life-blood and vital energy, their amputation may well follow. That is precisely how these ferocious, bestial monsters in human form ought to be severed from the body of mankind.

Such are the problems which beset our efforts to define obligations which may arise in particular circumstances. And this is the sort of theme which I believe Panaetius would have dealt with if some accident or distraction had not altered his plan. Indeed, plenty of rules bearing on precisely this sort of question had emerged from the earlier parts of his work. Those rules already suggest which courses of action have to be shunned as wrong, and which can be tolerated as right.

*

Well, the structure of my book is still not complete, but completion is not far off: now for the topmost stone. Mathematicians often simplify their arguments by leaving out the proofs of certain propositions and requiring that a number of conclusions should be taken for granted; and I shall adopt the same procedure. I shall invite you, my son, to concede to me (if you feel you can) that we must aim at nothing other that what is right. And even if Cratippus forbids such a concession,[1] at least you will grant me this: that right is more worth aiming at, for its own sake, than anything else. Either of these assumptions is enough for my purpose. Sometimes the one alternative may seem more convincing, sometimes the other; and no solution apart from these two has any probability at all.

Before going on, I must refute a charge against Panaetius. He never made the improper assertion that advantage could in certain circumstances conflict with right. What he said was that *apparent* advantage could do so. But he frequently asserted that nothing can be advantageous unless it is right and nothing right unless it is advantageous; and he comments that no greater plague has ever visited mankind than the attitude of mind which has regarded the two things as separable. So the conflicts that he postulated were not real but only apparent ones. Far from permitting us ever to allow advantage priority over right, he was thinking of occasions when we should have to distinguish

1. As a Peripatetic he admitted 'natural goods' (health, honour, etc.) in addition, though as inferior, moral goods. But the Stoics regarded all that was not morally good as 'indifferent'.

whether advantage or right were truly present, or whether their apparent presence was illusory; and his intention was to help us to reach such decisions correctly. However, as I have pointed out, Panaetius did not after all discuss this subject of apparent clashes. Accordingly in my treatment of the matter – which is now to follow – I shall be unsupported and fighting my own battle. True, I have seen studies on this theme by writers subsequent to Panaetius, but personally I have not found them satisfactory.

When we encounter advantage in some plausible form, we cannot help being impressed. But close examination may reveal something morally wrong with this apparently advantageous action. In such a case the question of abandoning advantage does not arise, since it is axiomatic that where there is wrong there can be no true advantage. For nature demands that all things should be right and harmonious and consistent with itself and therefore with each other. But nothing is less harmonious with nature than wrong-doing: and equally, nothing is more in harmony with nature than what is truly advantageous. So advantage cannot possibly coexist with wrong. Take it for granted, then, that we are born – that our nature impels us – to seek what is morally right. In that case, whether we adopt Zeno's view that this is the only thing worth trying for, or Aristotle's opinion that it is at any rate infinitely more worth trying for than anything else, then one must conclude that right is either the only good or at least the highest of all goods. Being identified, therefore, with good – which is certainly advantageous – right is advantageous too.

A man who has in mind an apparent advantage and promptly proceeds to dissociate this from the question of what is right shows himself to be mistaken and immoral. Such a standpoint is the parent of assassinations, poisonings, forged wills, thefts, malversations of public money, and the ruinous exploitation of provincials and Roman citizens alike. Another result is passionate desire – desire for excessive wealth, for unendurable tyranny, and ultimately for the despotic seizure of free states. These desires are the most horrible and repulsive things imaginable. The perverted intelligences of men who are animated by such feelings are competent to understand the material rewards, but not the penalties. I do not mean penalties established by law, for these they often escape. I mean the most terrible of all punishments: their own degradation.

Away, then, with the whole wicked, godless crowd of people who hesitate which course to follow – the course they know to be right, or deliberate immersion and self-pollution in sin and crime! For the mere fact of their indecision is an offence: some courses of action are wrong even to consider – merely to pause over them is evil. Nor will it help the vacillator to expect or hope for his offence to be covered by secrecy or privacy. For if we have learnt any philosophy at all, this at least we ought to appreciate: all the secrets we may be able to keep from any and every god and human being do not in the least absolve us from the obligation to refrain from whatever actions are greedy, unjust, sensual, or otherwise immoderate.

V

TEST CASES IN MYTH AND HISTORY

Plato illustrates this truth by telling the well-known story of Gyges.[1] Once upon a time, after heavy rainfalls, the earth opened asunder. Gyges went down into the chasm, and there he came upon a horse made of bronze, with a door in its side. He opened the door, and found inside the body of a dead man of superhuman stature, wearing a gold ring. Gyges took off the ring, and placed it upon his own finger.

Later, he went to a meeting of the king's shepherds, of whom he was one. There he found that by turning the bezel of the ring inwards – in the direction of the palm of his hand – he became invisible, though he himself continued to see perfectly; and he only became visible again by turning the ring back into the previous position. So he exploited the opportunities thus given him. He seduced the queen, and with her help murdered his royal master. Then he removed everyone whom he believed to stand in his way. In these crimes he remained entirely undetected. By using the ring in this way, he quickly rose to be king of Lydia.

Now picture this same ring in the hands of someone who is truly wise. He would not consider that its possession entitled him to do wrong any more than if it did not belong to him. For to act secretly is not what a good man aims at: what he wants to do is to act rightly.

1. Murdered King Candaules, married his widow, and succeeded him as king of Lydia (c. 685–657 B.C.). The story is in Book II of Plato's *Republic*.

Certain philosophers, who are not ill-intentioned but can hardly be very clever, declare that the story is a fiction invented by Plato. But that is to make Plato claim veracity, or at least possibility, for his tale – as he does not. The point of the ring and its story is this. Imagine yourself doing something in order to acquire excessive wealth or power, or tyranny, or sensual satisfaction. Suppose that no one were going to discover, or even suspect, what you had done: on the contrary, that neither gods nor men would ever have an inkling. *Would you do it?*

The philosophers I have just mentioned are content to reply that this could never happen. True enough – but what I want to know is this. If, in spite of their certainty, such a situation *could* arise, what would they do? By persisting, with boorish determination, in their repeated denials of the mere possibility, they are refusing to understand the significance of my supposition: which is this. When we inquire what they would do if they could escape detection, we are not interested in knowing whether such an escape would be practicable. What we are instead doing, metaphorically, is to put them on the rack. For if they answer that, assured of impunity, they would obey the dictates of their own selfishness, then they are admitting to a criminal attitude. A denial, on the other hand, that they would act in any such way would be tantamount to a proper rejection of any and every action that is by nature morally bad.

But I must return to my subject.

Plausible semblances of advantage are often confusing. I do not now refer to problems of sacrificing what is right in favour of some highly attractive apparent advantage, for there the immorality is beyond question. I refer to occasions when we have to decide whether the action involved in obtaining an apparent advantage may, in fact, not be morally wrong at all.

For example, when Lucius Junius Brutus deposed his fellow-consul Lucius Tarquinius Collatinus,[1] this action might well have been regarded as unjust. For Collatinus had been his fellow-planner and his associate in the expulsion of the royal house. However, the leading men of Rome had decided to eliminate all the relatives of King Tarquin the Proud, along with the very name of the Tarquins and every other reminder of the kingship. That being so, then the advantageous

1. Traditionally believed to have been the colleague of Lucius Junius Brutus as first consul after the expulsion of King Tarquin the Proud (509 B.C.).

course of action, namely the patriotic course, was so manifestly right that even Collatinus himself had to acquiesce. Here, then, advantage prevailed because of its rightness – the indispensable prerequisite of advantage.

The case of the king who founded Rome is different. He thought he saw advantage in reigning alone instead of with a colleague, so he killed his brother. But the semblance of advantage that prompted him was entirely unreal. In order to secure what he believed, wrongly, to be advantageous, he counted brotherly love and human feelings for nothing. His excuse that Remus had leapt over the wall was a mere specious show of rectitude, as unplausible as it was inappropriate. So his action was sinful – he must give me leave to say so – whether we are to call him the god Quirinus [1] or the man Romulus.

That does not mean that we are bound to sacrifice our own vital interests to other people. On the contrary, in so far as we can serve our interests without harming anyone else, we should do so. Chrysippus puts the point with his usual aptness: 'A man running a race in the stadium ought to try his best and exert himself to the utmost in order to win. In no circumstances, however, should he trip up his competitors or impede them with his hand.' The same applies to the struggle of life. Anyone may fairly seek his own advantage, but no one has a right to do so at another's expense.

But the field in which a man's obligations are most liable to confusion is friendship. For if, on a friend's behalf, you omit to do all that you properly could, that is to fail in an obligation; yet if you help him in some improper fashion, then that too is failure. However, this whole problem is governed by a short and simple rule. Apparent advantages for oneself, such as political success, wealth, sensual gratification, and so on, must never be given preference over friendship. On the other hand no man of integrity will, for the sake of a friend, act against his own country, or his honour, or his oath.

Even if someone has to sit in judgement over his friend in a lawsuit, the same will still be true: when he assumes the part of judge, he vacates the role of friend. The only legitimate concessions to friendship will then be these – to hope that his friend's cause is right, and, in so far as the law permits, to help him to fix the hearing at a time that

1. The mythical Romulus was deified under the name of this god of the Sabines worshipped from a very early date on the Quirinal Hill.

suits his convenience. When, however, the judge has to pronounce his sworn verdict, he must remember that his witness is God – in other words (according to my interpretation) his own soul, which is the most godlike thing that God has given to man. So I wish we still maintained the noble custom, bequeathed by our ancestors, of appealing to the judge *to do whatever he can without breach of honour*. This form of appeal is relevant to my discussion of what a judge can legitimately concede to a friend. For a relationship in which a friend's every wish had to be carried out would rank not as a friendship but as a conspiracy. (I am, of course, speaking of ordinary, everyday friendships. Among men who were ideally wise, and faultless, no such situation could arise.)

There is a story about the remarkable friendship between Damon and Phintias, the followers of Pythagoras. One of them had been condemned to death by the tyrant Dionysius, and the day of his execution was appointed.[1] The condemned man asked for a few days' grace so that he could arrange for the care of his loved ones; and the other went bail for him, on the understanding that if the prisoner did not return he himself would die in his place. But, on the appointed day, his friend duly came back. Full of admiration for their loyalty to one another, the tyrant asked to be allowed to become a partner in their friendship.

That is a further illustration of my point: when we are weighing up what appears to be advantageous against the morally right course, even in matters affecting friends it remains true that the apparent advantage should be disregarded in favour of the right. And when friendship's demands transgress what is right, they must yield precedence to scruples and honour. That is how we shall achieve our purpose of choosing successfully between apparently conflicting obligations.

Another field in which plausible semblances of advantage very often cause wrong actions is that of international politics. Our destruction of Corinth [2] is an example. An even worse atrocity was committed by the Athenians when they decreed that the people of Aegina,[3] whose strength depended on their fleet, should have their thumbs cut off.

1. According to another version the whole proceedings were intended by Dionysius (I, *c.* 430–367, or II, 367–345 B.C.) of Syracuse as a jocular test of their friendship.
2. By Lucius Mummius in 146 B.C.
3. Subjected to Athens 456, population expelled 431 B.C.

This seemed to the Athenians an advantageous measure, since their harbour the Piraeus was menaced by its neighbour Aegina. But cruelty can never be of advantage, seeing how inimical this is to nature, with which our actions have to be in harmony.

Wrong is likewise done by those who ban and eject foreigners from their cities, as Marcus Junius Pennus did in the time of our fathers and Gaius Papius [1] recently. True, non-citizens are not entitled to the rights of citizens: legislation to this effect was introduced by those outstandingly wise consuls Lucius Licinius Crassus and Quintus Mucius Scaevola. But the exclusion of aliens from the city's amenities is completely opposed to natural human relations.

*

There have been glorious instances of apparent, unreal advantage to a country being over-ridden in favour of what was morally right. Outstanding among many conspicuous examples in our own country's history was an incident that took place in the Second Punic War. The news of the disaster at Cannae was received at Rome more heroically than any victory and without the slightest signs of fear. Suggestions of peace did not exist – at the time they might have seemed advantageous, but so great is the potency of right that this can eclipse such specious appearances of advantage.

Again, when the Persians invaded Greece,[2] the people of Athens were not strong enough to stand against them; so they decided to abandon their city. Leaving their wives and children at Troezen, they proposed to take to their ships and defend the freedom of Greece at sea. Then a man named Cyrsilus proposed as an alternative that they should stay at Athens and admit Xerxes. But the Athenians stoned Cyrsilus to death. For any plausible advantage in what he said was entirely unreal, since right was on the other side.

After the victorious conclusion of the Persian War, Themistocles announced in the Athenian Assembly that he had a proposal to make

1. Marcus Junius Pennus and Gaius Papius were tribunes in 126 and 65 B.C. respectively. The most famous expulsion of aliens, directed by the consuls Crassus and Scaevola in 95 B.C., is here distinguished from the other occasions by Cicero, but was a blunder which probably helped to provoke the Italian cities to revolt in the Social (Marsian) war.

2. Before the battle of Salamis, 480 B.C.

which would be to the national advantage. But he added that its publication was inadvisable, and that the people should therefore nominate a representative to whom he might communicate his project. They appointed Aristides for this purpose. He learnt from Themistocles that the Spartan fleet, which had been hauled ashore at Gytheum, could secretly be set on fire – and the result would undoubtedly be the total destruction of Sparta's strength. After listening to the proposal, Aristides proceeded to the Assembly, where an expectant audience awaited him. He declared to them that the scheme proposed by Themistocles would bring great material advantage, but was the reverse of right. Thereupon, the Athenians came to the conclusion that, being wrong, the proposal could not be advantageous at all; and so, at the instance of Aristides himself, they rejected Themistocles' plan without even hearing what it was. They did better than us – we let pirates off taxes,[1] but impose them on our allies!

So let us regard this as settled: what is morally wrong can never be advantageous, even when it enables you to make some gain that you believe to be to your advantage. The mere act of believing that some wrongful course of action constitutes an advantage is pernicious.

But, as I remarked earlier, circumstances often arise in which advantage and right seem to clash. So an investigation is necessary – do they really clash in such cases? or can they be reconciled?

VI

TEST CASES IN BUSINESS

This is the type of problem. Suppose that there is a food-shortage and famine at Rhodes, and the price of corn is extremely high. An honest man has brought the Rhodians a large stock of corn from Alexandria. He is aware that a number of other traders are on their way from Alexandria – he has seen their ships making for Rhodes, with substantial cargoes of grain. Ought he to tell the Rhodians this? Or is he to say nothing and sell his stock at the best price he can get? I am

1. The pirates off south-eastern Asia Minor, suppressed by Pompey in 67 B.C., had revived during the Civil Wars; Antony was believed to have mobilized them against Brutus and Cassius. The 'allies' to whom Cicero refers are the people of Massilia and King Deiotarus of Galatia (pp. 142f.).

assuming he is an enlightened, honest person. I am asking you to consider the deliberations and self-searchings of the sort of man who
would not keep the Rhodians in ignorance if he thought this would
be dishonest but who is not certain that dishonesty would be involved.

In cases of this kind [1] that eminent and respected Stoic Diogenes of
Babylon habitually takes one side, and his very clever pupil Antipater
of Tarsus the other. Antipater says that all the facts must be revealed,
and the purchaser must be as fully informed as the seller. According
to Diogenes, on the other hand, the seller must declare the defects of
his wares as far as the law of the land requires, but otherwise – provided he tells no untruths – he is entitled, as a seller of goods, to sell
them as profitably as he can.

'I have brought my cargo, I have offered it for sale, I offer it as cheap
as other dealers – perhaps cheaper, when I am over-stocked. Whom
am I cheating?'

Antipater argues on the other side. 'What do you mean? You
ought to work for your fellow-men and serve the interests of mankind. These are the conditions under which you were born, these are
the principles which you are in duty bound to follow and obey – you
must identify your interests with the interests of the community, and
theirs with yours. How, then, can you conceal from your fellow-men
that abundant supplies and benefits are due to reach them shortly?'

'Concealing is one thing,' perhaps Diogenes will reply, 'but *not re-
vealing* is another. If I do not reveal to you, at this moment, what the
good are like – or the nature of the Highest Good – I am not *concealing*
that information (which would certainly be more useful to you than
the knowledge that wheat prices were down). I am not obliged to tell
you everything that would be useful for you to know.'

'Oh yes, you are,' Antipater will reply, 'if you remember that
nature has joined mankind together in one community.'

'I remember that,' the answer will be, 'but surely this community
is one in which private property exists? If not, nothing ought to be
sold at all – everything ought to be given away.'

In this whole argument, you will observe, neither party is saying 'I

1. These test cases are propounded by the successors of Panaetius in the head-
ship of the Middle Stoa. These philosophers of the second century B.C., who
were largely based on the commercial city-state of Rhodes, consequently sought
their illustrations from trade.

will perform this action, however wrong, because it is advantageous'. One side is claiming that the action is advantageous without being wrong, while the other urges that it *is* wrong, and should therefore not be committed.

Or suppose that an honest man wants to sell a house because of certain defects of which he alone is aware. The building is supposed to be quite healthy, but is in fact insanitary, and he is aware that it is; or the place is badly built and is falling down, but nobody knows this except the owner. Suppose he does not disclose these facts to purchasers, and sells the house for much more than he expected. Has he behaved unfairly and dishonestly?

'Certainly he has,' says Antipater. 'At Athens, not to set a man right when he has lost his way is penalized by general execration – and is it not precisely the same thing to let a purchaser make a mistake and ruin himself with a very heavy loss? That is even worse than not showing a man the way, since in this case the purchaser is being deliberately misled.'

'But he did not force you to buy, did he?' objects Diogenes. 'He did not even ask you to. He offered for sale something he did not want; you bought something you wanted. Seeing that people are not blamed when they advertise a bad, ill-constructed house as fine and well-built, still less ought they to be censured if they merely refrain from speaking in its praise. For when the purchaser can exercise his own judgement, what fraud can there be on the part of the seller? If you are not obliged to make good everything you say, how can you be responsible for what you do not say? It would surely be exceptionally stupid for a seller to enumerate the defects of what he is selling, and the height of absurdity for the auctioneer to proclaim, at the owner's request, *An Insanitary House for Sale!*'

*

These, then, are some of the doubtful cases in which one side takes a moral view, and the other cites advantage by asserting that it is not only right to do what seems to be advantageous but wrong to avoid so doing. Such conflicts between right and apparent advantage are frequent. But I must record my opinion about these cases; for I did not write them down merely to raise problems, but to solve them. I believe, then, that the corn-merchant ought not to have concealed the facts from the Rhodians; and the man who was selling the house should not have withheld its defects from the purchaser. Holding things back does not always amount to concealment; but it does when you want people, for your own profit, to be kept in the dark about something which *you* know and would be useful for *them* to know. Anyone can see the sort of concealment that this amounts to – and the sort of person who practises it. He is the reverse of open, straight-forward, fair, and honest: he is a shifty, deep, artful, treacherous, malevolent, underhand, sly, habitual rogue. Surely one does not derive advantage from earning all those names and many more besides!

If, then, mere suppression of the truth deserves censure, what must we think of people who have actually told lies? A Roman gentleman called Gaius Canius, quite a witty and cultured man, once went to Syracuse, not on business but on holiday; we owe him the story that follows. He often spoke of buying a little estate where he could invite his friends and enjoy himself without intrusion. When his intention became known, a Syracusan banker called Pythius disclosed his own possession of just such a property; this was not for sale, he said, but Canius could treat the place as his own if he wanted to. Pythius forth-with asked him to dinner there on the following day, and Canius accepted.

Now Pythius, being a banker, had people of all classes ready to oblige him. So he sent for some fishermen, and requested them to do their next day's fishing in front of his grounds; and he issued them full instructions. Canius arrived to dinner punctually, and Pythius gave him a sumptuous entertainment. Before their gaze there was a fleet of fishing-boats; each fisherman brought in his catch, which he then deposited at Pythius's feet. 'Tell me, Pythius,' said Canius, 'what does this mean? – all these fish and all these boats?' 'It is quite natural,' Pythius replied. 'All the fish and all the water in Syracuse are at this very spot; without this place of mine, the men could do nothing.'

Canius became excited and pressed Pythius to sell him the property. Pythius showed reluctance at first; but finally – to cut the story short – he gave in. Canius was rich and wanted the estate, and he paid what Pythius asked – and bought all its furnishings as well. Pythius clinched the agreement and entered the terms in his books.

On the following day Canius invited his friends to the house, and arrived early. As far as boats were concerned he saw not so much as a single thole-pin. He inquired from his next-door neighbour if there was some fisherman's holiday which accounted for their invisibility. 'I don't know of any,' was the answer. 'But nobody does fish here; so yesterday I couldn't think what had happened.'

Canius was furious. But what was he to do? For at that time my friend and colleague Gaius Aquilius Gallus [1] had not yet laid down the established forms of pleading in cases of criminal fraud. When Aquilius was asked what he meant by criminal fraud in this connexion, he used to answer: *pretending one thing and doing another* – a masterly reply, characteristic of a lawyer so expert at framing definitions.

So Pythius and everyone else whose actions belie their words are ill-intentioned, faithless, and dishonest. Nothing that such vicious people do can possibly be advantageous.

VII

SHARP PRACTICE AND THE LAW

If Aquilius's definition is correct, our lives ought to be completely purged of any misrepresentation or suppression of facts. The application of his ruling will mean that no decent person engaged in buying or selling can ever resort to invention or concealment for his own profit. Indeed, even before Aquilius's time, there were legal penalties against criminal fraud of this kind. For instance the Twelve Tables [2] apply them to wardship cases, and the Plaetorian Law to the defrauding of minors. In certain equity cases, too, the same purpose is served by the formula *as good faith requires*. Likewise, all other civil suits give prominence to phrases like this: in arbitrations about a wife's property *the fairer is the better*, in trust cases *honest dealing as between honest people*. Well, if we apply the formula *the fairer is the better*, how can there be any question of dishonesty? And the ruling *honest dealing as between honest people* again leaves not the slightest room for any fraudulent or unscrupulous action.

Moreover, as Aquilius points out, misrepresentation is the equivalent

---

1. Cicero's colleague in the praetorship (66 B.C.).

2. Earliest and fundamental Roman code of laws, ascribed to 451–450 B.C. The Plaetorian Law (c. 193–192 B.C.) first made a settled distinction between majors and minors (under 25 years of age).

of criminal fraud. In other words deception must be wholly eliminated from business transactions. For example, no seller must employ a sham bidder to raise prices; nor must the purchaser employ an agent to keep them down – and both of them, when they come to naming a sum, must state their price once and for all.

Quintus Mucius Scaevola,[1] son of Publius, wanted to buy a farm; and he requested that the seller should indicate his final price. When this had been done, Scaevola replied that he considered the farm to be worth more than the proposed sum; and he paid a hundred thousand sesterces over and above what had been asked. By so doing, as no one can deny, he proved the goodness of his character. However, his action has also been criticized as showing a lack of wisdom – just as much as if he had been selling the farm, and had accepted less than might have been offered. But what a pernicious doctrine! – implying, as it does, a denial that good men and wise men are identical. As Ennius relevantly says, 'if the wise man cannot benefit himself, his wisdom is vain.'[2] That is entirely true – if Ennius and I mean the same thing by 'benefit'!

Panaetius's pupil Hecato of Rhodes, in his work *On Duty* dedicated to Quintus Aelius Tubero,[3] makes a noteworthy remark on this subject. 'A wise man', says Hecaton, 'is justified in caring for his private interests, provided that this involves no action contrary to morality, law, or established institutions. For when we want to become rich, egotism is not all that prompts us: we feel this ambition for the sake of our children, our relations, and our friends – and most of all for our country, seeing that the nation's wealth is made up of the resources and fortunes of individuals.' So Scaevola's action, of which I am speaking, would not have met with the approval of Hecato, who regarded all profit-making as permissible unless it is of a kind specifically forbidden by law. But for a man who holds views like his we need not spare much commendation or gratitude.

Nevertheless, if criminal fraud includes concealment of the facts as

---

1. Consul 95 B.C., and chief priest; Cicero, who had been his pupil, described him as 'the greatest orator among the lawyers, the greatest lawyer among the orators'.

2. Quotation from Ennius's lost tragedy the *Medea*.

3. Praetor 123 B.C., jurist, nephew of Scipio Aemilianus, and friend of Panaetius.

well as positive misrepresentation, there are very few human dealings in which such fraud does *not* occur. Conversely, a good man will be far from easy to find – if, as I have said, we mean by this the person who helps all and hurts none. Yet, as I tried to show, bad actions can never be of advantage, because they are always morally wrong; goodness, being morally right, is invariably advantageous.

The laws in our civil code relating to real property stipulate that in a sale any defects known to the seller have to be declared. The Twelve Tables were content to require that defects explicitly indicated should be made good by the seller, and that a seller who denied them under questioning should pay twice their cost. Nowadays, however, our legislators have added suppression of the facts to the indictable offences, ruling that even if the seller has not declared all the defects he must make them good.

Once the augurs were proposing to take celestial observations from the Citadel. Tiberius Claudius Centumalus, who owned a house on the Caelian Hill, received instructions from them to pull down certain parts of the building which owing to their height obstructed the augurs' view. But Claudius responded by advertising the block for sale. Its purchaser was Public Calpurnius Lanarius, on whom the augurs then served the same notice; and he undertook the necessary demolition. At that juncture, however, Calpurnius learnt that Claudius had only offered the building for sale *after* the augurs had ordered its partial destruction. So he compelled Claudius to appear before an arbitrator, who was to decide *what indemnity he was obliged, in good faith, to deliver and make over to the other party.* The verdict was pronounced by Marcus Porcius Cato, father of our Cato (other men take their fathers' names, but he almost seems to take his from his glorious son!). His decision was as follows: 'Since the seller knew this fact at the time and did not divulge it, he must make good the purchaser's loss.'

Thereby Cato established the principle that good faith requires any defect known to the seller to be notified to the purchaser. If Cato's verdict was correct, then our grain-merchant and the seller of the insanitary house acted wrongly when they concealed the facts. Our civil laws naturally cannot handle suppression of the facts in all its forms. But with those aspects which come within their scope they deal severely.

Once my relative Marcus Marius Gratidianus [1] sold back to Gaius Sergius Orata a house he had purchased from the same man a few years earlier. In the terms of sale Gratidianus said nothing about the existence of a legal encumbrance to which any purchaser of the building would have to succeed. A dispute followed, and the matter came into court. Lucius Licinius Crassus [2] appeared for Orata, and Marcus Antonius [2] for Gratidianus. Crassus laid emphasis on the law requiring that the seller must make good the defects – which he had known but not disclosed. Antonius, on the other hand, appealed to equity. His argument was that Orata was already aware of the defect, seeing that the latter had himself sold the house to Gratidianus previously. Antonius therefore maintained that there had been no need to mention the liability involved in the purchase: since Orata knew of this already, he had not been the victim of any deception.

*

Why am I telling these stories? To show you that our ancestors would not countenance sharp practice!

Now law and philosophy have their different methods of combating sharp practice. The law attempts its conquest by forcible coercion, the philosophers by reasoning and logic, which, they argue, make any employment of deception, pretence, or trickery out of the question. Well, surely setting traps comes under the heading of deception! – even if one does not intend to start the game or drive it into the traps; for whether someone is after the animals or not they often get caught in the traps all the same. Advertising a house for sale raises just the same point. Clearly you ought not to make your advertisement into a trap which you hope will catch some victim unawares.

Nevertheless, the standards demanded by public opinion are not so high as they were, and I find that nowadays actions of this sort are not normally regarded as wrong, or penalized by statute or civil law. But what forbids them is the moral law which nature itself has ordained. As I have said before – and it needs constant repetition! – there is a bond of community that links every man in the world with every other. Though this bond is universal in application, it is particularly

1. Praetor 86 B.C. (?), murdered by Sulla. His aunt or great-aunt married Cicero's grandfather (see Genealogical Table, p. 253).
2. See above, p. 121.

strong as a unifying link between people of the same race: between actual compatriots the link is closer still.

The existence of this natural bond of community between all human beings explains why our ancestors chose to make a distinction between the civil law of the land and the universal law. The law of the land, it is true, ought to be capable of inclusion within the universal law, but they are not synonymous since the latter is more comprehensive.

Not that we possess any clear-cut, tangible images to show us what true, authentic Law and Justice really look like! We only have outline sketches. And the extent to which we allow ourselves to be guided even by these leaves a great deal to be desired. For at least they have the merit of derivation from the finest models – those which have been vouchsafed to us by nature and by truth. Think of the nobility of that formula: *that I be not deceived and defrauded because of you and because of trust in you.* And that other golden phrase: *between honest men there must be honest dealing and no deception.*

But that still leaves big questions unanswered: who are the honest men? and what is honest dealing?

The chief priest Quintus Mucius Scaevola attributed special importance to all arbitration cases involving the expression *in good faith.* He attributed the widest possible validity to this formula, applying as it does to wardships, associations, trusts, commissions, buying and selling, hiring and letting: in fact, to all the transactions which make up our daily human relationships. According to Scaevola's view the assessment of one man's obligation to another in these spheres, with all the counter-claims that are frequently involved, demands a judge of outstanding calibre.

Sharp practice, then, must go. And so must every kind of trickery masquerading as intelligence, seeing that the two things are entirely different and remote from one another. The function of intelligence is to distinguish between good and bad; whereas trickery takes sides between them, actually preferring what is bad and wrong.

Real estate is not the only field in which our civil law, basing itself on the dictates of nature, penalizes trickery and deception. In the sale of slaves, for example, all deception on the part of the seller is again forbidden. For the aediles have ruled that if a man knows that a slave he is selling is unhealthy, or a runaway, or a thief, he must (unless the slave is one he has inherited) report accordingly.

This then is the conclusion to which we come. Nature is the source of law: and it is contrary to nature for one man to prey upon another's ignorance. So trickery disguised as intelligence is life's greatest scourge, being the cause of innumerable illusions of conflict between advantage and right. For extremely few people will refrain from doing a wrong action if they have the assurance that this will be both undiscovered and unpunished!

VIII

RESPECTED MEN AT FAULT

We can test that conclusion, if you like, by applying the principle to certain instances where public opinion is unlikely to see anything wrong. In the present context, then, there is no need to discuss cutthroats, poisoners, forgers of wills, thieves, and embezzlers of state funds: since the coercion which such people merit needs no philosophers' phrases and arguments but is clearly a matter for shackles and imprisonment. Let us inquire, on the other hand, into the actions of those who are commonly reputed to be good men.

Certain individuals once conveyed from Greece to Rome a forged will purporting to belong to the wealthy Lucius Minucius Basilus. In order to improve its credentials they associated with themselves, as fictitious heirs, two of the most powerful men of the day, Marcus Licinius Crassus [1] and Quintus Hortensius.[2] These dignitaries had their suspicions of the forgery, but, since they did not feel personally implicated in its perpetration, refrained from rejecting this contemptible gift which other people's criminal action had placed into their hands. Does the indirect nature of their responsibility suffice to absolve Crassus and Hortensius from guilt? Though I felt affection for one of them while he was alive, and am no enemy to the other now he is dead, I maintain that the answer is no. For Basilus's own intention had been to confer his name and inheritance upon his sister's son Marcus

1. The triumvir, killed at Carrhae 53 B.C.
2. The orator, Cicero's chief opponent in the Verres case (Chapter 1).

Satrius – I mean the man who is 'patron' [1] of Picenum and the Sabine country (what a sign of the times that regrettable title is!). That the property, therefore, should instead go to two of Rome's leading men, and that Satrius should succeed to nothing but the name, was an injustice.

In the first part of this treatise I argued that even a man who merely fails to prevent or repel wrongdoing is himself thereby committing a positive wrong. That being so, what must be thought of the man who not only fails to avert wrong but actually promotes its commitment? Indeed I personally do not regard even genuine inheritances as justified, if they have been secured by insincere flatteries, and by services emanating from selfish rather than altruistic motives.

Still, in such cases, it does sometimes happen that one course *looks* right and another advantageous. Yet this must always be a delusion: because right and advantage are, by definition, identical. Once let a man fail to understand that, and no species of fraudulence or crime will come amiss to him. If he argues 'one course is certainly right, but the other is to my advantage', he will be tearing asunder two things which nature has joined together. And such misguided audacity leads to every sort of deception, crime, and sin.

Suppose that, by snapping his fingers, a good man could assume the power to insert his name into rich men's wills. Even if he could be absolutely certain that no one would ever suspect him, he still would not avail himself of a power like that. But imagine Marcus Licinius Crassus, on the other hand, being granted this capacity to snap his fingers and come into an inheritance which had not, in fact, been left him. In such a cause, believe me, Crassus would even have been prepared to dance in the Forum! On the other hand the just man, the good man as we understand the term, will never, for his own profit, take anything away from anybody. Whoever finds this assertion surprising will have to confess his total ignorance of what being a good man means.

For there is an ideal of human goodness: nature itself has stored and

---

1. The ancient link between patron and client, with their mutual obligations sanctified by custom and religion, had been extended to whole communities. Cicero deplores the fact that states enjoying Roman citizen rights should need someone to safeguard their interests. Marcus Satrius was a supporter of Antony.

wrapped this up inside our minds. Unfold this ideal, and you will straightaway identify the good man as the person who helps everybody he can and, unless wrongfully provoked, harms none. Well, the dispossession of legitimate heirs by some sort of magic spell would surely be doing others harm!

One contrary theory is that a man is entitled to act as his own interests and profit dictate. But that is not a true supposition, for he has to understand that his interests could not be advanced by injustice of any kind whatever. Before anyone can become capable of achieving goodness, this is a lesson which he has to learn.

When I was a boy I used to hear my father tell a story about the ex-consul Gaius Flavius Fimbria. Fimbria was judge in a case concerning Marcus Lutatius Pinthia, a leading knight of great integrity. Pinthia had wagered that he would pay a forfeit *if he did not prove his own goodness in court.* But Fimbria refused under any circumstances to deliver a verdict on this case; since if he did so either he would deprive a respectable man of his reputation – for that would be the effect of an unfavourable decision – or he would seem to be pronouncing someone a good man, whereas true goodness depends on the performance of countless obligations and praiseworthy actions. To this dilemma Fimbria refused to commit himself. So even he – let alone Socrates! – was capable of identifying the good man as the person who can see advantage in nothing except what is right.

Such a man would not be afraid to make a public announcement of all his actions and even all his thoughts. How scandalous, then, that philosophers should entertain doubts – about matters which cause no hesitation even to farm-labourers! For the labourers were the men who originated the timeworn proverbial compliment to a man's honesty and integrity: 'he is someone you could play odds and evens [1] with in the dark.' This is clearly the same thing as saying that you can never derive advantage from an improper gain, regardless of whether this has been detected or not.

The proverb leaves no excuse for Gyges, or for the man we imagined to have the power of sweeping in everyone's legacies by a snap of the fingers. For nature, as well as denying that wrong actions

---

1. Modern Italian *morra*. One player quickly opens any number of his fingers, the other simultaneously tries to open the same number of his own.

can ever be advantageous, refuses to admit that a disguise can ever help them to become right.

*

An objection: *When the prize is really splendid, wrong-doing is excusable.*

Take the case of Gaius Marius.[1] More than six years after being praetor he was still languishing in the background. A consulship seemed out of the question; indeed it looked as if he would never even stand for one. But then Quintus Caecilius Metellus, the eminent personage on whose staff he was serving, sent him to Rome. There, addressing the national Assembly, Marius attacked Metellus himself – his own commanding officer – and charged him with deliberately prolonging the war. He himself however (continued Marius), if they made him consul, would rapidly deliver up the enemy king Jugurtha, dead or alive, into the hands of the Roman people. Accordingly, he was elected consul. But his action had been totally at variance with good faith and fair dealing. For he had brought public disfavour upon a noble and greatly respected Roman who was his commander and was responsible for his mission; and he had achieved this by a false accusation.

Even my relative Marcus Marius Gratidianus[2] once failed to act as a good man should. While he was praetor, the tribunes of the people invited the board of praetors to meet them in order to decide jointly upon a standard for the currency; for at that time the value of money was so unstable that no one knew how much he was worth. So they drafted a joint declaration, including provision for penalties and judicial procedures in case of infringement. They then agreed to reassemble in the afternoon of the same day, when they would appear together on the official platform. And so the meeting dispersed. Gratidianus, however, went straight from the tribunes' benches to the official platform and published their jointly drafted statement as if he were solely responsible. And I have to add that his action made him a

1. The great Marius – victor over Jugurtha king of Numidia and the Germans, seven times consul, d. 86 B.C. But the true conqueror of Jugurtha was believed by the conservatives to be Metellus (consul 109 B.C.).

2. See p. 184: to counteract financial panic due to the issue of plated coins purporting to be silver, Gratidianus devised means (? the affixation of small stamps) of distinguishing good from bad money.

very famous man! His statues were in every street, with incense and candles burning before them. No one has ever been so popular.

This is the sort of case which can sometimes be perplexing: when the lapse from integrity does not appear to be particularly serious, whereas the favourable consequences of the action look extremely significant. For Gratidianus's theft of popularity from his fellow-praetors and the tribunes did not appear to him to be so terribly wrong; on the other hand his election to the consulship – which was what he was aiming at – seemed greatly to his advantage. But that was a mere delusion: for there are no exceptions to our rule. I hope this rule is now completely familiar to you: what appears advantageous can only be so if no wrong action is involved – if the contrary is the case, the action cannot be advantageous after all.

To conclude then – can we regard either the great Marius or Marius Gratidianus as a good man? Work the problem out! Examine your conclusions, and note the ideal of a good man that emerges from them. Will a good man lie for his own profit, will he slander, will he grab, will he deceive? He will do nothing of the kind.

Surely the reputation and the glory of being a good man are too precious to be sacrificed in favour of anything at all, however valuable and desirable in appearance. No so-called advantage can possibly compensate for the elimination of your good faith and decency and the consequent destruction of your good name. For if a human exterior conceals the savage heart of a wild beast, their possessor might as well be beast instead of man.

Again: assume that someone is prepared, for the sake of power, to ignore all that is right and good. That, surely, is a perfect description [1] of the man who wanted to marry a certain person's daughter, and then proposed to exploit his father-in-law's ruthlessness in order to achieve dominance for himself. As he saw the matter, there was advantage in gaining immense power in such a way as to arrange for its unpopularity to fall upon someone else. What he failed to see was that this damaged his country – and was therefore utterly wrong.

As for the father-in-law, he was fond of a quotation from the *Phoenician Women* of Euripides. Here is the best translation I can manage, crude perhaps but intelligible: *If right may ever be infringed,*

1. Pompey in 59 B.C. had married Caesar's daughter Julia, as part of the agreement of the First Triumvirate (see Genealogical Table, p. 254).

this can be done for the sake of kingship: in all else be god-fearing. The man who allowed himself a single exception of such a kind deserved his death! Criminality could go no further. Why trouble to list minor crimes – forged legacies, business deals, fraudulent sales? For here you have someone who actually aspired to be absolute monarch of Rome, indeed master of the whole world – and that purpose he achieved! No one but a lunatic could describe such an ambition as honourable. For its approval is tantamount to applauding the annihilation of law and freedom and glorying in the loathsome and dreadful act of their suppression.

Consider the paradox of a person who admits the wickedness of tyrannizing a country which was once free, and ought to be free still, but who nevertheless sees advantage in himself becoming its tyrant if he can. In the attempt to rescue him from that delusion there must be no limit to our reproaches and appeals. Who, in God's name, could possibly derive advantage from murdering his country? Of all murders that is the most hideous and repulsive: even when its perpetrator is hailed, by the citizens he has trodden underfoot, as 'Father of his Country'.[1]

The only yardstick of advantage, then, is moral right. Indeed the sole discoverable difference between the two terms, advantage and right, is a matter of sound. In meaning they are one. True enough, if we follow the standards of public opinion, no greater advantage can be imagined than to be an absolute ruler. But when we apply the standard of truth instead, the man who has achieved this position by wrongful means proves to have acted entirely at variance with his own interests. Agonies of anxiety, terrors day and night, a life of incessant plots and dangers, cannot possibly bring any advantage. 'To the throne many are hostile, many disloyal, and few friendly,'[2] wrote Accius. But the monarchy to which he was referring had been legitimately handed down from Tantalus and Pelops. Whereas our own autocrat was hated on a far, far, wider scale. For he had actually used the armies of Rome to crush the people of Rome; he had converted our nation – a land which had been not only free in itself but the ruler of other nations – into servitude to his own person.

1. See above, p. 116.
2. From an unidentified tragedy of Accius concerning the House of Agamemnon – the grandson of Pelops, who was the son of Tantalus.

Think of the corruptions and sores which must scar that man's conscience and his heart! How can anyone derive benefit from his own life, if unheard-of popularity and glory can be won by its destruction? Power on this scale *looks* extremely advantageous. But the loads of shame and sin weighing it down deny that this is so, and afford a further proof that nothing which is not right can be of advantage.

IX

IS HONESTY ALWAYS NECESSARY?

Testimonials to the conclusion I have just stated exist in abundance. A conspicuous example was provided during the war against Pyrrhus,[1] by Gaius Fabricius Luscinus (then consul for the second time) and our Senate. Without provocation, Pyrrhus had declared war on Rome. The stake was imperial supremacy – and our enemy was a powerful, illustrious monarch. One day a deserter from the army of Pyrrhus presented himself at Fabricius's camp and undertook, on promise of a reward, to return to Pyrrhus's camp as secretly as he had come, and kill the king by poison. But Fabricius had the man taken back to Pyrrhus; and our Senate applauded his decision. Yet, suppose the semblance of advantage – the popular conception of advantage – were all that we were looking for. Then a terrible war, and a formidable enemy of our rule, would both have been eliminated at one blow through the agency of this single deserter! On the other hand, the prize of the war was glory: and the employment of crime instead of courage as our conquering weapon would have been a dreadful scandal and disgrace.

What Aristides[2] had been to Athens, Fabricius was to Rome. Our Senate always identified advantage with principle. So one can see why they preferred to fight the enemy with battle-weapons rather than with poison. If the struggle is for supreme power, and the incentive is glory, then there must be no crimes, since out of crime glory cannot come. Indeed, even when gains are sought for reasons other than

1. King of Epirus; fought the Romans in south Italy 280–275 B.C.

2. Statesman and soldier, commanded the Athenian army at Plataea (479 B.C.); political opponent of Themistocles.

glory, the same remains true: if shameful means have been employed to acquire them, they can bring no advantage.

This applies, for example, to the proposal of Lucius Marcius Philippus, the son of Quintus. Acting in accordance with a decree of the Senate, Sulla had exempted certain communities [1] from taxation upon their payment of a lump sum. Philippus recommended that their exemptions should be cancelled, but that the payments they had made to secure them should not be reimbursed; and the Senate accepted this proposal. What a disgrace to our government! On this occasion even a pirate could have improved upon the Senate's good faith.

The argument of the other side is that since Philippus's measure meant an increase in our revenues, the result would be advantageous. But will people for ever incorrigibly see advantage in what is wrong? Governments cannot do without a splendid reputation and the good-will of their allies. So how can unpopularity and infamy possibly be to their advantage?

On this subject I frequently disagreed even with my friend Marcus Porcius Cato. He seemed to me to be carrying his vigilance over the treasury and its revenues to the point of obstinacy. In consequence, he turned down every request from the tax-farmers and a great many from our allies: [2] whereas our correct course would have been to treat the allies generously and the tax-farmers as if they were our own tenants. This was particularly desirable seeing that harmony between the different grades of our society was essential to our national well-being.

Gaius Scribonius Curio the elder, too, was wrong when, while admitting that the demands of the Transpadanes [3] were justified, he nevertheless invariably added: *Let advantage prevail!* He would have

1. Probably cities taken from King Mithridates VI of Pontus by Sulla during the First Mithridatic War (88–85 B.C.).

2. Cato the younger (p. 212) consequently frustrated Cicero's policy of assisting the knights (p. 10), who sponsored the tax-farmers. In the absence of a civil service, these bought from the Roman state for a lump sum the farming of provincial revenues (especially in Asia = W. Asia Minor), but sometimes (as now, in 61 B.C.) when they found they had paid too much they petitioned the Senate for a rebate. Cicero's reference to the allies alludes to Cato's stern action against the brother of Ptolemy 'the Flute-Player' in Cyprus when Cato annexed the island in 58 B.C.

3. Residents in Italy north of the Po had obtained half-way status towards citizenship during the Social (Marsian) War (89 B.C.), but only obtained the full franchise from Caesar in 49.

done better to argue that these claims were not justified, because they were not to our national advantage, than to admit their justice but deny their advantage.

*

The sixth book of Hecato's work *On Duties* is full of questions like this: 'When food is extremely scarce, is a decent man entitled to let his slaves go hungry?' Hecato gives both sides of the case, but finally bases his decision on advantage, as he interprets the term, rather than on human feeling.

Here is another of his problems: 'If there is a storm at sea, and cargo has to be thrown overboard, should a man prefer to lose a valuable horse or a valueless slave?' In this case his pocket pulls one way, human feeling the other.

Another question was this: 'If the ship has sunk and some person of little intelligence has grabbed a plank, will a wise man take this away from him if he can?' 'No,' says Hecato, 'that would be wrong.'

'What about the man who owns the ship, then? Will he take the plank away?'

'Certainly not – any more than he would propose to throw a passenger overboard in deep water. For until the ship reaches the port for which it was chartered it does not belong to the owner, but to the passengers.'

'Well, then, if there were only one plank, and two shipwrecked people – both men of true wisdom! – should each of them try to seize this single plank for himself, or should one give way to the other?'

'One should give way; the plank should be left with the man whose life is more valuable to himself or his country.'

'But what if both lives are equally valuable in both respects?'

'Then they will not compete, but one will give way to the other, as though the matter were decided by lot or by the game of odds and evens'.[1]

'Again, suppose a man's father were stealing from temples or digging an underground passage to the Treasury – ought his son to report him to the authorities?'

'No, that would be a sin. Indeed, if the father were charged, his son ought to defend him.'

1. See above, p. 188.

'So patriotism does not, then, come before all other obligations?'

'Yes, it does indeed, but our country will benefit by having sons who are loyal to their parents.'

'Then if a man's father tries to seize autocratic power or betray his country, will his son say nothing?'

'Of course he will; he will beg his father not to. If this appeal fails, he will reproach his father and even threaten him, and if, finally, national ruin seems imminent, he will put his country's safety before his father's.'

Hecato also asks: if a wise man inadvertently accepts a counterfeit coin, will he, on discovering his mistake, pass the piece off to someone else as good, in payment of a debt? Diogenes says yes, Antipater says no – and I agree with him.

And then, if a man knows that the wine he sells is going bad, ought he to disclose the fact? Diogenes says he need not, Antipater thinks an honest man should. The Stoics discuss problems of this kind like disputed points of law. Again, 'when you are selling a slave ought his defects to be declared – not only those which there is a legal obligation to declare (otherwise the transaction is liable to be cancelled), but also the fact that he is a liar or gambler or thief or inebriate?' One of the philosophers maintains that you ought to declare such facts, the other says you need not.

'If someone thinks he is selling brass when he is really selling gold, should an honest man tell him the metal is gold, or buy it at one-thousandth of its value?'

But it is clear by this time where the two philosophers disagree – and what my own opinion is.

*

However, assuming that an agreement or promise *has not been obtained by force or by criminal fraud* (as the praetors put the matter), does this undertaking always have to be kept?

Suppose one man present another with a cure for dropsy and stipulates that, if the treatment is successful, the recipient must never use the same cure again. The patient duly recovers; some years later, however, there is a recurrence of the complaint. But this time the man who previously agreed to help him refuses to let him have the remedy again. What ought the sufferer to do? My answer is that the owner of the cure, who would lose nothing by agreeing to its further employment, is inhuman to refuse, so the sick man is entitled to take whatever steps are necessary to safeguard his life and health.

Again: imagine that a wise man is going to be left a hundred million sesterces. But first the testator insists that his prospective beneficiary should perform a dance publicly in the Forum, in broad daylight. The wise man promises to comply, because otherwise he will lose the legacy: should he then keep his promise or not? Now, first of all, I think it is a pity he promised! A refusal would have been more dignified. However, we are assuming that the promise was given. Well, then, if he considers dancing in the Forum morally wrong, he will do better to break his promise, even if he gets not a penny from the legacy, than to keep the promise, and pocket the fortune. Unless, maybe, he contributes the money to the state during some crisis. For if the country is going to benefit, even dancing in the Forum could not be wrong.

Again, promises which are contrary to the interests of those to whom they are given need not be kept. To quote an instance from mythology, the Sun-god once told his son Phaethon to make any request he liked, and it would be granted. His request was that he should be allowed to ride in his father's chariot. The wish was granted. But while Phaethon was still riding in the heavens, a flash of lightning burnt him up. In this case how much better it would have been for his father to break his promise!

And then there was Neptune's promise to Theseus, which Theseus insisted should be kept. Neptune had offered him three wishes,[1] and Theseus, suspecting his wife's relations with his own son Hippolytus (who was her stepson), wished for his son's death. The wish was granted, and Theseus was overwhelmed with grief. Again, when Agamemnon had vowed to sacrifice to Diana the most beautiful creature born that year in his kingdom, this proved to be his own daughter Iphigenia; so he sacrificed her.[2] But, rather than commit such an appalling crime, he ought to have repudiated his vow.

1. According to the myth, Theseus was granted the following three wishes: safe return from Hades, release from the Labyrinth, and the death of Hippolytus.

2. According to a less savage version Diana substituted a stag for Iphigenia, whom she made priestess of her temple in Tauris (Crimea).

That is to say, promises do not always have to be honoured – and trusts do not always need to be made good. Suppose someone, while in his right mind, leaves his sword in your care; then he becomes insane, and demands the sword back. But compliance now would be criminal and you must refuse. Or suppose that a man who has entrusted you with a sum of money intends to take treasonable action against your country: should you return him his money? In my opinion you should not, for this would be against the interests of your country, which ought to be dearer to you than anything else in the world.

In special circumstances, then, a number of things which look natural and right may turn out not to be right after all. If the original advantage which prompted an undertaking, or agreement, or trust no longer exists, then its fulfilment may cease to be right and become wrong.

And now I feel I have said enough about courses of action which look intelligent and consequently advantageous, yet are the reverse of right.

X

OBJECTIONS TO HEROISM

In the first part of this treatise I deduced our moral obligations from the Four Cardinal Virtues,[1] or subdivisions of right. So let us now apply the same classification in order to emphasize this conflict between what is right and what displays the false appearance of advantage. I have discussed wisdom – which cunning seems to mimic. I have also dealt with justice, which can never fail to be advantageous. So there remain two Cardinal Virtues. One of them can be described as heroism or fortitude; and the other as the shaping and regulation of the character by temperance and self-control.

First, fortitude. Ulysses believed that the trick he played was to his

1. Cicero's Four Cardinal Virtues (adapted from the Stoics) are wisdom, justice, fortitude, and temperance. Augustus, going back to an earlier formulation (by Gorgias), established as the official slogans of his regime 'virtue' (*virtus* also means 'valour'), clemency, justice, and piety.

advantage. So, at least, say the tragic poets [1] – though in Homer, our best authority, this reflection on his conduct is not found. The tragedians, however, represent Ulysses as deliberately evading military service by simulating madness. Such a scheme evidently cannot be described as morally right! But it could, perhaps, be interpreted as advantageous, seeing that it enabled him to keep his throne and go on living at ease in Ithaca with his parents, wife, and son. A life so peaceful, the argument could run, is better than any of the glory which days filled with toil and danger might provide.

My own view, however, is that peacefulness of such a kind must be spurned and rejected, because it is wrong and therefore cannot be advantageous. Imagine if Ulysses had persisted in his pretence of madness; how he would have been criticized! Even as matters were, in spite of his subsequent deeds of heroism in the war he was attacked by Ajax in the following terms: [2] 'As you all know, Ulysses was the man who instigated the leaders to swear their oath – yet he alone broke that oath, when he began feigning madness to avoid joining up! And if Palamedes, with his shrewd sense, had not seen through this deceitful effrontery, Ulysses would have evaded the fulfilment of his vow for ever!'

Ulysses' battles against the enemy, and even his battles against the waves, were nobler than this abandonment of the union of all Greece against the barbarians.

*

But we have had enough of myths, and of foreign parts. Let us turn to our own country, and to real history.

In Africa, while Marcus Atilius Regulus [3] was consul for the second time, the enemy captured him by a trick; the Carthaginian commander was Xanthippus the Spartan, serving under Hannibal's father

1. Euripides, especially, represents Odysseus (Ulysses) as sly and cowardly.
2. Perhaps from *The Test of Arms* of the tragic dramatist Pacuvius (220–c. 130 B.C.). The story was that Palamedes proved the madness fictitious by placing the baby Telemachus in front of the ox and ass which Ulysses had yoked to a plough to sow salt. Ulysses stopped the plough.
3. Consul during the First Punic War in 267 and 256 B.C., captured 255. The story that follows, repeated by Horace, may be apocryphal, invented to justify the torture and murder of Carthaginian prisoners by Regulus's widow.

Hamilcar.[1] The enemy authorities then dispatched Regulus to Rome. His instructions were to meet the Senate, and request the return of certain aristocratic Carthaginian prisoners. In case, however, he should fail in his mission, he placed himself under oath to return to Carthage.

When Regulus arrived in Rome, the superficially advantageous course was obvious enough to him. But he rejected the advantage as unreal: as subsequent developments were to show. His interests *seemed* to require him to stay in his own country, at home with his wife and children – retaining his high position as consul, and treating the defeat he had suffered as a misfortune which anyone might experience in time of war. And what do you think refuted the supposition that these were advantages? I will tell you: his heroism and his fortitude. And no more impressive authorities could be imagined. For the whole point of these virtues is that they reject fear, rise above all the hazards of this life, and regard nothing that can happen to a human being as unendurable.

So what did Regulus do? He entered the Senate, and reported his instructions. But at first he refused to express his own opinion in the matter, because, as long as he was still bound by an oath sworn to the enemy, he refused to consider himself a member of the Senate. What happened next will cause him to be criticized for foolishness in acting against his own advantage. For he then proceeded to advise the Senate that the Carthaginian prisoners should not be sent back, since they were young men and capable officers whereas he himself was old and worn out. His advice prevailed, and the prisoners were not released.

So Regulus returned to Carthage. Even his love for his own homeland and his dear ones was not strong enough to hold him back. Yet he knew full well the refinements of torture which a ruthless foe had in store for him. Nevertheless he believed that he had to obey his oath. When he rejoined his captors, they gave him no sleep until death came to him. But even so he was better off than if he had stayed at home – an aged ex-consul who had fallen into the enemy's hands and then perjured himself.

The opposite thesis runs like this. 'Still, to argue explicitly against the release of the prisoners was foolish of Regulus. He would have done enough if he had merely refrained from advocating their release.'

1. Cicero is wrong in identifying this Hamilcar with Hannibal's father of the same name.

But how could what he did be foolish? If his advice furthered our national interests, where is the foolishness then? No course which is harmful to the state can possibly benefit any of its individual citizens.

People who argue that advantage is one thing and right another are uprooting the fundamental principles laid down by nature. Obviously we all aim at our own advantage: we find that irresistibly attractive. No one can possibly work *against* his own interests – indeed no one can refrain from pursuing them to the best of his ability. But seeing that our advantage can only be found in good repute, honour, and right, priority and primacy must be accorded to these. The advantage that goes with them should be interpreted as their indispensable accompaniment rather than as a glorious objective in itself.

But here are further arguments against Regulus's action. 'What is the significance of an oath, anyway? Surely we are not frightened of Jupiter's anger! We have no reason to be, since all philosophers maintain that God is never angry and never hurtful: on this point those [1] who teach that God is himself free from cares and does not inflict them on others, and those who hold that he is ever active and at work, are in full agreement. Besides, even if Jupiter had been angry, how could he possibly have damaged Regulus more than, as things turned out, Regulus damaged himself? So there could be no justification for allowing scruples to overrule the advantages of the opposite course.'

Another criticism is this. 'Was fear of doing wrong his motive? If so, he was misguided, for the following reasons. First, the proverb rightly insists that one should "choose the least among evils", and the breach of faith which he would have committed by staying was not so bad as the torture which he suffered because of his return. Secondly, remember those lines from Accius: "Have you broken your faith? But I never pledged it – to the faithless I pledge no faith." [2] Though the king who spoke those words was evil, the sentiment that they record is none the less admirable.'

The next point raised by Regulus's detractors goes as follows. Just as we maintain that certain things seem advantageous but are not, so they maintain that certain things seem right but are not. 'In this case, for instance,' they say, 'it *looks* as though Regulus did right in going back to be tortured for the sake of his oath. But his action proves not

1. The Epicureans. Those quoted as holding the opposite view are the Stoics.
2. From Accius's tragedy the *Atreus*.

to be right all the same, because an oath extracted forcibly by an enemy need not be honoured.'

Then their final objection is to the effect that something exceptionally advantageous often turns out to be right, contrary to first appearances.

So these are the principal lines of attack on Regulus's action. Let me deal with them in turn.

First, the argument that there was no need to be afraid of anger and harm from Jupiter, because Jupiter is never angry or harmful. Now this is only valid as a criticism of Regulus in so far as the same argument applies to any and every oath. But when we swear an oath, what we ought to have in mind is not so much fear of possible retribution as the sanctity of the obligation we have incurred. For an oath is backed by the whole force of religion: a promise you have solemnly made, with God as your witness, you must keep. This is not a question of the anger of the gods, which does not exist, but of right dealing and good faith. 'Gracious Faith, borne on wings; and oath sworn in Jupiter's name,' [1] is the fine phrase of Ennius. So whoever breaks his oath violates Good Faith: for which – as a speech of Marcus Porcius Cato the Censor tells us – our ancestors chose a dwelling on the Capitol itself, *next to the Temple of Jupiter the Best and Greatest.*

One of the other objections was that even if Jupiter had been angry he could not have damaged Regulus more than Regulus damaged himself. Correct – if pain were the only evil! But philosophers of the highest authority [2] assert that, on the contrary, pain is not even the greatest among evils: in fact it is not an evil at all! Regulus is our witness to this truth, and let us not disparage the force of his evidence. On the contrary, he seems to me the best of all possible witnesses. I can think of no more significant testimony than that of a leading Roman who insisted on doing his moral duty even to the extent of submitting to torture.

Then there was the criticism, *choose the least among evils.* But surely that cannot mean 'do wrong to keep out of trouble', seeing that the worst of all evils is wrongdoing. For since even an outward blemish such as a physical deformity is not very agreeable, a degeneracy of the soul itself faces us with something that is truly hideous and repellent.

1. Probably from Ennius's tragedy, the *Thyestes.*
2. The Stoics.

That is why the more rigorous school of philosophers go so far as to say that moral wrong is the only evil – and even those who are less strict [1] do not hesitate to call it the worst of evils.

Well, as to that quotation, *I never pledged my faith: to the faithless I do not pledge it.* The poet found the phrase apt because he had to make the words fit the character of Atreus [2] who appeared in his play. But anyone who sets out to argue that a pledge given to someone who is faithless need not be honoured should take care, or he may, by his proposition, merely be opening the door to perjury.

Indeed, even warfare has its legal obligations: an oath that you have sworn to an enemy very often has to be honoured. That is to say, if you swore with the clear intention of keeping your word, then you must do so. If, on the other hand, you had no such idea, then breaking the oath is no perjury.

Imagine, for example, that you have been captured by pirates, and you agree with them to pay a ransom for your life. Yet even if your agreement had been on oath, your failure to deliver the ransom would not count as fraudulent. For a pirate does not come into the category of regular enemies since he is the enemy of all the world – as far as he is concerned, good faith and oaths do not come into the picture at all.

For perjury is not simply swearing to what is false. It is the failure to honour an oath which, according to the traditional phrase, you have sworn *upon your conscience.* About the other sort of oath Euripides aptly writes: 'With my tongue I swore: my mind remains unsworn.'[3] Regulus, on the other hand, was not entitled to perjure himself by renouncing the terms and conditions of warfare agreed with the enemy. For our operations against them originated from a regular, formal declaration of war, and relations with enemies thus defined are governed by our whole code of warfare as well as by many international laws.

This is proved by the action taken on certain occasions by our Senate in handing over distinguished Romans, manacled, to our enemies. During the second consulships of Titus Veturius and Spurius Postumius we were defeated by the Samnites in the battle of the

1. The Peripatetics – the 'more rigorous school' being the Stoics (p. 19).
2. After pretending to be reconciled with his brother Thyestes, Atreus served up to him at a banquet the flesh of his (Thyestes') children.
3. From the *Hippolytus* of Euripides.

Caudine Forks.[1] Our legions were compelled to go under the yoke, and the consuls made peace. But because neither the Assembly nor the Senate had authorized them to do so, they were handed over to the enemy. So, at the same time, were Tiberius Numicius and Quintus Maelius, then tribunes of the people, since they had favoured the conclusion of peace: which their delivery to the Samnites was intended to repudiate. Moreover, the handing over of these men was actually urged and supported by Postumius himself, although he was one of their number.

Many years later the same thing happened to Gaius Hostilius Mancinus.[2] He had made a treaty with the people of Numantia without the Senate's sanction. Lucius Furius Philus and Sextus Atilius Serranus moved that he should be given up to the Numantines – and Mancinus himself spoke in favour of that proposal. The motion was passed, and he was surrendered to the other side. Quintus Pompeius Rufus acted less honourably, on another occasion, when he spoke against a similar proposal and secured its rejection. This was a case of abandoning the right course in favour of an apparent advantage. In the former instances, on the other hand, the false appearance of advantage was outweighed by what was right.

Another argument against Regulus was that an oath extorted by force need not be honoured. As if force could influence a hero!

Again: 'If Regulus only proposed to urge the Senate not to release the Carthaginian prisoners, why did he make the journey at all?' There you are complaining about the finest feature of his action! He subordinated his own judgement to the Senate's; the purpose of his mission was to enable the Senate to judge the matter for itself. True, without his advice, the prisoners would certainly have been returned to the Carthaginians, and in that event Regulus would have remained safe in his own country. But he did not think this was to his country's advantage, and he felt it right to say so – and suffer accordingly.

And then his critics argued that what is exceptionally advantageous often turns out to be right. However, they presumably mean 'is'

1. Between Capua and Beneventum, 321 B.C.
2. As consul, 137 B.C. After many years of resistance Numantia, centre of Spain's resistance to Rome, fell to Scipio Aemilianus in 133. Quintus Pompeius Rufus, consul 140 B.C., had concluded and then disowned a treaty with the Numantines.

right, not 'turns out to be' right – seeing that nothing can be advantageous unless it is right already! Things are advantageous *because* they are right.

So all the exemplary actions of the past could hardly supply a more splendid and noble deed than that of Regulus.

However, probably the most praiseworthy feature of the whole glorious incident is his own initiative in arguing against the release of the prisoners. True, his return to Carthage also seems to us admirable; but at that epoch he could not have done otherwise, so the merit belongs to the times rather than to the individual. For our ancestors believed that no guarantee of good faith was more powerful than an oath. That is proved by the Twelve Tables, the Sacred Laws,[1] and the treaties insisting on good faith even with an enemy.

*

Inquiries and penalties from the censors [2] tell the same story: cases relating to oaths were those for which they reserved their most rigorous judgements. The dictatorship of Lucius Manlius Capitolinus Imperiosus,[3] son of Aulus, provides an instance. Marcus Pomponius, tribune of the people, announced an indictment of the dictator because he had prolonged for a few days his tenure of office. Pomponius also accused Manlius of banishing his own son Titus (Titus Manlius Torquatus, as he was called later), and compelling him to live in the country away from all human society. But when Titus heard of his father's predicament, he hastened to Rome, the story goes, and early one morning called at Pomponius's house. When his presence was reported, Pomponius assumed that the motive for the young man's visit was an angry determination to bring fresh evidence against his father. The tribune rose from his bed, cleared the room of witnesses, and gave orders that the visitor should be admitted. But Titus no sooner entered than he drew his sword and vowed to kill Pomponius on the spot unless he promised, on oath, to withdraw the charge against the elder Manlius. Terrified, Pomponius did as he was told. Later, reporting the incident in the Assembly, he explained that because of what had hap-

1. Laws placing their transgressor under the ban of a divinity. For the Twelve Tables, see above, p. 181.

2. See Appendix C, p. 258.

3. Dictator 363 B.C.

pened he was obliged to abandon the case; and so he withdrew the charge against the dictator.

Such was the reverence felt for an oath in those days!

The young man in that story was the same Titus Manlius who at the battle by the Anio [1] was challenged to single combat by a Gaul. He killed the Gaul and pulled off his collar (*torques*), thus acquiring the surname Torquatus. Later, when consul for the third time, this exceptionally distinguished man defeated and routed the Latins near Veseris. He had shown remarkable indulgence towards his father – although to his own son he behaved with ruthless severity.

When we praise Regulus for keeping his oath, we must censure ten Romans concerned in another occurrence. After the battle of Cannae Hannibal dispatched ten of his Roman prisoners on parole as envoys to the Senate. If the story that they omitted to return to the Carthaginians is true, they were gravely at fault, since, in the event of failure to arrange an exchange of prisoners, they had sworn to go back to the camp and to the enemy who were now its occupants. Their subsequent behaviour is variously described. Polybius,[2] an outstandingly reliable authority, reports that nine out of the ten aristocratic envoys duly returned to Hannibal when their mission to the Senate had proved unsuccessful, but that the tenth found a reason for remaining at Rome. Shortly after his initial departure, this man had turned back and re-entered the camp on the pretext that he had forgotten something; and now he argued that by this 'return to the camp' he had released himself from his oath. But he was wrong. Far from rehabilitating perjury, deliberate deception makes things worse. So his cunning was merely foolishness, perversely masquerading as intelligence. He was a sly rogue – and the Senate directed that he should be taken back to Hannibal in chains.

But the most significant part of the story is this. The eight thousand prisoners in Hannibal's hands had not been captured by him in battle, and had equally not fled from the battle to save their lives: the consuls Marcus Aemilius Paullus and Gaius Terentius Varro had left them

1. Against the Latins. The story of the *Torques* is probably an aetiological myth to explain the name Torquatus. The (? unauthentic) battle near Veseris ('battle of Vesuvius') in the same war is celebrated for the self-immolation of the elder Publius Decius Mus (p. 230). The Latin towns submitted in 338 B.C.
2. The great Greek historian of Rome (204–122 B.C.).

behind in the camp. Their ransom could have been cheaply arranged. Yet the Senate did not take this step, owing to a desire to implant in our soldiers the lesson that they must conquer or die. Polybius described the effect of this news on Hannibal; such heroic courage displayed by the Senate and people of Rome in the face of disaster plunged him into despair. Here, then is another case of right outweighing apparent advantage. (However, Gaius Acilius,[1] the writer of a Roman history in Greek, gives another version. According to him, not one but several of the envoys played this trick of re-entering the camp in the hope of releasing themselves from their oaths, and they incurred the deepest ignominy from the censors.)

So let us conclude this discussion. Obviously, no action performed in a timid, base, degraded, crushed spirit can be a source of advantage – because such actions are immoral, offensive, and wrong. And that would have been the proper description for what Regulus had done if his advice concerning the prisoners had been influenced by his own seeming advantage, and his desire to stay at home, rather than by the interests of his country.

XI

THE FALLACY OF PLEASURE

There still remains our fourth Good Quality. This comprises propriety, moderation, decorum, restraint, and self-control.

How can anything which conflicts with such a chorus of virtues possibly be advantageous? Yet the Cyrenaic followers of Aristippus, and the philosophical school named after Anniceris,[2] used to interpret pleasure as the one and only good. Virtue, they held, is praiseworthy only to the extent that it produces pleasure. These doctrines are out of date nowadays; but Epicurus is in fashion, and the view which he strongly advocates is very much the same as theirs. And yet if we are determined to maintain and stand up for what is right, these beliefs must be resisted by main force. Metrodorus,[3] too, identifies advantage,

1. A Roman Senator who interpreted in the Senate for a delegation of Greek philosophers in 155 B.C.

2. For Aristippus, Anniceris, Epicurus, see above, p. 18.

3. Metrodorus of Lampsacus was the most distinguished pupil of Epicurus (who described him as unoriginal).

and indeed a happy life in general, with good physical health and the firm expectation of its continuance. But such an interpretation of advantage – and what is being defined here is the *supreme* advantage – cannot escape clashing with what is right.

Take wisdom first of all: where can a system like this possibly find room for such a quality? I suppose wisdom will be assigned the function of hunting up pleasures wherever they can be found! But what a depressing servitude for wisdom, the synonym of virtue – slaving for pleasure. Its job, I suppose, will be to make an intelligent choice between one pleasure and another. But granted that this prospect has its superficial attractions, would not such a task be degrading in the extreme?

And then if people argue that pain is the supreme evil, I cannot see what role they can assign to that other Cardinal Virtue, fortitude – seeing that this means disregard for pains and troubles. It is true that Epicurus, in his observations concerning pain, frequently displays a respect for fortitude. But such sayings lack significance beside the fundamental question: what place can fortitude logically occupy in a system which identifies good with pleasure and evil with pain?

The same applies to restraint and self-control. Reading Epicurus one finds, scattered about his works, many references to these good qualities. But *the stream is clogged*, as the proverb goes. For instance, if he regards pleasure as the highest good, how can he recommend self-control? – seeing that pleasure is served by the passions, and self-control is their adversary.

So when they come to the three Virtues of wisdom, fortitude, and self-control, these Epicureans have to hedge; though they do it ingeniously enough. Wisdom finds a place in their system as the knowledge by which pleasures are procured and pains removed. For fortitude, too, they make some sort of a case, as the quality which enables people to make light of death and to endure pain. They even bring in self-control – not very easily, one must admit, but as well as they can – by claiming that pleasure in its highest form amounts to the absence of pain and nothing more.

However, the fourth Cardinal Virtue, justice, makes only a tottering appearance in their doctrine – or rather, its condition is one of collapse. And so are all the other good qualities which are concerned with our daily lives and with the association between one human being and another. Integrity, generosity, and courtesy: these, and friendship too, cannot exist if they are pursued, not because they are desirable in themselves, but for the sake of pleasure and self-interest.

Let me recapitulate briefly. First I tried to show that nothing opposed to right can be advantageous. Then I pointed out that this wrongful category includes all sensual indulgence. That is why, in my opinion, Calliphon and Dinomachus [1] deserve particular censure for their attempt to solve this problem by coupling pleasure with right: which is like coupling a man with an animal! The highest good, being of necessity homogeneous, cannot be a composite mixture of contradictory qualities.

But I have dealt with the highest good elsewhere – and it is a large subject! So back to our present discussion. I have treated in some detail the problem of deciding what to do when right and apparent advantage conflict. A place among apparent advantages may certainly be claimed for sensual pleasures. Yet with right they have nothing in common. To pleasures of such a kind, one concession only can be made – perhaps they add a certain spice to life! But they certainly provide no real advantage.

*

Here then, Marcus my son, is your father's present to you. Personally I consider it a substantial one! But that will depend on the use you make of it. I should like you to think of these three parts of my work as three welcome guests among your notes of Cratippus's lectures.

I should certainly have come to Athens myself, if my country had not unmistakably called me back when I was already on my way. [2] If I had come, I am sure you would, from time to time, have given me your ear. Instead, I have to be represented by my voice: in the shape of these volumes. So do please give them as much time as you can – which means as much as you want to. And when I have heard that

1. Calliphon and Dinomachus tried to follow a middle path between the Stoics and Epicureans (third century B.C.).

2. See above, p. 94. Cicero, who wrote this treatise at his villa at Puteoli, never saw his son again.

you are enjoying your study of these subjects, I hope we shall soon be discussing them together. Meanwhile, we are separated, and our talks must be at a distance.

Goodbye, then, my son. My affection for you is very great, as you know. And it will be a good deal stronger still if this sort of advice and instruction meets with your favour!

CHAPTER FIVE

CATO THE ELDER ON OLD AGE

(ON OLD AGE)

He gives one an appetite for growing old.

MONTAIGNE

Cicero wrote this famous essay at the beginning of 44 B.C., completing its revision some six months later, and dedicating it to his friend Atticus. This is one, slighter and more rapidly written than On Duties *(Chapter 4), of the astonishingly numerous philosophical or semi-philosophical works which he produced at this time of his enforced political inaction during the dictatorship of Caesar and its unsatisfactory aftermath.*[1]

In his discussion on old age, that 'seductive combination of increased wisdom and decaying powers', as E. M. Forster calls it, 'to which too little intelligence is devoted', Cicero anticipates Schopenhauer and modern gerontological research. The Wisdom of Solomon *was unknown to him, but he drew upon a number of Greek treatises on the same subject – he mentions a certain Aristo as the author of one, and Theophrastus was another writer on this theme. However, the discussion which he pretends to reproduce here is staged at Rome in 150 B.C. The main speaker is Marcus Porcius Cato the Elder, known as 'the Censor' – farmer, soldier, statesman, orator, writer, and stern patriotic moralist, aged 84 at the time of this imaginary conversation. Cicero was a great admirer of Cato (whom Seneca was to recognize as the historical embodiment of the Stoic sage), and had already mentioned him at least sixty times in his previous writings. Though Cicero admits that Cato may not have been so profoundly Hellenized as he appears here, he was likewise not the rough and aggressive anti-Hellenic rustic presented by Greek writers: he was no peasant but a capitalist who thought like other Senators, though more effectively than most of them.*

With Cato are Scipio Aemilianus (Lucius Cornelius Scipio Africanus the younger), patron of letters and writer – aged 35 at the time – who was to destroy Carthage in the Third Punic War four years later; and his friend Gaius Laelius, known, like Cato himself, as 'the wise'. Scipio and Laelius

---

1. For a list of these writings, see below, pp. 251 f.

also appear in On the State, *and Laelius is the chief speaker in* On Friendship. *Scipio – unlike the leading orators of his day – admired the Greek philosophical ideal, and his circle helped decisively to introduce this and other aspects of Greek culture into Roman education.*

Cicero, writing under an autocrat who had profited from disharmony, makes his idealized Cato – a 'new man' like himself – the spokesman for an unspoilt Republican past in which, allegedly, leading politicians had been friends with one another.

> The Romans were like brothers
> In the brave days of old.

This picture, dwelling upon the happy relations between Cato and Scipio Aemilianus, draws a veil over an earlier period in which Cato had determinedly opposed the elder Scipio Africanus after the latter's successful conclusion of the Second Punic War.

Cicero's many illustrations from the history of Rome and other countries – derived from many sources, including a genealogical work by Atticus and various treatises by Varro (including perhaps one on Old Age) – display Cicero at his unsurpassed best as raconteur and anecdotist; the tone is somewhat reminiscent of Hellenistic discussions on popular philosophy such as the 'Diatribes' ('leisure hours') of Bion of Borysthenes (c. 325–255 B.C.).

Cicero's reflections on immortality come from the heart because of the recent death of his beloved daughter Tullia. He himself, when he composed this essay, was sixty-two, and one of his aims, as he fretted in retirement, may have been to show that he was still capable of playing an important part in affairs of state. Furthermore, by giving the chief role to Cato the Elder, he indirectly compliments his own austerely Republican contemporary Cato the Younger (the elder Cato's great-grandson), who had killed himself at Utica in North Africa after the failure of the Republican cause at Thapsus (46 B.C.). Even if Cicero often disagreed with Cato's politics (p. 193), he greatly respected his high principles – and had recently written him a flattering obituary, to which Caesar replied with an Anti-Cato (though each praised the style of the other's pamphlet).

INTRODUCTION

'If I can give you any help, Titus, if I can lighten the cares which are implanted in your breast and are roasting and turning you on the spit, what will be my reward?'[1]

Our poet Ennius attributed those words to 'that man of little wealth but rich in loyalty', as he described Titus Quinctius Flamininus. I take leave to copy them, Atticus, and address them to yourself. I am certain, however, that you cannot be described, like Flamininus in the same passage, as 'full of anxiety day and night'. For I know you are a moderate even-tempered man – who have imported more than just your surname from Athens! You have brought back a civilized, intelligent point of view as well. Nevertheless, I suspect that at times you too are more than a little disturbed by the events which are causing me such grave anxiety today. However, the search for comfort in these troubles would be too great a task for now, and must be left for another time.

My present intention, instead, is to write you an essay on Old Age. For this is a burden which you and I share;[2] if not already imminent, age cannot fail to be upon us before long. What I shall try to compose for you – as well as for myself – is a consolation for this prospect. True, you face it, I know, and you will continue to face it, with philosophical calm. That is why, when I thought I would write something about old age, I felt you deserved its dedication! The book was to be

---

1. From the *Annals*, epic of the elder Cato's close friend Ennius (239–169 B.C.): a shepherd of Epirus is addressing Titus Quinctius Flamininus, conqueror of Philip V of Macedon at Cynoscephalae (197 B.C.). Titus is also the first name of Atticus (T. Pomponius Atticus).

2. Cicero was 62, Atticus 65.

something that we should have in common. I have so greatly enjoyed its composition that the task has rid me of any thought of the irritations which age will bring, and has even made the condition seem agreeable and attractive.

No praise, then, is too great for philosophy! – which enables this period in her obedient disciples' lives, like every other period, to be lived without anxiety.

Other aspects of philosophical study I have dealt with elsewhere, at length – and I shall do so again on other occasions – whereas the book I am sending you now will concentrate on old age. When Aristo of Chios [1] wrote on this theme, he made Tithonus his spokesman. I have not followed his lead because a myth seems too insubstantial. I have instead put my sentiments in the mouth of the aged Marcus Porcius Cato (the Censor), so that his personality may confer authority upon the discussion. At Cato's house, I shall imagine Gaius Laelius and Publius Cornelius Scipio Aemilianus. They are expressing wonder at the ease with which their host endures being old, and Cato explains why this is. And if his arguments may seem to show greater learning than was habitually displayed in the books he wrote, the credit must go to Greek literature – which he is known to have studied extensively in his last years.

That is all I shall say at this point. From now on you will hear my views on old age from Cato's lips.

I

CATO AND HIS FRIENDS

SCIPIO : Laelius and I often express admiration for you, Cato. Your wisdom seems to us outstanding, indeed flawless. But what strikes me particularly is this. I have never noticed that you find it wearisome to be old. That is very different from most other old men, who claim to find their age a heavier burden than Mount Etna itself.

1. It has been disputed whether Cicero is referring to a Stoic philosopher Aristo of Chios or to a Peripatetic of the same name from Ceos. Tithonus, son of the Trojan king Laomedon, was, through the favour of Eos (Dawn), granted by Jupiter eternal life, but not eternal youth: tired of senility, he was transformed into a grasshopper.

CATO: You are praising me for something which, in my opinion, has not been a very difficult achievement. A person who lacks the means, within himself, to live a good and happy life will find any period of his existence wearisome. But rely for life's blessings on your own resources, and you will not take a gloomy view of any of the inevitable consequences of nature's laws. Everyone hopes to attain an advanced age; yet when it comes they all complain! So foolishly inconsistent and perverse can people be.

Old age, they protest, crept up on them more rapidly than they had expected. But, to begin with, who was to blame for their mistaken forecast? For age does not steal upon adults any faster than adulthood steals upon children. Besides, if they were approaching eight hundred instead of eighty, they would complain of the burden just as loudly! If old people are stupid enough, then nothing can console them for the time that has gone by, however great its length.

So if you compliment me on being wise – and I only wish I lived up to your estimate and to the name people have given me! – my explanation is this. I regard nature as the best guide: I follow and obey her as a divine being. Now since she has planned all the earlier divisions of our lives excellently, she is not likely to make a bad playwright's mistake of skimping the last act. And a last act was inevitable. There had to be a time of withering, of readiness to fall, like the ripeness which comes to the fruits of the trees and of the earth. But a wise man will face this prospect with resignation, for resistance against nature is as pointless as the battles of the giants against the gods.

LAELIUS: Yes, Cato, but I have a special request to make; and I can speak for Scipio too. We hope and desire to live long enough to see old age. Could you therefore not tell us now, well in advance, how its oncoming can best be made endurable? If you can, you will be doing us a very great favour.

CATO: If you both really want me to give you my advice, I will.

LAELIUS: You have already travelled far on the long road for which we also are destined. If, therefore, this is not asking too much of you, we should like to hear your impressions of the place to which you have come.[1]

1. Here, as in other passages of this section, Cicero closely follows the discussion in Plato's *Republic* between Socrates and the aged Cephalus.

CATO: Then I will do the best I can.

When I talked with my contemporaries – and the ex-consuls Gaius Livius Salinator and Spurius Postumius Albinus, who are almost my age ('Like consorts with like,' says the old proverb) – how they used to grumble! They had lost all material pleasures, they said, and without those life was not life at all. They also complained that people who had once been attentive to them were now neglectful. But I felt they were not directing the blame where this belonged. For if the troubles which they lamented were due to age, then I and all other veterans would be suffering the same experiences; whereas I have known many old men who had no complaints about their age or its liberating release from physical pleasures, and who were by no means treated with contempt by their associates. When you hear protests of this kind, the trouble is due to character, not age. If a man controls himself and avoids bad temper and churlishness, then he can endure being old. But if he is irritable and churlish, then any and every period of his life will seem to him tiresome.

LAELIUS: You are undoubtedly right, Cato. All the same, the objection might be raised that what helps you to find age more tolerable is your money and property and position – advantages which few others possess.

CATO: There is something in that, but it is not the whole story. Remember that anecdote of the man from Seriphos: [1] he was quarrelling with Themistocles, whose fame this Seriphian attributed to his country's greatness, not his own. 'Quite right,' answered Themistocles; 'I should certainly not have been famous if I had come from Seriphos; nor would you if you had come from Athens!' You might say the same sort of thing about age – even the wisest man would not find it pleasant to be old if he were very poor, and even the richest man would not find it particularly tolerable if he were very stupid.

Old age has its own appropriate weapons: namely the study, and the practice, of decent, enlightened living. Do all you can to develop these activities all your life, and as it draws to a close the harvest you reap will be amazing. That is partly for the very important reason that you can go on living in this fashion until your dying day. Besides,

1. A small, insignificant island in the Aegean. Themistocles (c. 528–462 B.C.), victor of Salamis, was the creator of Athenian sea-power.

there is great satisfaction in the knowledge of a life well spent and the memory of many things well done.

When I was a young man Quintus Fabius Maximus, who captured Tarentum,[1] was already old. Yet I was as fond of him as if we had been contemporaries. His natural dignity had a sociable streak, and age had not changed his character. True, when I first knew him, he was by no means extremely old, though he was already getting on in years. He had been consul in the year after I was born; and in his fourth tenure of that office I was a very young private soldier in his army marching on Capua – and then, five years afterwards, on Tarentum. Four years after that, in the consulships of Publius Sempronius Tuditanus and Marcus Cornelius Cethegus (when I was quaestor), Fabius, by now really old, spoke in support of the Cincian Law [2] on gifts and rewards.

Even in quite advanced years he fought his wars with as much determination as any young man. What wore down Hannibal's youthful exuberance was the patience Fabius showed. My friend Ennius wrote splendidly about him: 'One man, by delaying, restored our fortunes: he reckoned the talk of his critics as of less account than the safety of his country. So now his glory waxes even more splendidly thereafter.' What vigilance and strategy he displayed in the recapture of Tarentum! I myself heard Marcus Livius Salinator, who had lost the town and taken refuge in the citadel,[3] boasting to him; 'You would not have recaptured Tarentum without me.' 'Very true,' replied Fabius with a laugh; 'if you had not lost the place first I should never have recaptured it.'

And he was as distinguished a statesman as a soldier. During his second term of office as consul, the tribune Gaius Flaminius [4] was

1. The leading Greek town of south Italy, captured in the Second Punic War (209 B.C.) by Quintus Fabius Maximus 'the Delayer', five times consul, twice dictator (d. 203 B.C.).

2. The Cincian Law forbade gifts which might defeat justice, and certain donations above a given amount (204 B.C.).

3. A slip by Cicero (or Cato); it was Salinator's relative Marcus Livius Macatus who held the citadel.

4. This apparently democratic statesman and soldier proposed a law for the settlement of citizen-farmers on the public lands south of Ariminum confiscated from the Gauls. The date was not 228 B.C., as given by Cato here, but 232.

trying to allot land in Picenum and Cisalpine Gaul as small-holdings, in defiance of a ruling from the Senate. The other consul Spurius Carvilius did not raise his voice, but Fabius made every effort to oppose Flaminius. Again, when Fabius was augur, he had the courage to pronounce that if an action were for the good of the state then the favourable quality of the auspices need not be doubted; and conversely, when any action was opposed to the national interests the auspices could not fail to be bad.

There were many remarkable things about that great man, as I can vouch from personal knowledge. But I know of nothing more admirable than the way in which he received the death of his son, who was a distinguished former consul. The father's funeral oration is extant for us to read, and when we do, every philosopher is put to shame. However, the greatness Fabius showed before Rome's public gaze was less notable than his achievements in the privacy of his own home. As a talker, as a moralist, he excelled; in history, too, and augural law, his knowledge was outstanding. He was also, for a Roman, very well read: his mind was stored with information about all the wars our country has ever fought, and about wars between foreign countries as well. My absorption when I listened to his talk was prophetic, you might have said, of the time to come – when he had died and I had no one left to learn from.

Why have I said so much about Fabius Maximus? Because you must see how wrong one would be to describe an old age like his as unhappy. True, not everyone can be a Scipio or a Maximus and remember the cities he has captured, the battles he has fought on land and sea, the triumphs he has won. But there is another sort of old age too: the tranquil and serene evening of a life spent in peaceful, blameless, enlightened pursuits. Such, we are told, were the last years of Plato, who died in his eighty-first year while still actively engaged in writing. And then there was Isocrates,[1] who informs us himself that he was rising ninety-four when he finished his *Panathenaicus*; and he lived for another five years after that. His teacher, Gorgias of Leontini, had reached his one hundred and seventh birthday without ever relaxing from his studies and his labours. When someone asked him why he chose to stay alive so long, he replied: 'Old

1. Athenian orator and teacher of rhetoric, 436–338 B.C. Gorgias, the most famous of the 'sophists', is stated to have lived from 485 to *c.* 378.

age gives me no cause for complaint.' A fine answer, worthy of a scholar!

The evils for which ignorant people blame old age are really their own faults and deficiencies. Ennius, whom I mentioned just now, did not make that mistake when he compared himself, as an old man, to a gallant, victorious race-horse: *like a courageous steed which has often won races in the last lap at Olympia, and now, worn out by years, takes his rest.* Probably you can both remember Ennius quite clearly. He died in the year when Gnaeus Servilius Caepio and Quintus Marcius Philippus were consuls (the latter's second tenure), only nineteen years before the assumption of office by our present consuls, Titus Quinctius Flamininus and Manius Acilius Balbus. I was sixty-five at the time, and I made a speech in favour of the Voconian Law,[1] with the full force of my still powerful lungs. Ennius lived until he was seventy, and at that age he had to endure two of what are regarded as men's heaviest burdens – poverty and age. But he bore them so remarkably well that you might almost have thought he was enjoying them.

When I think about old age I can find four reasons why this is regarded as an unhappy time. First, because it takes us away from active work. Secondly, because it weakens the body. Thirdly, because it derives us of practically all physical pleasures. And fourthly, because it is not far from death. If you like we will go over these reasons one by one, and see how much truth there is in each of them.

II

ACTIVITIES FOR THE OLD

'Old age takes us away from active work.' From what sort of work? Presumably from the sort which needs youth and strength. But surely there are also occupations fitted for old men's minds and brains even when their bodies are infirm. There were occupations enough for Fabius, as well as for your father,[2] Scipio – Lucius Aemilius Paullus Macedonicus, whose son-in-law was my beloved son. And then there were those others who used the experience and authority of their

---

1. Concerning inheritance by women (169 B.C.).
2. Conqueror of King Perseus of Macedonia at the battle of Pydna (168 B.C.).

advancing years for the protection of their country: Gaius Fabricius Luscinus, Manius Curius Dentatus,[1] Titus Coruncanius. Surely they could not be described as doing nothing!

Old age made Appius Claudius[2] blind. All the same, when our Senate was inclining towards a peace pact with king Pyrrhus, Appius did not hesitate to utter the words that Ennius later put into verse: 'What is this madness that has turned your minds, until now firm and strong, from their course?' And so on, in the most impressive terms, for you know the poem – and indeed Appius's speech itself has come down to us. He delivered it seventeen years after his second tenure of the consulship, and since ten years had elapsed between his two consulships and he had been censor before the first of them, you can see that by the time of the war with Pyrrhus he was a very old man. Nevertheless, that was his vigorous intervention, as our fathers recorded it for us.

So people who declare that there are no activities for old age are speaking beside the point. It is like saying that the pilot has nothing to do with sailing a ship because he leaves others to climb the masts and run along the gangways and work the pumps, while he himself sits quietly in the stern holding the rudder. He may not be doing what the younger men are doing, but his contribution is much more significant and valuable than theirs. Great deeds are not done by strength or speed or physique: they are the products of thought, and character, and judgement. And far from diminishing, such qualities actually increase with age.

Now I have fought all kinds of wars in my time. First I was a private soldier, then a junior officer, then a commander, and finally consul. Well, I am not fighting wars any longer, so perhaps I seem to you to be taking my ease. Yet mine is the advice the Senate listens to about which wars to fight, and how to fight them. At present I am looking well ahead and planning for war against Carthage:[3] my suspicions of that city will never come to an end until I am certain it

1. See pp. 235. Titus Coruncanius, consul 280 B.C., triumphed over the Etruscans, and was the first plebeian chief priest and an early jurist.

2. (Caecus): consul 307 and 296 B.C., the earliest Roman prose-writer and 'first clear-cut personality in Roman history'. His speech was attributed to a meeting of the Senate in 280 or 278 B.C.

3. Scipio Aemilianus was to end the Third Punic War by destroying Carthage in 146 B.C. Cato had repeatedly said 'Carthage must be destroyed'.

has been totally destroyed. And may the gods save for you, Scipio, the honour of completing your grandfather's achievement! He died in the year before I became censor, nine years after my consulship (during which he was elected to his second tenure of the same office). Nearly thirty-three years have gone by since then, but his heroic memory will remain in the minds of men for time everlasting.

If he had lived to be a hundred, would he regret his age? Surely not. True, he would not spend his time running and jumping, or throwing spears or swords. But he would still be employing his wisdom and logical powers and judgement. If old men did not possess those qualities, our ancestors would not have named their highest council the 'Senate' – which means the assembly of old men. The Spartans, too, call the holders of their chief state offices the 'elders', which is just what they are. And if you choose to read, or have read to you, the histories of foreign countries, you will find that the greatest states were overturned by young people and restored by the old. 'Tell me, how did you lose your great nation so speedily?' they ask in Naevius's play *The Game*.[1] And the most significant answer is this: 'Because new public speakers came forward – silly young men.' Early adulthood is naturally rash; sound sense only comes with advancing years.

Another objection to age is that this weakens the memory. Certainly, if you fail to give it exercise, or if you are not particularly intelligent. Themistocles had learnt by heart the names of all his fellow-citizens: do you suppose then when he had become old he would be likely to mistake the son Aristides for the father Lysimachus? My own acquaintance is by no means limited to those who are living today, since I remember their fathers and their grandfathers. I often read their epitaphs, and the act of reading about the dead brings them back to my mind, so I am not at all afraid of losing my memory, as they say happens. Besides, I never heard of an old man forgetting where he had buried his money! Old people remember what interests them: the dates fixed for their lawsuits, and the names of their debtors and creditors.

And what about elderly lawyers, priests, augurs, and philosophers? They remember a great many things. Provided the old retain their concentration and application, they stay sound of mind. And that not only applies to well-known public figures, but is equally true of people

1. *The Game* if *Ludo* is correct – *Lupo* (The Wolf) is a variant reading.

living quietly in retirement. Sophocles went on writing tragedies
until he reached a very great age. His preoccupation with this literary
work created the impression that he was neglecting his family's
finances. So his sons took him to court, urging that he was weak-
minded and should have the family property taken out of his control
(like us they had laws empowering such action in cases of mismanage-
ment). The story goes on, however, that the aged Sophocles read
aloud to the magistrates from the play that he had just written and was
still working on, the *Oedipus at Colonus*. Then he asked them if they
would describe its author as weak-minded. After listening to his
recitation they voted his acquittal. Clearly, then, his activities were
not silenced by old age! The same is true of Homer, Hesiod,
Simonides,[1] and Stesichorus, and the two I mentioned earlier, Isocrates
and Gorgias, not to speak of outstanding philosophers such as Pythagoras, Democritus, Plato, and Xenocrates, or their successors Zeno
and Cleanthes, or Diogenes the Stoic whom you have both seen at
Rome. Every one of them remained actively at work until his dying
day.

But, leaving aside superhuman pursuits such as these, I can name
you elderly Roman farmers in the Sabine country, my own friends
and neighbours, who are practically never out of the fields during the
major farming operations such as sowing and reaping and storing
the crops. True, their work on the annual harvests deserves less comment than the rest, since no one is too old to think he has another year
to live. Yet these men are also working at things which they know
they will not live to see. 'He plants trees for the use of another age', as
our poet Caecilius Statius says in his play *Comrades in Youth*. If you ask
a farmer for whose benefit he is planting, however advanced his age
he will unhesitatingly reply: 'For the immortal gods, who have
ordained that I should receive these things from my ancestors, and
hand them on to my descendants.'

Now, in making that observation about an old man providing for
ages to come, Caecilius wrote to better purpose than when he made a
character say: 'By heaven, Old Age, it would be enough if you

1. Simonides of Ceos, *c.* 556–468 B.C., Greek lyric and epigrammatic poet;
Xenocrates, 397–315/13, head of the Academy; Diogenes the Stoic, see above,
p. 178; for both the other philosophers mentioned here, see above, pp. 17 ff.
The tragedian Sophocles is believed to have lived from *c.* 496 to 406 B.C.

brought with you no evil but this: that a person by living long sees many things he does not want.'[1] But perhaps the same man also sees much that he likes! And, after all, even youth has to look at some things it does not care for.

An even worse sentiment, again expressed by Caecilius, was this: 'The unhappiest thing, in my belief, about being old is feeling that other men find you wearisome.' On the contrary: they are much more likely to enjoy your company. An old man is well advised to favour the society of promising young people. If the young cultivate and like him, he will find age more tolerable – and youths welcome an old man's advice, which helps them to work at living good lives. I like to think you enjoy my company as much as I enjoy yours!

So old age, you see, far from being sluggish and feeble, is really very lively, and perpetually active, and still busy with the pursuits of earlier years. Some people never stop learning, however old they are. You can see Solon,[2] for example, boasting in his poems that while he grows old he continues to learn something new every day. That is what I have been doing, too! In my later years I have learnt to read Greek. I have fastened upon this study with the greed of a man trying to satisfy a long-endured thirst. And that, incidentally, is how I know the Greek passages you have heard me quoting. Socrates learnt to play that favourite instrument of the ancients, the lyre, and when I hear of the progress he made I wish I could do the same; but at any rate I have worked hard at literature.

III

CONSOLATIONS FOR LOST STRENGTH

Nowadays I do not miss the powers of youth – that was the second point about the failings of old age – any more than when I was young, I felt the lack of a bull's strength or an elephant's. A man should use what he has, and in all his doings accommodate himself to his

1. From *The Little Necklace*, comedy by Caecilius (d. 168 B.C.). 'The unhappiest thing': from his play *Ephesio*.
2. Athenian statesman, lawgiver, and poet (7th–6th century B.C.).

strength. There is a story about Milo of Crotona,[1] in his later years, watching the athletes train on the race-course. With tears in his eyes he looked at his own muscles, and said a pitiable thing: 'And these are now dead.' But you are the one who is dead, not they, you stupid fellow, because your fame never came from yourself, it came from brute physical force.

Very different were the men who instructed their fellow-citizens in the law and remained expert jurists until their dying breath: Sextus Aelius Paetus Catus,[2] and at an earlier date Titus Coruncanius,[3] and more recently again Publius Licinius Crassus Dives. It is true that a public speaker's powers diminish when he becomes old, because his profession depends on the strength of his lungs and physique as well as on his brain. Nevertheless, advancing years have a way of bringing out a fine melodious quality of delivery. I myself still have something of this, and you can see how old I am. But the oratorical style appropriate for later years is peaceful and restrained: a mild, elegant speech from an old but skilful speaker very often secures a favourable hearing.

Or even if you cannot achieve this yourself, you can instruct a Scipio or a Laelius! I can think of nothing more agreeable than an old age surrounded by the activities of young people in their prime. For surely at the very least we must concede age the capacity to teach and train young men and fit them for jobs of every kind; and no function could possibly be more honourable than that. I used to think, Scipio, of the good fortune of your great-grandfather Publius Cornelius Scipio and his brother Gnaeus Cornelius Scipio Calvus, and your grandfathers Lucius Aemilius Paullus and Publius Cornelius Scipio Africanus – because they had leading young Romans as their companions. However infirm with age a man has become, if he is imparting to others a liberal education he cannot fail to be accounted happy.

In any case, when failures of bodily vigour do occur they are to be blamed upon youthful dissipations more often than upon old age. A

1. In the later 6th century B.C. six times victor in wrestling at the Olympian Games and six times at the Pythian.

2. Consul 198 B.C., author of *Tripertita* which contained the Law of the Twelve Tables and an account of its development.

3. For Coruncanius, see p. 220. Crassus Dives was consul in 205 B.C., chief priest, and censor.

youth spent in immoderate debauchery transmits to later years a body that is already worn out. The aged Cyrus the elder,[1] on the other hand, declared in his deathbed speech (quoted by Xenophon) that he had never felt feebler in age than he did as a young man. And then consider Lucius Caecilius Metellus, who four years after his second consulship became chief priest and retained the post for twenty-two years; when I was a boy I remember that he was still so vigorous, in spite of extreme old age, that the loss of youth meant nothing to him.

I need not remind you of my own case! – though old men like me are allowed the privilege of doing so: look at Homer's Nestor, and how he constantly proclaims his own good qualities! Nestor saw before him the third generation of men, and yet he did not need to be afraid of seeming unduly conceited or garrulous if he paid truthful tribute to himself. 'Speech sweeter than honey flowed from his tongue,' says Homer. Now, this sweetness in no way depended upon physical strength – and yet the great leader of the Greeks never prays for ten men like Ajax, but for ten men like Nestor: if he had them, added Agamemnon, he knew full well that Troy would quickly fall.

But to return to myself: I am in my eighty-fourth year, and I wish I could make the same boast as Cyrus! I must admit, however, that I no longer have the energy I had as a private soldier and then a quaestor in the Second Punic War, or later as consul in Spain; or as military tribune four years later, serving in the Thermopylae campaign [2] under the consul Manius Acilius Glabrio. Still, this I can say: age has not altogether shattered or undermined me – as you yourselves can see. For the Senate and the platform, for my friends and dependants and guests, my strength is still always available. I never agreed with that much-praised ancient proverb which advises taking to old age early, if you want it to last long. Personally, I should rather stay old for a shorter time than become old prematurely! Consequently, I have never yet refused an appointment to anyone who wanted to see me.

True, I have less physical strength than either of yourselves. But neither have you the strength of the centurion Titus Pontius. So

1. Founder of the Persian empire (559–529 B.C.). According to another account he was killed fighting against the Scythians.

2. In which the Seleucid monarch Antiochus III 'the Great' was defeated (191 B.C.).

does that make him the better person? A man must husband his powers properly and exert himself in accordance with their capacity, and then he will never find them very deficient. Milo is said to have walked from end to end of the race-course at Olympia with an ox on his back; well, which would you prefer to be given, Milo's physical vigour, or the intellectual might of Pythagoras? In short, enjoy the blessing of strength while you have it, and have no regrets when it has gone – any more than young men should regret the end of boyhood, or those approaching middle age lament the passing of youth. Life's course is invariable – nature has one path only, and you cannot travel along it more than once. Every stage of life has its own characteristics: boys are feeble, youths in their prime are aggressive, middle-aged men are dignified, old people are mature. Each one of these qualities is ordained by nature for harvesting in due season.

I expect you sometimes hear news of Masinissa,[1] Scipio. He is ninety now, yet once he has started a journey on foot, he still never mounts a horse; and having set out on horseback he never dismounts. Even on the coldest and stormiest days he goes bareheaded. With his extra-ordinary physique, he carries out all his royal duties and functions in person. That shows how exercise and self-control enable a man to preserve a good deal of his former strength even after he has become old.

So advancing years bring a certain diminution of vigour? But vigour is not even expected of them. That is why law and custom exempt men of my age from public duties requiring bodily strength. In fact, we are not only spared duties that are beyond us, we are even excused functions which would be within our powers. For many old men are supposed to be too infirm to engage in activities, public or otherwise. But weakness of such a kind, far from being peculiar to age, is a product of poor health in general. Your adoptive father,[2] Scipio – the son of Publius Cornelius Scipio Africanus – was completely enfeebled by ill-health, indeed his health practically did not exist. If that had not been so, he would have been the second glory of our nation: for he possessed his father's heroic qualities, and a wider range of learning besides. Since, therefore, even the young cannot

1. c. 240–194 B.C., king of the Numidians and enemy of Carthage.

2. Publius Cornelius Scipio, orator and historian. For the relationships of the Scipios, see Genealogical Table, p. 257.

always escape physical infirmity, we should not be surprised if old men are sometimes sufferers too.

Age has to be fought against; its faults need vigilant resistance. We must combat them as we should fight a disease – following a fixed régime, taking exercise in moderation, and enough food and drink to strengthen yet not enough to overburden. However the mind and spirit need even more attention than the body, for old age easily extinguishes them, like lamps when they are not given oil. And whereas exercises can wear the body out, they stimulate the mind. When Caecilius Statius writes of 'foolish old men in comedies',[1] he is referring to the credulous, forgetful, and slovenly type. But these are faults not of old age in general but only when it has allowed itself to become slack, sluggish, and somnolent. The same applies to the bad qualities of youth. Wrongheadedness and sensuality are more prevalent in young men than in old; yet they are not found in all young men, but only in youths of inferior character. Likewise senile imbecility, what is called 'dotage', does not occur in all old men but only in those of feeble mind.

Appius Claudius was blind and aged, yet he maintained control of four vigorous sons, five daughters, a great household, and a host of dependants. For instead of inertly capitulating to old age he kept his mind as taut as a boy. He not only directed his home, he ruled it; his slaves feared him, his children venerated him, he was loved by everyone, and beneath his roof prevailed ancestral custom and discipline. Age will only be respected if it fights for itself, maintains its own rights, avoids dependence, and asserts control over its own sphere as long as life lasts. For just as I like a young man to have something old about him, so I approve of the old man who has a touch of youth. If that is his aim, whatever the age of his body, in spirit he will never be old.

I am at work on the seventh book of my *Origins*.[2] This involves collecting all the records of our early history. And what I am particularly engaged upon at the moment is the revision of all the speeches I have delivered in famous cases. I am also preparing a treatise on augural, pontifical, and civil law. I am an active student of Greek literature; and to keep my memory in training I adopt the practice of

1. From a play imitating Menander's *Heiress*.
2. A history (now lost) of Rome from its foundations until 150 B.C.

227

the Pythagoreans and, every evening, run over in my mind all that I have said and heard and done during the day. That is my intellectual exercise, my running-track for the brain – and while I sweat and toil at the task I do not greatly miss my bodily strength. I also give my friends legal assistance, and I often attend the Senate, where after long and careful thought I offer topics for discussion and argue my point of view concerning them.

All this is done by strength of mind, not of body. And even if the effort were more than I could manage, I should still find satisfaction at my reading-couch: I could lie on this and think about the activities which were now beyond me. That they are not beyond me is due to the life I have led. For the man whose whole life consists of study and activity of this kind does not notice old age creeping up on him. Instead, he grows old by slow stages, imperceptibly; there is no sudden break-up, only a gradual process of extinction.

IV

THE PLEASURES OF AGE

Next we come to the third allegation against old age. This was its deficiency in sensual pleasures. But if age really frees us from youth's most dangerous failing, then we are receiving a most blessed gift.

Let me tell you, my dear friends, what was said years ago by that outstandingly distinguished thinker, Archytas[1] of Tarentum, the city at which I heard of his words when I was a young soldier serving under Fabius. 'The most fatal curse given by nature to mankind', said Archytas, 'is sensual greed: this incites men to gratify their lusts heedlessly and uncontrollably, thus bringing about national betrayals, revolutions, and secret negotiations with the enemy. Lust will drive men to every sin and crime under the sun. Mere lust, without any additional impulse, is the cause of rape, adultery, and every other sexual outrage. Nature, or a god, has given human beings a mind as their outstanding possession, and this divine gift and endowment has no worse foe than sensuality. For in the realm of the physical passions

1. Pythagorean philosopher, mathematician, astronomer, and statesman; a friend of Plato.

there can be no room for self-control; where self-indulgence reigns, decent behaviour is excluded.

'This can be made clear', continued Archytas, 'if you think of someone enjoying the most delightful sensual pleasure imaginable. It will be generally agreed that during the process of enjoyment he is incapable of any rational, logical, or cerebral process. The consequence is that such pleasures are exceptionally repulsive and harmful. Indeed their substantial, prolonged indulgence will plunge the whole light of the spirit into darkness.'

Nearchus, a steadfast friend of Rome with whom I was staying at Tarentum, told me of the tradition that Archytas had put forward these views in conversation with Gaius Pontius the Samnite, father of the man who defeated our consuls Spurius Postumius and Titus Veturius Calvinus at the Caudine Forks.[1] Nearchus added that the Athenian philosopher Plato was among those who heard the pronouncement; and I have verified that Plato [2] did come to Tarentum, in the year when Lucius Furius Camillus and Appius Claudius Crassinus were consuls.

Now, why have I gone into all this? To prove to you that, if logic and intelligence did not already enable us to avoid lustful pleasures, we ought to feel very grateful to old age for removing the desire to do what is wrong. For such feelings cloud a man's judgement, obstruct his reasoning capacity, and blind his intelligence: let sensuality be present, and a good life becomes impossible.

When I had to eject Lucius Quinctius Flamininus from the Senate,[3] this caused me great regret. He was brother of the famous Titus, and had been consul seven years previously. But an action of his, prompted by a sexual impulse, seemed to me to necessitate this degradation. At the time when he was consul in Gaul, a certain man convicted of a capital offence was in prison there. During a party, Lucius was urged by his mistress to execute this man; and he did as she asked him. While his brother was censor (immediately prior to my own tenure), Lucius avoided punishment. But since his scandalous capitulation to sensual pressure had dishonoured Roman rule as well as wronging an

1. See above, p. 203.
2. Cicero (or Cato) ascribes his visit to 349 B.C.; his last visit to Italy is usually attributed to 361.
3. As censor in 184 B.C.

individual, Marcus Valerius Flaccus and myself felt quite unable to condone what he had done.

I was often told by my elders – who in turn claimed to have heard the story from old men when they were boys – that Gaius Fabricius Luscinus was deeply impressed by something which, while on a mission to King Pyrrhus, he had learnt from Cineas the Thessalian.[1] What Fabricius had been told was that there was an Athenian,[2] professing philosophical insight, who asserted that the standard by which all our actions should be judged was pleasure. When Fabricius reported this to Manius Curius Dentatus [3] and Titus Coruncanius, they expressed the hope that the Samnites, and Pyrrhus himself, would accept this doctrine – for then they would abandon themselves to self-indulgence and become easier to defeat! Curius had been a close friend of Publius Decius Mus who, while consul for the fourth time (five years before Curius held the office), had sacrificed his life for his country. Fabricius and Coruncanius knew him too, and all of them, to judge from the lives they led and from that deed of Decius, were convinced that certain things are naturally fine and noble in themselves and are sought after for their own sake; and that every decent man pursues such aims, and spurns and rejects material indulgence.

Why then do I have so much to say about pleasures of this kind? Because the weakening of temptation to indulge in them, far from supplying a pretext to reproach old age, is a reason for offering it the most cordial compliments. Age has no banquets, no tables piled high, no cups filled again and again. So it also avoids drunkenness, and indigestion, and sleepless nights!

However, the allurements of pleasure are admittedly hard to resist; they are 'the bait of sin',[4] as Plato brilliantly calls them, which catch men like fish. If, then, we have to make them some concession, there is no reason why old age, though spared extravagant feasting, should not gratify itself with entertainments of a more modest nature. While

1. A pupil of Demosthenes and famous orator, employed by Pyrrhus to negotiate with the Romans.

2. Epicurus (p. 18).

3. For Manius Curius Dentatus, Titus Coruncanius, Publius Decius Mus: pp. 235, 220, 164.

4. From Plato's *Timaeus*.

I was a boy, I often saw how old Gaius Duellius,[1] Marcus's son – the first person ever to defeat the Carthaginians in a sea-battle – when he was returning home after a dinner-party used to enjoy being escorted by men carrying torches and playing flutes. Such behaviour from a private citizen was unprecedented, but his glorious reputation gave him that much licence.

But enough of others – let me return to myself! Now, to begin with, I have always had my friends at the club. I was quaestor at the time when the clubs were first established at Rome in honour of Cybele[2] and her newly introduced Idaean worship. I used to dine with these friends, quite modestly, and yet with a good deal of enjoyment, since I was young in those days; such delights became less vivid with advancing years. However, the gastronomic pleasures of those parties did not appeal to me so much as the company and conversation of my friends. The word our ancestors invented for a meal where friends meet was *convivium*, a 'living together', and they were quite right, because of its essential quality of a social reunion. The Greek terms 'a drinking together' and 'feasting together' are less satisfactory since they emphasize what is the least significant aspect of such occasions.

Personally, I am so fond of conversation that I even enjoy afternoon parties. At these I like meeting not only my contemporaries – of whom very few remain – but yours too, and you yourselves. I actually feel grateful to old age, because this has increased my enthusiasm for conversation but eliminated the desire for food and drink. However, since nature does perhaps authorize material pleasures within limits, I must not give the appearance of declaring war on them outright! Well then, granted that food and drink do appeal to some people, I see no reason why these tastes need be wholly lacking in the old.

I myself appreciate our long-established formalities of appointing toastmasters for such entertainments, and of starting the conversation at the head of the table after the wine has been brought in. I enjoy cups that are small enough 'to bedew rather than drench', as Xenophon

1. (Duilius.) Defeated the Carthaginians off Mylae in Sicily during the First Punic War (260 B.C.).

2. The 'Great Mother of the Gods', whose worship was introduced to Rome from Pessinus (Galatia) in 203 B.C. 'Idaean': from Mount Ida in Phrygia, a centre of the cult.

put it in his *Symposium*; and I like my drinks well-cooled in summer and warmed in winter by sunshine or fire. Even when I am in the Sabine country I go to gatherings of this sort. Every day I take a meal with my neighbours; we talk on all manner of subjects, and prolong the party as late as possible into the night.

But the objection is that old people are no longer so enjoyably tickled by their senses. I agree – but they do not want to be either! No deprivation is any trouble if you do not miss what you have lost. When Sophocles was already well advanced in years someone asked him if he still made love. 'Good heavens, no,' he replied: 'I have gladly made my escape from that barbarous, savage master.'[1] Covet such things, and the lack of them may well be tiresome and annoying; but if you have had enough of them and are replete, to lack becomes more pleasant than to possess! Or rather, if you do not miss their absence, you cannot be said to lack them – and that is why I say that not missing them is best of all.

However, let us admit that youth exceeds age in its enjoyment of this particular kind of pleasure. Then two points need to be made. First of all, as I have already said, such pleasures are unimportant; and secondly, in any case, even if old age does not possess them in abundance, it is not wholly deficient in them. The spectators who appreciate Lucius Ambivius Turpio's[2] acting most are those in the front row; but the back row also enjoys his performance. The same applies to the pleasures of sex: young people, who look on them at close quarters, may well find them more exciting, but old people too obtain as much satisfaction as they need by viewing them from afar.

When its campaigns of sex, ambition, rivalry, quarrelling, and all the other passions are ended, the human spirit returns to live within itself – and is well off. There is supreme satisfaction to be derived from an old age which has knowledge and learning to feed upon. I saw Gaius Sulpicius Gallus[3] – your father's friend, Scipio – engaged until his dying day in measuring, you might say, the whole heavens and the earth. Often at night he would begin constructing some chart, and dawn would surprise him still at work – or night would overtake him

1. The story is from Plato's *Republic*.

2. Acted and produced the comedies of Terence (*c.* 195–*c.* 159 B.C.).

3. Served in the campaign of Pydna (168 B.C.), during which he predicted an eclipse of the moon to the army.

at a task he had begun as long ago as daybreak. He used to have the satisfaction of forecasting to us, far in advance, the eclipses of the sun and the moon.

Others, again, were engaged, during their later years, in intellectual work which, though less exacting, nevertheless required keenness of brain. Naevius, for instance, was happily absorbed in his *Punic War*,[1] Plautus in *The Savage* and *The Cheat*. I myself saw Livius Andronicus [2] when he had reached a considerable age. He brought out a play six years before I was born – when Gaius Claudius Cento and Marcus Sempronius Tuditanus were consuls – but lived on until after I was grown up. And there is no need for me to recall to you Publius Licinius Crassus Dives,[3] active in priestly and civil law, and our own Publius Cornelius Scipio Nasica Corculum,[4] who was appointed chief priest only a few days ago. I have seen every one of them enthusiastically engaged in these pursuits of theirs when well advanced in years. Marcus Cornelius Cethegus,[5] again, whom Ennius rightly described as 'the marrow of persuasiveness': I can vouch myself for his technique as a public speaker, even after he had become an old man.

What pleasures from eating banquets or watching shows or consorting with mistresses are comparable with delights of such a kind? If a man is sensible and well-educated, his taste for intellectual pursuits like these increases with the years. So there is truth in that verse I just quoted, in which Solon observed that as he grew old he learnt much that was new every day. And surely the satisfactions of the mind are greater than all the rest!

V

THE JOYS OF FARMING

Now I come to the pleasures of farming. These give me an unbelievable amount of enjoyment. Old age does not impede them in the least, and in my view they come closest of all things to a life of true

---

1. An epic on the First Punic War.
2. *c.* 284–*c.* 204 B.C. Composed and acted in first Latin comedy and tragedy (240 B.C.) (with Greek models and metres); wrote official expiatory hymn (207), and first Latin epic the *Odyssia*. 3. See above, p. 224.
4. Consul 162 (abdicated) and 155, censor. 5. Consul 204.

wisdom. The bank, you might say, in which these pleasures keep their account is the earth itself. It never fails to honour their draft; and, when it returns the principal, interest invariably comes too – not always very much, but often a great deal.

But what delights me is not only the product, but the productivity and nature of the Earth herself. First, the scattered corn-seed is taken within her soft, subjugated lap. For a time it remains hidden – *occaecatum* is our word, from which comes *occatio*,[1] harrowing. Then, warmed by the moist heat of her embrace, the seed expands and brings forth a green and flourishing blade. Supported by the fibres of its roots, this blade gradually matures. Within its sheath it stands firm upon a jointed stalk; this is its adolescent stage. Then, bursting out from the sheath, the blade puts forth the ears of corn, the ordered rows of grain with their palisade of spikes protecting them from the beaks of the smaller birds of the sky.

To give an account of the vine – its beginnings, its cultivation, its expansion – would be out of place here. But I must tell you that this is the recreation and satisfaction of my old age: my delight in the vine is insatiable. First, a general point, which I pass over briefly. In every product of earth there is an inborn power. This is the power by which a minute fig-seed, or a grape-stone, or the tiniest seeds of any crop or root, are transformed into vast trunks and branches. Cuttings of vines or trees, young twigs springing from a branch, plants formed by dividing roots and lodging an unsevered shoot – who could fail to be amazed and delighted by the products that emerge from these? The natural disposition of vines is to fall to the earth; but give them a prop, and they will embrace it with hand-like tendrils to raise themselves aloft. Far and wide they twist and turn, until the farmer's skilful knife lops them in case they turn to wood and spread too luxuriantly.

When spring has started, the branches that have been left on a vine put forth their buds at every joint, and these buds are transformed into freshly growing grapes. At first very bitter to the taste, the moisture of the earth and the rays of the sun mature them, so that they sweeten to ripeness, wrapped round by young foliage which tempers the heat and keeps away the too powerful rays of the sun. What could be more delicious to the taste or more attractive to the eye?

Nor, I repeat, is the usefulness of the vine all that delights me. There

1. *Occatio* comes not from *occaecatum*, but from *occa*, a hoe.

is also the manner of its cultivation and the very nature of the vine itself: the rows of stakes, the joining of the vine-tops to trellises, the tying down of the shoots, their propagation by slips; as well as the pruning of certain branches, such as I have already mentioned, and the liberation of others.

Then – but I cannot go into this now – there is the fertilization of the soil, by means of irrigation, ditching, and intensive hoeing. The uses of manure I shall again leave undescribed, since you will find them set out in my book *Agriculture*.[1] When the learned Hesiod [2] wrote about farming, he did not mention manure. But Homer, whom I believe to have lived many centuries earlier, tells how Laertes consoled his longing for his absent son Ulysses by tilling his lands and manuring them well.

Cornfields, meadows, vineyards, woods, all give added pleasure to the cultivator's life. And so do orchards, cattle-pastures, bees in their swarms, and flowers in their infinite variety. Planting, too, is a delight, and so is agriculture's most ingenious operation, grafting.

I could go on at length about the numerous attractions of the farmer's life; but I realize I have spoken rather too long already. However, I know you will excuse me. My enthusiasm for the subject has carried me away – and I must not acquit old age of every fault: it does tend to be long-winded!

Such, then, was the life in which Manius Curius Dentatus,[3] after his triumphs over the Samnites and the Sabines and Pyrrhus, spent his last years. His country house is not far from my own – and when I look at the place I am overwhelmed with admiration for that man's self-control and the disciplined spirit of his times. He was sitting by his fireside once when certain Samnites entered, bringing him a massive gift of gold. He rejected this, however, with the comment that possessing gold is not so glorious as dominating its possessors. A man with as noble a character as that must have been capable of finding happiness in old age.

1. Most of Cato's *De Agricultura* (*De Re Rustica*) survives.
2. In his poem *Works and Days*. Homer (*Odyssey*, Book XXIV) actually says that Odysseus found his father 'alone on the vineyard terrace digging round a plant'.
3. Four times consul, censor, ended Samnite War (290), conquered Sabines (290), Senonian Gauls (284), Pyrrhus (275), Lucanians (274), triumphed 290, 275.

But I want to talk about my own affairs, so let us return to the farmers. In those days Senators (that is *senes*, 'elders') lived on their farms – if we are to believe the story that the men sent to tell Lucius Quinctius Cincinnatus [1] of his appointment as dictator found him at the plough. His were the orders, as dictator, upon which his Master of the Horse, Gaius Servilius Ahala, caught Spurius Maelius attempting to make himself king, and put him to death. Manius Curius Dentatus, too, and other veterans, when they were summoned to the Senate-house, came from their farms; and that is why the messengers sent to fetch them were called *viatores*, 'travellers'.

Surely men like these, who delighted in being farmers, cannot have been unhappy when they were old. Personally I incline to the opinion that no life could be happier than the farmer's. To begin with, the services which he performs by his cultivation of the soil are beneficial to the entire human race. And then there are the delights of which I have spoken, and his abundant and plenteous production of all things that are needed for the worship of the gods and the sustenance of mankind.

Seeing that such material considerations are important to some people, I hope this reference to them will bring me back into favour with the hedonists! For an efficient and industrious farmer keeps his wine-cellar, his oil-store, and his larder always full. His whole house has a prosperous appearance: within its rooms are stored generous supplies of pork, goat's meat, lamb, poultry, milk, cheese, and honey. There is also his garden, which farmers call their 'second leg of pork'. The relish of all these good things is sharpened by labours for time of leisure, such as hawking and hunting.

The greenness of the meadows, the ordered rows of trees, the lovely spectacle of vineyards and olive groves – these are themes which, in the interests of brevity, I must pass over. A well-kept farm is the most useful thing in the world, and also the best to look upon. And age, far from impeding enjoyment of your farm, actually increases its pleasures and fascinations. For nowhere else in the world can an old man better find sunshine or fireside for his warmth, or shade and running water to keep himself cool and well.

Others may have their weapons, horses, spears, foils, and balls, their hunting, and their running. Out of all the sports that exist, just leave

1. Traditionally venerated as dictator and conqueror of the Aequi in 458 B.C.

us old men our two kinds of dice, the oblong and the cube – if you choose to, that is, for even without them old age can still be happy!

The writings of Xenophon are in many ways extremely informative, and I recommend you to read them carefully; indeed I know that you already do. His book *On Estate Management* [1] is packed with the praises of agriculture: devotion to farming seemed to him the most royal of pursuits. He emphasizes this by a story he makes Socrates tell Critobulus. The younger Cyrus, a Persian prince of outstanding intelligence and rank, was visited at Sardis by Lysander. This enlightened Spartan brought Cyrus gifts from their allies, and was given a kindly and hospitable reception. Among other attentions, Cyrus showed Lysander an elaborately planted park. His visitor complimented the prince on the lofty trees, planted in patterns of five, and on the clean well-tilled soil and the fragrance of the flowers; and what impressed him, added Lysander, besides the hard work which had been devoted to its growth, was the ingenuity with which the whole park had been planned and marked out. Cyrus replied that the planning was all his own: the rows were arranged, the lay-out designed, by himself. On hearing this Lysander gazed at his host's purple robe, and resplendent good looks, and the Persian magnificence of his abundant golden ornaments and jewels, and declared: 'people are right to call you happy, Cyrus, because you are not only good, you are fortunate too.'

Well, this good fortune of practising agriculture and horticulture is one which an old man is able to enjoy: the cultivation of the soil is one of the activities which age does not impede up to his very last days. Tradition records, for example, that Marcus Valerius Corvinus [2] worked on his farm at an extremely advanced age, indeed until he was a hundred. His first and his sixth consulships were forty-six years apart – in other words his public career lasted for what our ancestors

1. By Xenophon (*c.* 430–*c.* 354 B.C.). Cicero translated this in his youth. Cyrus, the younger son of the Persian king Darius II, was killed at Cunaxa (401); Xenophon's mercenaries were his allies. His cooperation with the Spartan general and statesman Lysander (d. 395 B.C.) had contributed to the defeat of Athens in the Peloponnesian War.

2. Marcus Valerius Corvinus (or Corvus) – six times consul 348–301 B.C., dictator 342, 301, believed to have defeated the Gauls (349), Volscians (346), Samnites (343), people of Cales (335), Aequi (300), and Etruscans (299).

reckoned to be the duration of a man's life exclusive of old age. And the last part of his life was happier than the middle, because he was held in greater respect, and had less work to do.

VI

HONOURS AND FAULTS

To be respected is the crowning glory of old age. Lucius Caecilius Metellus, for instance, received enormous respect. So did Aulus Atilius Calatinus: [1] 'many nations agree', said his epitaph, 'that this was the noblest man of his country.' But you know the whole epitaph, because it is inscribed on his tomb. The unanimity of the praises that he received shows how greatly he deserved this veneration. I myself knew Publius Licinius Crassus Dives, who was high priest, and his successor Marcus Aemilius Lepidus.[2] What great personalities they were! Of Lucius Aemilius Paullus, and Publius Cornelius Scipio Africanus, and Quintus Fabius Maximus there is no need to speak; about Fabius I have said something already. Men such as these displayed authority not only in what they said but by their merest nod, and the authority which belongs to old age, especially when enhanced by a distinguished record, is more precious than all the pleasures of youth.

But please bear in mind, throughout this discussion, that to deserve all these compliments of mine, old age must have its foundations well laid in early life. Which means (as I once said in public, amid general approval) that an old age in need of self-justification is unenviable. White hairs and wrinkles cannot suddenly usurp authority, since this only comes as a final result of well-spent earlier years. When such authority has arrived, we find signs of respect which at first sight, perhaps, seem unimportant and ordinary – morning visitors and applicants for interviews; people making way for a man and rising at his approach; escorting him to the Forum and back, and asking for his advice. All these are practices which we observe most scrupulously; and so do all other civilized societies.

Lysander the Spartan, of whom I was speaking just now, is credited

1. Consul 258 and 254, dictator 249, censor, was a hero of the First Punic War.

2. Consul 187 and 175, censor 179, leader of the Senate for 27 years.

with the observation that the most honourable home for old people was Sparta, seeing that its inhabitants treated age with greater respect and deference than any other community. At Athens, on the other hand, when an old man came into the theatre to see a play, the story goes that not one of his fellow-citizens in the crowded auditorium offered him a place. When, however, he reached the section occupied by certain Spartans, who had places assigned to them because they were official delegates, each one of them rose and invited the old man to have his seat. This was applauded loud and long by the whole gathering. But one of the Spartans commented: 'The Athenians know what good behaviour is – but they do not put their knowledge into practice!'

Among the many fine customs practised by your Board of Augurs a particularly relevant one to our present subject is this: precedence in debate goes by age, which takes priority over official rank, so that even the highest functionaries yield place to augurs older than themselves. Surely the rewards of authority are incomparably superior to bodily pleasures! I suggest that those who have made good use of such rewards have acted life's drama nobly to the end. Not for them is the sort of incompetent performance which breaks down in the last act!

However, old people are also complained about as morose, and petulant, and ill-tempered, and hard to please; and on inquiry some of them prove to be avaricious as well. But these are faults of character, not of age. Besides, moroseness and the other faults I have mentioned have a substantial, if not wholly adequate, excuse: old men believe themselves despised, ignored, and mocked – and a weak body is sensitive even to the lightest blow. In any case, however, a decent, enlightened character can keep such faults under control. This can be seen in real life, not to speak of the Brothers in the play [1] of that name, of whom one is highly disagreeable, the other very pleasant. For the fact is that not every personality, any more than every wine, grows sour with age. Austerity in old men seems to me proper enough; but like everything else I want this in moderation – without any sourness. Besides, I cannot see the point of old men being miserly. Is it not the height of absurdity for a traveller to think he needs more funds for his journey when it is nearly over?

1. Terence's *Adelphi*.

VII

DEATH HAS NO STING

Now we must consider the fourth objection to being old: one which might be thought well calculated to worry and distress a man of my years. I refer to the nearness of death. When a man is old, there can obviously be no doubt that it is near. Yet if, during his long life, he has failed to grasp that death is of no account he is unfortunate indeed. There are two alternatives: either death completely destroys human souls, in which case it is negligible; or it removes the soul to some place of eternal life – in which case its coming is greatly to be desired. There can be no third possibility. If, then, after death I shall either lack unhappiness or even be positively happy, I have nothing whatever to fear.

Besides, even the youngest of men would be rash to feel any confidence that he will still be alive this evening! Indeed, young people are actually more liable to accidental deaths than old: they fall ill more easily, their illnesses are more severe, and their convalescences are more painful. That is why few of them reach old age. If so many people did not die young, there would be more examples of decent and sensible living. For the people who have sense and prudence and judgement are the old. Had it not been for old men, no state would ever have existed!

But to return to the imminence of death. This is not a fault to blame on age, since you can see that youth may suffer from the same disability. The loss of my dear son,[1] and of your two brothers, Scipio – both destined for brilliant careers – has underlined for both of us that death comes to all ages alike. Certainly you can argue that young men are entitled to hope for long lives, whereas old men are not. But such hopes are misguided, since it is unintelligent to mistake certainty for uncertainty, and untruth for truth.

The objector may go on to say that an old man has nothing even to hope for. Still, he is better off than his juniors, since what they are

1. Also called Marcus Porcius Cato. He was the Brother-in-law of Scipio Aemilianus.

hoping for he has actually achieved: they want long lives, and he has had one.

And yet, for goodness' sake, what in the whole human condition lasts for any length of time? Think of the longest of all possible lives; let us imagine we shall attain the age of that king of Tartessus – I have been reading about Arganthonius of Gades who reigned for eighty years and lived for a hundred and twenty. Even so, I suggest that nothing can be called long if it has an end. For when that end comes, then all that is gone before has vanished. Only one thing remains – the credit you have gained by your good and right actions. Hours, days, months, and years go by: once they have passed they never come again. And what is to come in the future we cannot tell. So whatever life is allotted to us, we ought to be content.

An actor need not remain on the stage until the very end of the play: if he wins applause in those acts in which he appears, he will have done well enough. In life, too, a man can perform his part wisely without staying on the stage until the play is finished. However short your life may be, it will still be long enough to live honestly and decently. If, on the other hand, its duration is extended, there need be no more sorrow than a farmer feels when the pleasant springtime has passed, and summer and autumn have arrived. For spring, the season of youth, gives promise of fruits to come, but the later seasons are those that reap the harvests and gather them in. And the particular harvest of old age, I repeat, is its abundant recollection of blessings acquired in earlier years.

All things in keeping with nature must be classified as good; and nothing is so completely in keeping with nature than that the old should die. When the same fate sometimes attacks the young, nature rebels and resists: the death of a young person reminds me of a flame extinguished by a deluge. But the death of the old is like a fire sinking and going out of its own accord, without external impulsion. In the same way as apples, while green, can only be picked by force, but after ripening to maturity fall off by themselves, so death comes to the young with violence but to old people when the time is ripe. And the thought of this ripeness so greatly attracts me that as I approach death I feel like a man nearing harbour after a long voyage: I seem to be catching sight of land.

Yet old age has no fixed limit: as long as a man remains able to live up to his obligations and fulfil them, reckoning death of no account, he is entitled to live on. That gives age an actual advantage over youth in courage and toughness – a conclusion which is illustrated by the answer Solon once gave Pisistratus. When the king asked what support Solon relied upon in maintaining such stubborn opposition to his rule, Solon replied: 'Old age.'

The best end to life is with mind unclouded and faculties unimpaired, when nature herself dissolves what she has put together. The right person to take a ship or house to pieces is its builder; and by that analogy nature, which constructs human beings so skilfully, is also best at their demolition. But a new structure is always hard to destroy, whereas old buildings come down easily.

So the aged ought neither to cling too greedily to their small remnants of life nor, conversely, to abandon them before they need. Pythagoras forbids us desert life's sentry-post till God, our commander, has given the word. Wise Solon wrote a couplet expressing the hope that when he was dead his friends would grieve and mourn. His purpose, no doubt, was to show how much he valued their affection. But I am inclined to prefer Ennius's version: 'Let no one weep in my honour, or utter lamentations at my last rites.' Ennius finds death no cause for grief, seeing that what comes thereafter is immortality.

The act of dying, it is true, may be accompanied by certain sensations, but if so these only last a very short time, especially when one is old. After death, feelings are either non-existent or agreeable. From our youth upwards we should bear that in mind, since the thought will encourage us to regard death as of no account, and without such a conviction we can have no peace of mind. For we cannot avoid dying: perhaps this very day. Since, therefore, death is an imminent possibility from hour to hour, you must not let the prospect frighten you, or you will be in a state of perpetual anxiety.

There is no need to argue this point at any length. It is enough to remember Lucius Junius Brutus, who fell in the struggle for his country's freedom, and the two Decii, who rode full speed deliberately to their deaths.[1] Or we may recall Marcus Atilius Regulus, who for the

1. Lucius Junius Brutus, Decii, and Regulus, see above, pp. 114, 164, 198. The two Scipios are: Publius (the father of Scipio Africanus the elder), consul 218 B.C., and Gnaeus Calvus, consul 222, who were separately cut off by the Carthaginians in Spain in 211 and killed. The colleague of Paullus at Cannae

sake of keeping his faith with the enemy went back to be the victim of their tortures – and the two Scipios, Publius and Gnaeus Calvus, who blocked the advancing Carthaginians with their own dead bodies. And then, Scipio, there was your grandfather Lucius Aemilius Paullus, who amid Cannae's shameful rout gave his life to atone for his colleague's unwisdom; and Marcus Claudius Marcellus, who was conceded funeral honours even by a merciless foe. But let us pass these by, and rather consider our own Roman legionaries. I have written of them in my *Origins*: marching again and again, with indomitable enthusiasm, to destinations from which they never expected to return. So what those uneducated, rustic young soldiers think nothing of should surely not terrify men of advanced education and years.

One has had enough of life, in my opinion, when one has had enough of all its occupations. Boys have their characteristic pursuits, but adolescents do not hanker after them, since they have their own activities. Then these too, in their turn, cease to attract the grown-up and middle-aged, seeing that they also have their special interests – for which, however, when their time comes, old people feel no desire, since they again, finally, have interests peculiar to themselves. Then, like earlier occupations before them, these activities fall away; and when that happens a man has had enough of life and it is time for him to die.

VIII

THE AFTER-LIFE

I will tell you [1] what I myself believe about death. I do not see why not, for the nearer this comes the better I feel I understand what it means.

I loved your illustrious father, Scipio, and yours too, Laelius; and I am certain that they are still alive – living the only life that is worthy of the name.

---

(216) was Gaius Terentius Varro. Marcellus captured Syracuse in 212 and was killed fighting against Hannibal in 208.

1. These sentiments are comparable to the more elaborate *Dream of Scipio* in Cicero's work *On the State* (p. 26).

As long as we remain within these bodily frames of ours, we are undergoing a heavy labour imposed on us by fate. For our human souls have come into our bodies from heaven: they have been sent down from their lofty abode and plunged, so to speak, into the earth, which is alien to their divine and eternal nature. As I believe, the reason why the immortal gods implanted souls in human beings was to provide the earth with guardians who should reflect their contemplation of the divine order in the orderly discipline of their own lives.

My own powers of logic and reasoning have not brought me to this conviction unaided. I have also relied upon the weighty and authoritative guidance of outstanding thinkers. For Pythagoras and his disciples – practically compatriots of ours, since they were known as the 'Italian philosophers' – never doubted, I am told, that each of our souls is a fraction taken from the divine universal Mind. Besides, I have studied the arguments concerning the immortality of the soul which Socrates advanced on the last day of his life;[1] and he was the man whom the oracle of Apollo had pronounced to be wiser than all others.

Human souls function at lightning speed, equally remarkable for their memory of the past and knowledge of things to come. Their capabilities, funds of knowledge, and powers of discovery are endless. Their simultaneous possession of all these talents means, I am convinced, that they cannot be mortal. Seeing that their unceasing motion was self-created and had no other originator but themselves, they can likewise have no end, because their self-elimination is inconceivable. Being, furthermore, homogeneous, with the admixture of no different or discordant element whatever, they are indivisible – that is to say, indestructible. The hypothesis that a considerable part of human knowledge is of prenatal origin is supported by a strong argument: even a small child can tackle the most difficult subjects and rapidly master innumerable facts about them. This suggests that he is not learning for the first time but only recollecting what is already in his memory.

That, more or less, is Plato's teaching. Xenophon tells us [2] that these problems were debated by the elder Cyrus on his deathbed. 'My dear sons,' he said, 'do not conclude that after I have left you I shall have

1. The last day of Socrates' life is described in Plato's *Phaedo*.
2. In *The Education of Cyrus*.

ceased to exist. Even while I have been with you, you have not seen my soul; you knew it was in this body because of the actions that I performed. In the future, too, my soul will remain invisible to you, but you should still be able to credit its existence just as you have hitherto.

'The renown of famous men would not survive their deaths but for the continued activity of their own souls in preserving their memory among us. I have never felt able to believe that, whereas souls remain alive while they are still in human bodies, they must perish after they have ceased to dwell in them – for since the soul and not the body does the thinking, why should its departure remove this capacity? On the contrary, I have preferred to believe that it is only after liberation from all bodily admixture has made them pure and undefiled that souls enter upon true wisdom. Furthermore, in a human being's dissolution by death, the destination of his corporeal elements is evident: each of them returns to its beginnings. Only the soul never appears at all, either when it is present or when it has departed.

'Again, the closest thing to death (as you can see) is sleep. But sleep is precisely the condition in which souls most clearly manifest their divine nature. For when they are in this liberated and unrestrained state, they can see into the future: and that gives us a hint of what they will be like when they are no longer earth-bound by the human frame.

'If I am right in believing in eternal life, then I am now turning into a god for you to worship! If, on the other hand, my soul is after all going to die with my body, still I know you will keep me in dutiful memory, reserving your worship for the gods who rule and watch over the beauties of the Universe.'

Those were the dying words of Cyrus. Now let us see about my own.

No one will ever convince me, my dear Scipio, that your father Lucius Aemilius Paullus Macedonicus, or your grandfathers Lucius Aemilius Paullus and Publius Cornelius Scipio Africanus, or the father or uncle [1] of that Africanus, or other famous men too numerous to be named, would have done such mighty deeds to be remembered by posterity, if they had not understood that posterity was theirs. And now let me say, as old men do, some boastful words about myself. You cannot suppose that I should have worked so hard, day and night,

1. Publius Cornelius Scipio and Gnaeus Cornelius Scipio Calvus (see p. 242).

in war and peace alike, if I had believed that my fame would not out-
last my life. In that event I should surely have done much better to
live in leisurely tranquillity, remote from labour and contention. Yet
somehow my soul seemed to understand that its true life would only
begin after my death: alertly, unceasingly, it fastened its gaze upon
the generations to come. The souls of our finest men engage in this
pursuit of immortal fame – and they would not feel this urge unless
immortality were really in store for them.

Besides, the wisest people are those who die with greatest equani-
mity, and the most stupid are the least resigned. This surely indicates
that the souls of the former, with their longer and clearer view, per-
ceive that they are on their way to a better world, whereas the others,
with their duller vision, do not realize that this is so.

I respected and loved your fathers; I long to see them both again.
But those whom I myself have known are not the only men I hope to
see. I look forward also to meeting the personages of whom I have
heard, and read, and written. So when I start on my journey towards
them, it will be extremely difficult for anyone to pull me back, or boil
me back to life as they did Pelias.[1] Indeed if some god granted me the
power to cancel my advanced years and return to boyhood, and wail
once more in the cradle, I should firmly refuse. Now that my race is
run, I have no desire to be called back from the finish to the starting
point!

For what is the advantage of life? – or rather, are not its troubles
infinite? No, there are advantages too; yet all the same there comes
a time when one has had enough. That does not mean that I am joining the large and learned body of life's critics! I am not sorry to have
lived, since the course my life has taken has encouraged me to believe
that I have lived to some purpose. But what nature gives us is a place
to dwell in temporarily, not one to make our own. When I leave life,
therefore, I shall feel as if I am leaving a hostel rather than a home.

What a great day it will be when I set out to join that divine
assemblage and concourse of souls, and depart from the confusion and
corruption of this world! I shall be going to meet not only all those of
whom I have spoken, but also my own son. No better, no more devoted man was ever born. He should have cremated my body; but I

1. It was not Pelias but his half-brother Aeson whom Medea was said to have
restored to youth by cutting him up and boiling him in a cauldron.

had to cremate his. Yet his soul has not gone from me, but looks back and fastens upon me its regard – and the destination to which that soul has departed is surely the place where it knew that I too must come. To the world I have seemed to bear my loss bravely. That does not mean that I found it easy to bear, but I comforted myself with the belief that our parting and separation would be of short duration.

You remarked, Scipio, that I appeared to you and Laelius to endure old age lightly; and I have told you why I find this no burden but actually enjoyable. Even if I am mistaken in my belief that the soul is immortal, I make the mistake gladly, for the belief makes me happy, and is one which as long as I live I want to retain. True, certain insignificant philosophers [1] hold that I shall feel nothing after death. If so, then at least I need not fear that after their own deaths they will be able to mock my conviction! And if we are not going to be immortal, well, even so it is still acceptable for a man to come to his end at his proper time. For nature, which has marked out the limits of all things, has marked out life's limits among them. When life's last act, old age, has become wearisome, when we have had enough, the time has come to go.

That is what I think about old age. May you both live to see the condition! Then you will be able to prove by experience that what I have told you is true.

1. The Epicureans.

APPENDIXES AND INDEX

LIST OF SURVIVING WORKS OF CICERO

c. 84 B.C.	On Invention I–III
81 B.C.	For Quinctius
80 B.C.	For Roscius of Ameria
?77 B.C.	For Roscius the Comic Actor
70 B.C.	Divination against Caecilius; Against Verres I, II i–v
69 B.C.	For Tullius; For Fonteius (incomplete); For Caecina
68–44 B.C.	Letters to Atticus (XVI books)
66 B.C.	For the Manilian Law (On the Command of Cn. Pompeius); For Cluentius
?60s B.C.	Translations of Aratus's Phaenomena (fragments)
63 B.C.	Against Rullus (On the Agrarian Law) I–III; For Gaius Rabirius; Against Catiline I–IV; For Murena
62 B.C.	For Sulla; For Archias
62–60 B.C.	Poem on his Consulate I–III (fragments)
62–43 B.C.	Letters to Friends (XVI books)
60–54 B.C.	Letters to his Brother Quintus (III books)
59 B.C.	For Flaccus
57 B.C.	After his Return, to the People; After his Return, in the Senate; On his Home
56 B.C.	On the Reply of the Diviners; For Sestius; Against Vatinius; For Caelius; On the Consular Provinces; For Balbus
55 B.C.	On the Orator I–III; Against Piso
54 B.C.	For Plancius; For Rabirius Postumus; For Scaurus (fragments)
c. 54 B.C.	The Divisions of Oratory
54–51 B.C.	On the State I–VI (incomplete)
52 B.C.	For Milo; On the Best Kind of Orators (fragment)
52 and 46–45 B.C.	On Laws I–?V (incomplete)
46 B.C.	For Marcellus; For Ligarius; Brutus; The Orator; Paradoxes of the Stoics
45 B.C.	For King Deiotarus; On the Greatest Degrees of Good and Evil I–V; Academics I–IV (incomplete); Translations of Plato's Timaeus and Protagoras (fragments); Consolation (fragments); Hortensius (fragments)

APPENDIX A

44 B.C.   Tusculan Disputations I–V; On Divination I–II; On Auguries (fragments); On Fate (part); On Glory I–II (fragments); Cato the Elder, On Old Age; Laelius, On Friendship; Topica (Methods of Drawing Conclusions); On Duties I–III; On Virtues (fragments); On the Nature of the Gods I–III

44–43 B.C.   Letters to Brutus (books I–IX; two books of these dates survive)

44–43 B.C.   Against Antony, Philippics I–XIV

A number of these works are translated in other volumes in this series, *Cicero: Selected Political Speeches*, *Cicero: Murder Trials*, and *Cicero: On the Good Life*. These volumes also include lists of modern works about Cicero.

GENEALOGICAL TABLES

I. CICERO

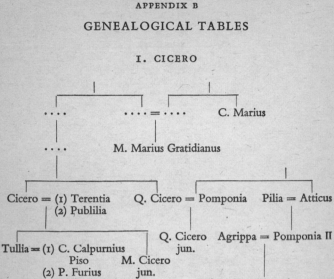

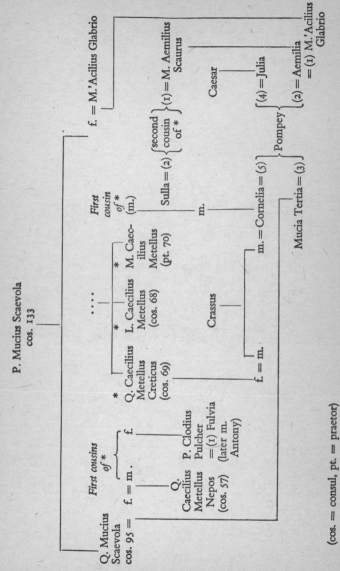

(cos. = consul, pt. = praetor)

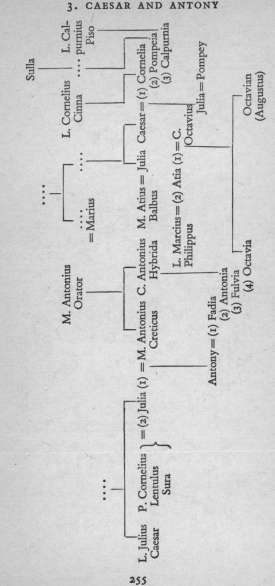

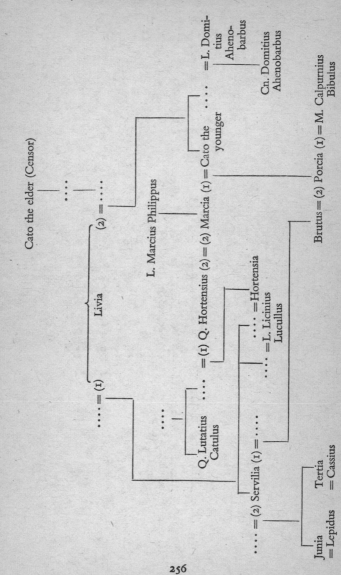

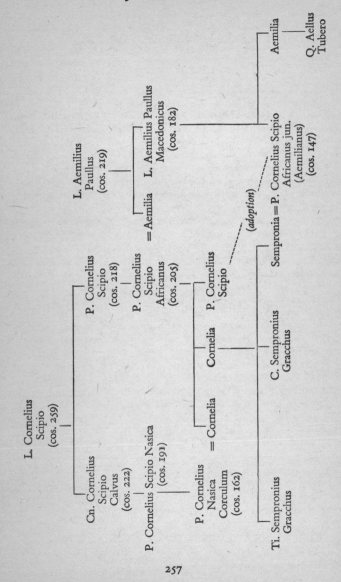

KEY TO TECHNICAL TERMS

AEDILES. Officials ranking above quaestors and below praetors (*q.v.*), concerned with the care of the city of Rome, its corn-supply, and its Games.

ASSEMBLY. An Assembly of the Roman people, i.e. citizens summoned in groups (centuries or tribes, *q.v.*) by a senior official. The Assembly enacted laws, elected officials, and declared war and peace.

AUGURS. The official Roman diviners, one of the four Orders of Priesthood. They took the auspices (*q.v.*) at the request of a magistrate (*q.v.*).

AUSPICES. Certain types of divination – particularly from birds – officially practised at elections, inaugurations of office and entrance into a province, as well as in the conduct of wars.

CENSORS. Officials appointed every five (earlier every four) years to draw up and maintain the list of citizens (*census*) and revise the list of Senators.

CENTURIES. The units of one hundred men by which voting was organized in the Assembly (*q.v.*) for some of its most important business, notably the election of the principal magistrates (*q.v.*).

CHIEF PRIEST. Head of the Pontifices, one of the four Orders of Priesthood; and head of the whole state clergy.

CONSULARS. The ex-consuls, traditionally an inner ring of the Senate.

CONSULS. The supreme civil and military officials (magistrates) of Republican Rome, two in number, holding office for one year, and giving their names to that year.

DICTATOR. Originally a temporary, extraordinary, supreme office for an emergency, restricted to six months. Sulla retained the power for two years, and Caesar, after three renewals, assumed it permanently at the end of his life.

FORUM. The chief public square, surrounded by important temples and halls.

GOVERNORS of provinces, usually ex-consuls or ex-praetors (*q.v.*), were normally sent to them for one year, but their tenures could be renewed.

IMPERATOR. A genetic title for Roman commanders, became a special title of honour by which they were saluted by their soldiers after a victory.

JUDGES. The permanent criminal courts for trying specific offences (mostly directed against the state) were composed of thirty or more

KEY TO TECHNICAL TERMS

judges (or jury-men) under the presidency of a praetor (*q.v.*). C.
Gracchus (123–122 B.C.) had admitted knights (*q.v.*) to their membership, Sulla restored the Senate's monopoly of this, and L. Cotta (70
B.C.) divided it among both Orders and a third less wealthy than
either.

KINGS. Traditionally the earliest rulers of Rome. The last, the autocratic
Tarquinius Superbus, was believed to have been expelled in 510 B.C.

KNIGHTS. A powerful Order with financial interests (minimum property qualification 400,000 sesterces) outside the Senate and at this
period often conflicting with it.

LEGATE. A Senator, often of high rank, on the staff of a governor or
general. Caesar employed them to command legions.

MAGISTRATES. The leading civil and military officials of the state.

MASTER OF THE HORSE. An official nominated by a dictator (*q.v.*) to
represent him either on the field of battle or at Rome.

PATRON. A 'client' was a free man who had entrusted himself to the
care of a 'patron' and received protection in return – a traditional institution supported by the law. By an extension of this custom, important Romans became patrons of whole communities in Italy and the
provinces.

PRAETORS. The state officials next in importance to the consuls, largely
concerned with the administration of justice. From one in the fourth
century B.C. (the city praetor) their number was gradually raised to
the Sullan figure of eight.

QUAESTORS. The lowest office of state in the Senator's official career:
the quaestors, twenty in number since Sulla, were young men (often
concerned with finance) who stood almost in a filial relationship to
the consuls or governors with whom they served. They were appointed to provinces by lot.

SENATE. The chief Council of the state, its numbers raised to 600 by
Sulla and 900 by Caesar. Sulla made admission depend mainly on tenure of the quaestorship (*q.v.*). Technically an advisory body, but with
great traditional influence over the executive Assembly (*q.v.*).

SESTERCE (*sestertius*). A unit of currency, containing four *asses*. At this
time, however, neither sesterce (earlier a tiny silver coin) nor *as*
(originally a bronze piece declining in size from 1 Roman lb. to ½ oz.
in 89–86 B.C.) was issued, the principal coin being the silver *denarius*
of 16 *asses* and 4 sesterces.

TREASURY. The main state Treasury was in the Temple of Saturn below the Capitol, and was controlled by quaestors (*q.v.*).

TRIBE. All Roman citizens were registered in one of the thirty-five
territorial tribes (four urban and the rest 'rustic'), which were the

units for voting on certain matters in the Assembly (e.g. in the election of tribunes and one sort of aedile), and for census, taxation, and the military levy. The tribes also elected to the augurship one of two persons nominated by the augurs (*q.v.*).

TRIBUNES OF THE PEOPLE possessed ancient revered 'democratic' powers entitling them to 'protect the people' by intercession and veto. The Gracchi revived these long obsolete powers, Sulla again abolished them but they reappeared in the years 70–49 B.C.

TRIUMPH. The processional return of a victorious Roman general, when he sacrificed to Jupiter on the Capitol. Triumphs were awarded by the Senate.

TRIUMVIRS. The informal, autocratic First Triumvirate was formed by Pompey, Caesar, and Crassus in 60–59 B.C., and the formal Second Triumvirate, with dictatorial powers, by Antony, Octavian, and Lepidus in 43 B.C.

MAPS

THE ROMAN

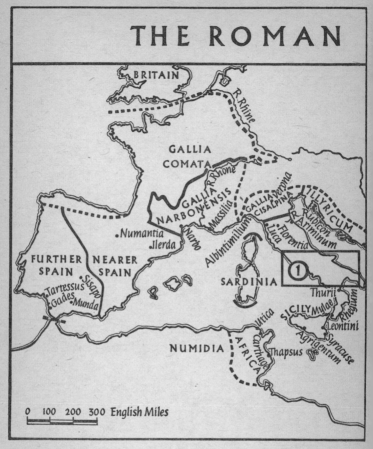

For detailed map of inset (1) see p. 264.

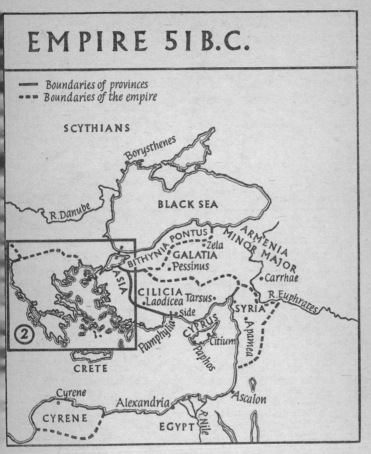

EMPIRE 51 B.C.

—— Boundaries of provinces
--- Boundaries of the empire

SCYTHIANS

Borysthenes

R. Danube

BLACK SEA

ARMENIA
MINOR MAJOR

PONTUS
BITHYNIA
Zela
GALATIA
Pessinus
ASIA

CILICIA
Laodicea
Tarsus
Side
Pamphylia
CYPRUS
Citium
Paphos

Carrhae

R. Euphrates

SYRIA
Apamea

②

CRETE

Cyrene
Alexandria
Ascalon
CYRENE
EGYPT
R. Nile

For detailed map of inset (2) see p. 264.

CENTRAL ITALY

Places where Cicero owned house or rest-house

ETRURIA
R. Tiber
PICENUM
Cosa
SABINES
AEQUI
*ROME
R. Anio
Corfinium
Lanuvium
Anagnia
*Tusculum
Trebula
Arpinum
Arpinum
SAMNITES
*Antium
Casinum
LATIUM
Interamna
*Astura
Teanum Sidicinum
APULIA
Cannae
Circeii
Cales
*Fundi
Casilinum
Beneventum
Canusium
*Formiae
Capua
*Minturnae
Caudine Forks
Appian Way
Brundusium
Sinuessa
CAMPANIA
Cumae
*Miseno
Puteoli
*Pompeii
Mt Vesuvius
Tarentum
LUCANIA

0   50   100 English Miles

①

GREECE AND WEST OF ASIA MINOR

Dyrrhachium
EPIRUS
MACEDONIA
Philippi
Thessalonica
Pydna
Troy (Ilium)
THESSALY
Mt Ida
Larissa
Cynoscephalae
ASIA
Pharsalus
Pitane
LYDIA
Thermopylae
AEGEAN SEA
Smyrna
Sardis
Parnes
Chios
Leucas
IONIAN ISLANDS
Plataea
ATTICA
Samos
Pantias
Corinth
Athens
ACHAIA
Mycenae
Ceos
PELOPONNESE
Pagae
Seriphos
Olympia
Troezen
Cos
Sparta
Gythium
Rhodes

0   50   100 English Miles

②

ANCIENT ROME

○ Blocks of flats owned by Cicero

--- City-wall

Flaminian Way (To Red Rocks)

FIELD OF MARS

QUIRINAL HILL

VIMINAL HILL

Theatre of Pompey
(Caesar murdered)

CAPITOLINE HILL

CITADEL

Temple of Concord

Temple of Ops
Minucian Portico

Treasury

Rostra

Senate-House

Temple of Julius

ESQUILINE HILL

FORUM

Temple of Tellus

R Tiber

Temple of Jupiter Stator

Arch of Fabius

PALATINE HILL

(Cicero's House)

CAELIAN HILL

AVENTINE HILL

CIRCUS MAXIMUS

Appian Way

0 ⚹ 1 English Mile

265

INDEX OF PERSONAL NAMES

Romans are shown here under the name of their family (*gens*); a few, who are best known under another name, are given a second reference.

Gorgias, 197, 218, 222
Gracchus. See Sempronius
Gregory the Great, Pope (c. 540–604), 25
Grey, William (d. 1478), 28
Guarino da Verona (1374–1460), 28
Guicciardini, Francesco (1483–1540), 27

Hamilcar, 199
Hannibal, 159, 198, 205 f., 243
Hastings, Warren (1732–1818), 30
Hecato, 182, 194 f.
Herbart, J. F. (1776–1841), 30
Herbert, Edward (1583–1648), 29
Herennius, 26
Herennius, C., 51
Herodotus, 17
Herophilus, 148
Hesiod, 222, 235
Hieronymus, 163. See also Jerome
Hippias, 129
Hirtius, A., 65, 100
Homer, 222, 225, 235
Hooker, Richard (1554–1600), 29
Horace, 19, 198
Hortensius, Q., 36, 43, 51, 53, 104, 108, 186
Hostilius Mancinus, C., 203
Hume, David (1711–76), 30
Humphrey, Duke. See Gloucester
Huysmans, J. K. (1848–1907), 32

Isocrates, 17, 218, 222

Jefferson, Thomas (1743–1826), 30
Jerome, St, 25
John of Salisbury. See Salisbury
Johnson, Dr Samuel (1709–84), 30
Jugurtha, 189
Julia, 62, 71, 190
Julius Caesar, C., 7, 10, 59, 62 ff., 66 f., 69, 71, 77 f., 81–5, 87–93, 96, 101–8, 112–18, 121, 124–7, 129, 132–46, 148–52, 158, 165, 190 f., 193, 212

Julius Caesar, L., 97, 109
Junius, C., 48
Junius Brutus, Dec., 93, 96 f., 99, 147
Junius Brutus, L., 87 f., 114, 151, 173, 242
Junius Brutus, M. (Q. Caepio Brutus), 27, 58, 79, 87 f., 91–5, 98, 100 f., 105, 114–17, 143, 147, 177
Junius Pennus, M., 176
Junius Silanus, Dec., 108
Juvenal, 25, 102
Juventius Laterensis, M., 63 f.

Kant (1724–1804), 30
Komensky. See Comenius

Laco, 147
Lactantius, 25
Laelius Sapiens, C., 62, 137, 165, 211 f., 214 ff., 224
Lepidus. See Aemilius
Lepta, 77
Licinius Crassus, L., 121, 176, 184
Licinius Crassus, M., 7, 36, 53, 62, 67, 69, 71, 74, 105, 108, 186 f.
Licinius Crassus Dives, P., 224, 233, 238
Licinius Lenticula, 127
Licinius Lucullus, Cn., 92
Licinius Lucullus, L., 56, 108
Licinius Murena, L., 108
Linacre, Thomas (c. 1460–1524), 28
Lincoln, Abraham (1809–65), 31
Livius Andronicus, L., 233
Livius Macatus, M., 217
Livius Salinator, C., 216
Livius Salinator, M., 217
Livy, 25
Locke, John (1632–1704), 29
Longinus, 20
Louvet, J.-B. de C. (1760–97), 30
Lucceius, L., 60
Lucullus. See Licinius, Terentius
Lutatius Catulus, Q., 53, 69, 108
Lutatius Pinthia, M., 188
Luther, Martin (1483–1546), 29